CONTENTS

PREFACE

Because of our history, Ireland can be said to have a common law legal system. The central feature of such a system is that principles of law are enunciated by the judges in actual cases rather than being formulated by a law making body. It can be said with some certainty that, despite the enactment of a written Constitution and a more forceful role played by the Oireachtas in law-making, the bulk of our legal principles are to be found in the decisions of the judges. Whether this is appropriate or not is another question and whether this continues to be so with the increased importance of EC Community Law remains to be seen.

Because these decisions are found in a diverse number of law reports, many old or unavailable, and at a time when the court system and legal procedures were very different, the practitioner and the student need an accessible method of reaching these cases. This difficulty is further compounded by the fact that not every novel point of law leading to a decision by the superior courts is reported in the law reports.

The answer is the casebook: a collection of the relevant cases under a single cover. By judicious editing of each judgment with a short synopsis of the facts, followed by a clear statement of the actual decision, a two-fold effect is achieved. First, the principle of law is expounded in each case and secondly, the subject locks together into a cohesive body of law.

A casebook generally complements a textbook. As regards business law it is essential to have to hand a number of statutes, such as the *Sale of Goods Act 1893*, the *Sale of Goods and Supply of Services Act 1980* and the *Hire-Purchase Act 1946*. While the legislature has left the development of contract law principles to the judges it is noticeable that with specific business contracts the legislature has considered it necessary to set forth some regulatory measures. The law invariably trails behind business in that the commercial sector invents some novel practice and only later will the law intervene, generally to protect the weaker party to the contract. This casebook illustrates that phenomenon in areas such as sale of goods and hire-purchase.

It has taken this country many years to learn the lesson that for our society to survive and be vibrant we must be skilled in the many facets of business, in both domestic and foreign markets. To survive in the business world a knowledge of business law is crucial. The fact that we are becoming a business-oriented community is proven in this book in that the bulk of the cases cited are of fairly recent origin, many within the past decade. This must be a trend which is set to continue, particularly with the approach of 1992.

I must express my appreciation to the Librarian of the King's Inns, Jonathan Armstrong (and his staff), and to the Librarian of the Law Society, Margaret Byrne (and her staff) for their assistance. A special word of thanks to Bridget Lunn for her considerable editorial expertise.

I wish to thank the Incorporated Law Reporting Council of Ireland for permission to reproduce extracts from the *Irish Reports*, and to the Round Hall Press for permission to reproduce excerpts from the *Irish Law Reports Monthly*. My thanks are due to the judges, both past and present, for permission to reproduce their endeavours.

Brian Doolan
Law Library
Four Courts
Dublin
July 1989

ABBREVIATIONS

A.C./App.Cas	Appeal Cases
All E.R.	All England Reports
B./BB.	Baron/Barons
C.	Chancellor
C.B.	Chief Baron
Ch.	Chancery
Ch.App.	Chancery Appeal
Ch.D.	Chancery Division
C.J.	Chief Justice
Eq.	Equity
I.L.R.M.	Irish Law Reports Monthly
I.L.T.R.	Irish Law Times Reports
I.R.	Irish Reports
I.R.C.L.	Irish Reports—Common Law
I.R.C.L.R.	Irish Common Law Reports
I.R.Eq.	Irish Reports—Equity
Ir.L.R.	Irish Law Reports
J./JJ.	Mr Justice/Miss Justice
L.C.	Lord Chancellor
L.C.J.	Lord Chief Justice
L.J./L.JJ.	Lord Justice/Lord Justices
L.R.H.L.	Law Reports—House of Lords
L.R.Ir.	Law Reports Ireland
L.T.	Law Times
M.R.	Master of the Rolls
P.	President of the High Court
Q.B.D.	Queens Bench Division
S.C.	Court of Sessions—Scotland
Sol.Jo.	Solicitors' Journal
unrep.H.C.	unreported judgment of the High Court
V.C.	Vice Chancellor
W.L.R.	Weekly Law Reports

TABLE OF STATUTES

TABLE OF CASES

xi

PART ONE

AGENCY

For practical and commercial reasons the common law permitted a person to act through an agent. The maxim *qui facit per alium facit per se*: he who does something through another does it through himself, was applied. Agency is the relationship which arises when one person, called the agent, acts on behalf of another person called the principal, thus affecting the legal position of the principal with regard to third parties.

A universal agency occurs where a principal appoints an agent to handle all of the principal's affairs. A general agency occurs where the principal appoints the agent to represent the principal in all matters of a particular kind. A special agent is appointed by the principal for a particular purpose and the agent's authority is confined to matters directly affecting that purpose. No multiplication of acts as a special agent converts a special agent into a general agent: *Foley v Carden* (Case 1) and *Barrett v Irvine* (Case 2).

CHAPTER 1.
CREATION OF AGENCY

Agency may be created in a number of ways. The obvious way to create an agency is to do so expressly. Or, an agency may be implied or apparent from the circumstances of the case: *Kilboggin Mink & Stud Farms Ltd v National Credit Co.Ltd* (Case 3).

Should a properly appointed agent exceed his or her authority, or a person having no authority purport to act as an agent, the principal incurs no liability on the contract allegedly made on the principal's behalf. But in such circumstances the principal may ratify the transaction and thereby become liable and bound by it. It is, in a sense, a case of express authority given after the event has occurred: *Barclay's Bank v Breen* (Case 4), and *Brennan v O'Connell* (Case 5). Where some formality must be observed, such as the giving of authority under seal, ratification cannot occur where there is an absence of such formality: *Athy Guardians v Murphy* (Case 6).

Case 1. Foley v Carden
King's Bench (1903) 4 New Ir.Jur.Rep. 198

The defendant arranged to have a bull consigned by ship from Glasgow, via Dublin, to his Templemore farm. On the bull's arrival in Dublin the shippers, who had no through rates to Templemore, asked a third party to take delivery of the animal. This third party had on previous occasions received specific instructions to take delivery of cattle for the defendant but on this occasion he had no such instruction. When the bull was being transported by the third party's employee to the third party's premises it broke loose due to the employee's negligence and injured the plaintiff who sued the defendant for damages alleging that the third party was acting as the defendant's agent.

Held that there was no evidence from which a general agency could be inferred and that since there had been no specific instruction from the defendant to the third party to take delivery of the bull there was no agency relationship between the parties and the action must be dismissed.

Gibson J.:

. . . Then it was said that the third party was a general agent for the defendant. On the evidence it seemed that he was a special agent acting on specific instructions given in each case, and no multiplication of acts done by him as special agent could alter the character of the agency, or authorise him, as general agent, to impose liability for the consequence of his unauthorised intervention. His act could not turn an officious courtesy into a contract of agency. I could not assent to the suggestion of the Lord Chief Baron [in the trial court] that the shippers were, by the necessity of the situation, justified in what they did, and that the defendant might, by this imputation of agency, be made liable. Assuming that the third party was not a general agent, and that the shippers had no instructions or duty as to forwarding the bull, they occupied the position of bailees, and were bound to communicate with the defendant, whose address they knew. Meantime, they were under an obligation to do what was reasonable in keeping and maintaining the animal at the defendant's expense. They were not entitled to make delivery of the bull to a third person, and in giving up

the bull they renounced the character of bailees, relying on the credit and
responsibility of the third party . . .

Boyd J. concurred.

Case 2. Barrett v Irvine
Court of Appeal [1907] 2 I.R. 462

The plaintiff sold a horse to a minor on the representation that his
mother would pay for it. The minor had, on former occasions, to the
knowledge of the plaintiff, purchased horses for which his mother
afterwards paid. In an action by the plaintiff against the mother for the
price of the horse, it was contended that the conduct of the mother in
relation to her son's former purchase transactions constituted the son
her general agent for the purchase of horses.

Held that no multipication of acts as special agent can convert a
special agent into a general agent so as to bind a principal in a
transaction of this kind. The facts proved did not amount to evidence
of general agency in the son. The action was dismissed.

Lord O'Brien L.C.J.:

If this case is deemed worthy of a place on our law books, or is made the
subject of story in any metropolitan or local magazine, it may be well
entitled 'The Enfant Gâté of Roscarberry'. A fond mother paid some
money—the price of horses which her son, a spoilt boy, had bought, and it
is argued that she thereby held him out to the world as, and constituted
him, her general agent to buy horses on her credit to any extent his
juvenile fancy might suggest. That, in fact, if another Waterloo was to be
fought in defence of the liberties of Europe, this impulsive youth might
horse, at her expense, a brigade of Greys, Inniskillings, and 1st Royals, to
add another page to the history of chivalry. If the law permits this, the
man in the street, to whom I have so often referred as the embodiment of
common sense, may well regard Mr Bumble's famous *dictum* not merely as
historical, but true. The defendant is sued for the price of a horse called
'Easter Boy'—her son, the spoilt lad I referred to, bought him from the
plaintiff during the absence of his mother in Scotland. It is admitted she
knew nothing about the transaction—about the purchase—that she did not
in any way expressly authorise the purchase. Special authority to purchase
the particular animal is admitted not to have existed, but it is said that she
paid the price of some three or four other horses the boy bought, and that
therefore in some way she held him out as her general agent to buy horses.
This is an alarming doctrine. During the argument I put the following case
to counsel. Take, I said, the instance of a father who has a daughter who

hunts—who is fond of horses, buying them during an interval of some years, and the father pays for the horses, and keeps them at his expense for the daughter. Does that fact, the fact of the payment of the price of the horses by the father and the keep of them by him, supply any evidence that the father held out the daughter, constituted the daughter, as his general agent to buy as many horses as she pleased—to buy, for instance, all the horses at the Dublin Horse Show! This, in my opinion, would be the very extravagance of absurdity; but let me assume—which is not the fact—that there was in this case clearly proved an antecedent authority to buy from time to time some particular horses. It has been decided in this court that no multiplication of transactions, each of which depended upon particular special authorisation, can constitute general agency: see the case of *Foley v Carden* (Case 1), which was affirmed on appeal. However, it is argued that there are some additional circumstances in this case: there was a civil-bill decree obtained against the mother in relation to the price of another horse, and the fact that the Roscarberry hounds were kept in premises belonging to her. I do not think that the civil-bill decree was any evidence whatever of a general agency in the son. She had made a promise in the goodness of her heart in a particular transaction, and was decreed for the sum she promised to pay. As to the hounds, I cannot conceive how, allowing a subscription pack to be kept in some out-offices is any evidence that she authorised the Master of the pack to act as her general agent in the purchase of horses. . .

Gibson and Kenny JJ. delivered concurring judgments.

Case 3. Kilgobbin Mink & Stud Farms Ltd v National Credit Co.Ltd
High Court [1980] I.R. 175

In compromising ejectment proceedings instituted by the defendant against the plaintiff for recovery of possession of premises the parties agreed that the plaintiff would surrender its interest in the lease to the defendant in consideration of the payment of £8,500 by the defendant to the plaintiff. The plaintiff authorised its chairman to deliver possession of the premises to the defendant on a stated date. This was done by the chairman but he was allowed to remain in occupation of the premises as caretaker for the defendant for a limited period on the basis that the £8,500 would not be paid to the plaintiff until he had left the premises. The chairman directed the defendant to pay the £8,500 to a third company, which was a subsidiary of the plaintiff, and which was trading in the premises. The defendant wrote to the third company undertaking to pay that sum to that company when the chairman quit the premises. On the day the chairman quit the premises the defendant paid the third company. Three days previously a bank, which held a debenture over the assets of the plaintiff, appointed a receiver. The plaintiff sought a declaration that at the time of the receiver's appointment the defendant was indebted to the plaintiff in the sum of £8,500.

Held that having regard to the circumstances of the case the plaintiff's chairman had implied an ostensible authority to request the defendant to pay the sum in question to the third company and that the plaintiff was estopped from revoking that authority.

Hamilton J.:

. . . On behalf of the defendant, counsel submitted that L., as chairman and director of the plaintiff company, had actual authority to enter into the said agreement and to authorise the defendant to pay the balance of the consideration, namely, £8,500 to the credit of the third company in the Anglo-Irish Bank. Alternatively, he submitted that L. was held out by the plaintiff as having ostensible authority to do so and that the plaintiff is estopped from denying responsiblity for his acts.

In order to rely on the doctrine of ostensible authority, it is essential that the person who claims the benefit of it must (a) prove that that he relied upon the ostensible authority which he sets up and (b) show that he was not put upon enquiry as to whether the transaction was in order.

On behalf of the plaintiff, counsel submitted that the nature of the transaction was such as to put the defendant and its solicitor on enquiry as to whether the transaction was in order as it could not be considered to be an ordinary transaction where money due to one company was authorised to be paid to another company.

I have read and considered carefully all the authorities opened to me by counsel and found them of considerable assistance. The questions which I have to determine are partly questions of fact and partly questions of law. So far as the facts are concerned, it is clear from the evidence of the receiver that L. was the chairman of the plaintiff company which has an issued share capital of 50,000 shares; that L. held 49,999 of these shares and that McE. was the managing director of the plaintiff company and held the remaining issued share; that L. held the majority of the issued shares in the third company; and that that company was trading in the demised premises though the lease was held by the plaintiff company. It is clear from the evidence on behalf of the defendant that all the dealings between the plaintiff and the defendant were conducted by L. on behalf of the plaintiff. It is true that the resolution of the plaintiff company (required by defendant's solicitor because no deed of surrender was being executed) authorises L. to surrender the lease but is silent with regard to the consideration for the surrender and the manner of its disposal.

As stated by Willmer L.J. in *Freeman & Lockyer v Buckhurst Park*

Properties (Mangal) Ltd (1964) 'Actual authority might, of course, be either express . . . or it might be implied . . .' Though there is no resolution of the plaintiff company authorising L. to dispose of the £8,500 in the manner in which he did, I am satisfied, having regard to all of the evidence, that he did have such actual authority and that this can be implied from the facts that he was the chairman of the plaintiff company and one of the two directors of the company, that he was the holder of all but one of the issued shares of the company, and that he was the person expressly authorised by the plaintiff company to surrender the lease to the defendant. I am also satisfied that L. had ostensible authority to direct or authorise payment of the £8,500 in the manner in which he did authorise that payment, and that the defendant relied on such ostensible authority to make the payment in the manner in which it did.

While on the surface it may appear to be unusual that an amount due to the plaintiff company should be directed to be paid to the credit of another company, in the circumstances of this particular case it was not so unusual as to put the defendant on enquiry as to the extent of L.'s authority because, as appears from evidence on behalf of the defendant, the third company was trading in the premises which were being surrendered . . .

Case 4. Barclay's Bank v Breen
Supreme Court (1962) I.L.T.R. 179

The plaintiffs, executors of an estate, proposed to sell the deceased's farm and employed a local solicitor who was to have carriage of the sale. By letter the solicitor has been instructed by the plaintiffs to act on their behalf 'in dealing with any legal formalities in connection with our proof of title and ultimate disposal of the property'. The solicitor in reply said 'I shall be happy to act for you in putting the title in this matter in order and disposing of the lands'. The solicitor prepared the conditions of sale and sold the lands to the defendant who paid a deposit and later the balance for which the solicitor issued a receipt. The solicitor became insolvent after transferring only a part of the purchase price to the plaintiffs. The plaintiffs claimed that part of the purchase money which remained unpaid from the defendant. The defendant in return claimed that the purchase money had been paid by him to the solicitor as the plaintiffs' agent and sought specific performance of the contract.

Held that the intitial letter from the plaintiffs and the surrounding circumstances established that the solicitor had been authorised to act as the plaintiffs' agent to receive the purchase money and to give a receipt. Even if the solicitor had not such actual authority, the plaintiffs with knowledge of the facts had ratified the receipt of the purchase money by accepting payments out of it and by subsequent correspondence.

Lavery J.:

. . . The extent of an agent's authority is to be determined first by the express instructions given him and second on such implications as may arise from the conduct or situation of the parties or from necessity.

The express instruction is to be found mainly in the letter of 3 April 1950, which I have already quoted. It is argued that the instruction to deal with 'the ultimate disposal of property' and the reply thereto of 6 April—'I shall be happy to act for you . . . in disposing of the lands' gave the solicitor a wider authority than would arise from his mere appointment as solicitor with carriage of the sale, and in particular would authorise him to receive and give a discharge for the purchase-money.

It is said further that the relations between the plaintiffs and the solicitor, both prior to the date of the instruction to sell, and subsequent thereto, authorised him to act on behalf of the plaintiffs as executors in the winding up of the testator's Irish estate and again in particular to receive the purchase money and to make thereout such payments as might be necessary in the administration of the estate and in the completion of the title with the obligation of course when this had been done to remit the balance to the plaintiffs. The correspondence establishes that the solicitor was directed to arrange the sale of certain furniture in the dwellinghouse on the lands and certain other articles, namely galvanised iron, and to collect the proceeds of such sales and to collect certain rents.

The solicitor carried out these instructions and collected from the auctioneers, the rents of the property payable in a previous year and the proceeds of these sales, and remitted them to the plaintiffs.

I do not consider it necessary to extend this judgment by referring to the correspondence on these matters in detail.

It is further said that the fact undoubtedly is so that the preparation of the Conditions of Sale and its provisions were committed entirely to the discretion of the solicitor and that the plaintiffs did not at the time nor at any time thereafter make any enquiry about these Conditions or whether, as the fact was, the purchaser had on payment of the purchase money been put into possession of the lands . . .

It is the view of the court that the letter of 3 April and these surrounding circumstances establish that the solicitor was more than the solicitor for the vendors having carriage of the sale and that he was, in fact, authorised to act as the plaintiffs' agent in all respects in relation to the testator's Irish affairs and in particular to receive the purchase-money and give a discharge therefor.

The subsequent course of events which I shall have to examine in relation to the second issue goes far to support this conclusion.

It is agreed by counsel for the plaintiffs that these subsequent matters may be looked to to determine the nature and extent of the solicitor's actual authority.

This conclusion would be sufficient to determine the action in favour of the defendant and to entitle him to an order for specific performance on his counterclaim.

Nevertheless as the other issue raised, in the opinion of the court, so clearly leads to the same conclusion it is considered well to deal with it.

If, contrary to the view expressed, the solicitor had no actual authority on 12 December 1950 to receive the purchase money and give a discharge therefor it has to be considered whether on that date he purported so to do and if he did whether his action was subsequently ratified by the plaintiffs so as to bind the plaintiffs and effectively to discharge the defendants from payment of any part of the purchase price.

If these matters are established then the maxim *omnis ratihabitio retrotrahitur et mandato priori aequiparatur* [every ratification relates back and is equivalent to a prior authority] should be applied. The issue, as well as the one already dealt with, should be determined contrary to the view taken by the learned trial judge [in the High Court]. A court of appeal naturally gives great weight to the conclusions of fact and inferences of fact reached by a trial judge but in the present case where the transactions were entirely carried out by correspondence and no real question of credibility of witnesses arises, the appeal court is equally well able to examine the evidence and reach its own conclusions. It is true that the manager of the trustee department of the plaintiffs gave important evidence but while the court acquits him of any desire to misrepresent the position, we are bound to say that his evidence as to his state of mind at particular points is difficult to reconcile with the letters written by him and other officers of his department and where a conflict might seem to appear the contemporary record should be preferred.

The correspondence is extremely lengthy and the members of the court have read and considered it carefully. I shall have to refer to some of the more important letters but generally we consider the conclusion inescapable that up to the month of August 1953, the plaintiffs continued to regard the solicitor as their general agent to make such payments as might be necessary in the winding up of their testator's estate and that at no time did they question his authority to have received the purchase money on their behalf and to apply it.

On the second issue the first matters to be determined are whether in receiving this payment the solicitor, on the assumption that he had no actual authority, did represent to the defendant that he was claiming the balance of the purchase money as agent for the vendors, whether it was so paid, and whether he purported to give a discharge as agent for the vendors.

The defendant positively testified that he understood the letter of 4 December 1950, to be a demand by the plaintiffs as vendors, for the money and that he paid it to the solicitor as solicitor and agent for the vendors on the date fixed for closing which in his opinion was the date on which he was bound to pay it. We accept this evidence fully. He gave his reasons for making a payment which was said to be unusual because he was not obtaining an executed deed of transfer and these reasons satisfy the court. This of course would not be in itself sufficient, as the critical question is in what character was the payment called for and in what character was it received. I read the letter of 4 December 1950, which I have quoted as a demand on behalf of the plaintiffs and I certainly read the form of receipt as a receipt given by the solicitor for the balance of the purchase-money as agent for the vendors. An important feature of the case is that from 12 December 1950, till August, 1953, neither the solicitor nor the plaintiffs demanded any release of the whole or any part of the money from the defendant but treated it in the hands of the solicitor as the proper moneys of the vendors. I have mentioned that certain small payments were made by the solicitor on behalf of the vendors out of this balance of purchase money or at least were made without any other funds being available for their payment.

We conclude, therefore, that the solicitor did claim to act as agent for the vendors in receiving the money and in giving the receipt therefor.

The conditions necessary for ratification were fully discussed in argument but there is no doubt as to the principles applicable. The first is that at the time the act is done it should be done in purported exercise of an authority from the principal. As I have explained in the opinion of the court this condition is satisfied.

It is further necessary that in order that a person may be deemed to ratify an act done without his authority that, at the time of the ratification, he should have full knowledge of all the material circumstances in which the act was done unless he intended to ratify the act and take the risk whatever the circumstances may have been. But it is not necessary that he should have knowledge of the legal effect of the act or of collateral circumstances affecting the nature thereof. I quote this statement of the principle from Bowstead on *The Law of Agency* (10th edn), page 39. It was accepted as an adequate and correct statement.

The act done in this case was simply the receipt of the entire purchase-money of the lands sold and it seems to us that the only material circumstance was the payment. I cannot think that any other circumstance save perhaps the solvency and continued solvency of the agent need be considered. The solvency of a person who is allowed to receive money for a principal, or whose receipt of money is in purported exercise of an authority which is said to have been afterwards ratified, is no doubt an important consideration but can it be regarded as a material circumstance if the intention to ratify is established? Every person who allows another to receive moneys on his behalf and to retain them must be deemed to have satisfied himself of the solvency of such person or to have taken the risk, if risk there be, that the agent either by original appointment or by subsequent ratification may misappropriate the money or, when its payment is demanded, prove insolvent.

Passing over a number of letters between the plaintiffs and the solicitor on 5 October 1951, the plaintiffs wrote:

'We should be obliged if you could now let us have a portion, say half of the proceeds of the sale of land assuming that this money has been paid into your hands.'

This would appear to the court to be a recognition of the solicitor's original authority to receive the money but at least it is a ratification of his having received it on the plaintiffs' behalf if, in fact, he had done so.

On 17 November 1951, the solicitor wrote the plaintiffs—'I am still awaiting a clearance from the estate Duty Office in this case but for the present I enclose you cheque for £100 on account which will help the widow.'

In answer to an enquiry the solicitor wrote again on 22 November 1951, 'The payment I sent you is on account of the purchase of the lands.' It is to be noted that the solicitor had no funds belonging to the estate other than the purchase-money of the lands and that the plaintiffs asked for and obtained this payment in order to apply it for the benefit of the beneficiary of the estate.

On 29 January 1952, the plaintiffs wrote to the solicitor—'We should be glad if you would now advise us whether the proceeds of sale of the property are in your possession and, if so, we should be glad if you let us have a payment of say £500 on account of the final total'.

On 31 January 1952, the solicitor replied—'I have the balance purchase-money but it is on deposit. However I enclose you cheque for £500 on account as requested'. This seems to me to be an explicit statement that he has collected the balance purchase-money for the plaintiffs and I cannot accept the suggestion that the reference to it being on deposit could convey that he held it in some way in suspense for the vendor and purchaser pending completion. If he did so hold it he could not make the payment of £500 and as I have already pointed out there was no reference therein either by the plaintiffs or the solicitor to any right or interest of the defendant as purchaser to resist the application for the purposes of the estate of the money he had paid.

Passing over several other letters which evidence the same state of mind, the plaintiffs wrote on 27 March 1952—'It would greatly facilitate matters if you could let us have the balance of the moneys due together with a full statement and a statement of rents pending the issue of this certificate (i.e., a certificate of discharge from the Inland Revenue).' I forbear dealing with the subsequent correspondence save to note that a further payment of £100 was made by the solicitor to the plaintiffs on 10 May 1952, again without reference to any rights of the defendant as purchaser to resist such payment being made.

The court cannot understand the course of events in any sense other than that if the plaintiffs had not in fact authorised the solicitor to receive the balance of the purchase-money that they afterwards became aware that he had so received it and that with knowledge of this fact they ratified his action. In fact, they have received not only £700 directly paid to them but also credit for other payments due by them out of the balance of the purchase-money.

The conclusion, therefore, is that the defendant has established that he paid the balance of the purchase-money to the agent of plaintiffs', the vendors, that he was given a discharge therefor and that either because of an actual authority existing at the time or by subsequent ratification, he is entitled to claim that the purchase-money has been paid in full.

Accordingly, the title being in order and the plaintiffs being the registered owners discharged from equities, the defendant is entitled to an order for specific performance . . .

Maguire C.J., Kingsmill Moore, Ó Dálaigh and Maguire JJ. concurred.

Case 5. Brennan v O'Connell
Supreme Court [1980] I.R. 13

The defendant appointed auctioneers to procure a purchaser who was willing to purchase one of his farms. Having found the plaintiff, who was such purchaser, the auctioneers entered into a written contract on the defendant's behalf to sell the farm to the plaintiff. The auctioneer concluded that agreement without the defendant's authority. However, when the auctioneer informed the defendant of these events, he replied that he was well satisfied with what had been done. When the defendant expressed his approval he did not know that (a) on the day after the auctioneer had so contracted another person had inquired of the agent whether the farm in question and another of the defendant's farm could be sold as one lot and if so, the asking price, and (b) that the agent had replied in the affirmative and quoted a price, and (c) that the inquirer had commented that the quoted price was a lot of money. When the plaintiff sought an order of specific performance the defendant claimed he was not bound by the contract effected by the auctioneer.

Held that the defendant's subsequent approval of the acts of the auctioneer constituted a ratification by him of the contract made by the agent, provided that at the time of his approval the defendant knew of all facts which were known to his agent and of which it was objectively necessary for him to be aware in order to be able to decide whether or not to give his approval. The fact that at the time of his approval the defendant was not aware of the type of inquiry which was made did not invalidate his approval.

Henchy J.:

. . . Before a principal can be held to have ratified a contract made on his behalf by his agent, the principal must be made aware of all the material facts on which the contract is founded; that is well-established law. This stands to reason, for clearly it would be unfair to hold a man bound by the obligations of a contract made on his behalf if he was debarred by lack of factual information from being able to assess what a ratification would let him in for. The nature of the information that must be made available to the principal depends on the circumstances of the particular case. In the instance of a vendor and an estate agent, the vendor should not be held to have ratified a contract for sale which the estate agent has purported to make on his behalf unless the vendor is made aware of all facts in the knowledge of the estate agent which, in the particular circumstances and without the benefit of hindsight, could objectively be said to have been necessary to enable the vendor to decide if he should assent to the sale. Applying that test to the present case, the question at issue reduces itself to this. Before the defendant could be said to have been able to decide if he should approve of the sale to the plaintiff of the home farm for £25,000, should he have been told (a) that on the day after the purported sale an inquirer had inquired of the auctioneer if the two farms might be sold together and, if so, at what price, and (b) that, on being told that the two farms could be bought together for £45,000, the inquirer had merely replied that that was a lot of money?

In my opinion it was not necessary for the defendant to be given that information before he could be said to have been in a position to ratify the sale to the plaintiff for £25,000. The inquirer was a person who had made a qualified offer of £24,000 for the home farm a few days previously; that offer was rejected and he had made no further offer. His inquiry about the possibility of a sale of the two farms as one lot was no more than an inquiry. The evidence does not disclose that there was at the time any reason to expect that the inquirer's inquiry would lead to an offer from him for either or both farms. The inquiry was in character indistinguishable from the usual inquiries about properties on their books which it is the business of estate agents to elicit and to answer. In the absence of special terms in the contract of agency between a vendor and an estate agent, and so long as they remain mere inquiries, disclosure of such inquiries to the vendor could not be said to be necessary to enable him to decide whether or not to accept a particular offer. They would be objectively immaterial. So much so, that the estate agent and his staff might not even think it necessary to keep a record of them. Only facts which are material to the decision of acceptance or non-acceptance have to be disclosed for the purpose of ratification. The suggestion in the judgment of Pringle J. [in the High Court] that non-disclosure of material facts would not invalidate an alleged ratification cannot be supported.

The defendant insists that he would not have approved of the sale to the plaintiff if he had been told of the inquirer's inquiry. He points to the fact that after he learned of that inquiry he sought, and still seeks, to avoid being bound to sell to the plaintiff; he says that this shows that it was a material fact that was essential for a valid ratification by them. Viewed in the light of the subjective requirements of the defendant, that may be so; but an objective test of materiality must be applied. If information which, merely by the subjective standards of a particular vendor, is thought necessary to be disclosed before a sale can be approved, the contract of agency should provide for such disclosure. If that were not the law, a vendor could avoid an otherwise valid ratification, on which the estate agent may have acted, by claiming that the estate agent had withheld from him information which he (the vendor), for private and unpredictable reasons, considered necessary—such as the identity of the purchaser; or the nature of his race, religion or politics; or the way in which the property is to be used by the purchaser; or other purely personal or idiosyncratic considerations which would not reasonably be expected to be material to a decision to reject or to accept an offer to purchase.

The contract of agency should expressly, or by necessary implication, authorise the property owner to do so before he can avoid an otherwise valid ratification by relying on non-disclosure of a circumstance which, according to ordinary business standards, could not be said to be material to a decision to accept or reject a particular offer. No such term can be read into the agency here. As the mere fact that someone had made an inquiry about the terms on which the property migh be sold could not, without more, be held to be a consideration which might be expected in the ordinary course of business to affect a decision to assent to an otherwise acceptable offer, the non-disclosure of that inquiry cannot be held to avoid the ratification . . .

O'Higgins C.J. and Budd J. concurred.

Case 6. Athy Guardians v Murphy
Chancery [1896] 1 I.R. 65

A dispensary committee at a meeting agreed in writing to purchase for the plaintiffs a plot of land from the defendant. This committee had no authority from the plaintiffs to contract for the purchase of land. The defendant subsequently withdrew and refused to carry out the agreement. After the withdrawal and refusal the agreement came before the plaintiffs and it was approved by them. Neither the agreement nor approval was under seal. The plaintiffs sought specific performance.

Held that though a subsequent ratification may supply the want of authority in an agent at the time of the acceptance of an offer, it must be shown that there was a contract purporting to be made by and with the agent, which if the agent had authority, would be a valid binding contract. In this case there was nothing under the plaintiffs' seal to give effect to the agreement in the only way in which they could bind themselves. Therefore there was no contract which could be ratified so as to make this approval relate back to the date of the agreement and thus render the defendant's withdrawal inoperative. The action was dismissed.

Chatterton, V.C.:

. . . The question then is, was there ever a concluded agreement between the plaintiffs and the defendant? Mutuality is of the essence of every contract. The plaintiffs never bound themselves by this contract till at soonest 13 June 1894; never heard of it till 6 June, before which time the defendant had distinctly refused to perform it. As a general rule either party may withdraw from a contract till it has been conclusively entered into by the other contracting party. If this rule applies here, there never was a time when both the plaintiffs and the defendant were bound to this contract, so that there could never have been any mutuality between them.

But it was contended by the plaintiffs that there was a ratification by the plaintiffs which operated retrospectively on the principle expressed by the maxim, *omnis ratihabitio retrotrahitur et mandato aequiparatur* [every ratification relates back and is equivalent to a prior authority] and which covered by intendment of law the whole period from the time the document was signed by the chairman of the dispensary committee, and that this deprives the defendant of his right to withdraw his offer . . .

The case principally relied on by the plaintiffs was that of *Bolton Partners v Lambert* (1889) where an offer for purchase was made by the defendant to an agent of the plaintiffs, who had not authority to make a contract for sale, and was accepted by him on behalf of the plaintiffs. The defendant withdrew his offer, and after the withdrawal the plaintiffs ratified the acceptance of the offer by their agent. It was held that the ratification related back to the acceptance by the agent, and therefore the withdrawal by the defendant was inoperative, and judgment for specific performance was given. This decision appears to be at variance with the other cases I have mentioned, but assuming it to be a conclusive authority proposition that if there be a transaction between one of the parties to a contract with the unauthorised agent of the other party, it is capable of being validated by the principal ratifying the act of his agent, it remains to be seen whether it rules the present case. Cotton L.J., in his judgment said that he thought the proper view was that the acceptance by the agent did constitute a contract, subject to its being shown that he had authority to bind the company, that if that were not shown it would be no contract on the part of the company, but when and so soon as authority was given to the agent to bind the company, the authority was thrown back to the time when the act was done by the agent, and prevented the defendant from withdrawing his offer because it was then no longer an offer, *but a binding contract.*

Lindley L.J. assents to the proposition as an ordinary principle of law that an offer may be withdrawn before acceptance, but he goes on to say that the question is acceptance by whom; and whether, when there has been in fact an acceptance which is in form an acceptance by a principal through his agent, though the person assuming to act as agent has not been authorised, there can or cannot be a withdrawal of the offer before the ratification of the acceptance. He said that he could find no authority to warrant the contention that an offer made, and in fact accepted by a principal through an agent or otherwise, can be withdrawn; and that the true view on the contrary appeared to be that the doctrine as to the retrospective action of ratification is applicable. Lopes L.J. takes the same view and says that on the adoption of the contract of the agent, the doctrine of ratification applied and gave the same effect to the contract made by the agent as it would have had if the agent had been clothed with a precedent authority to make it . . .

From any decision of the English Court of Appeal I should of course not presume to differ. But I do not think that the cases there decided, to which I have referred, go father than deciding that the ratification may supply the want of authority in the agent at the time of his acceptance. Therefore it must be shown in any such case that there was a contract purporting to be made by and with the agent which, if the agent had authority, would be a valid binding contract. Has that been done here? In my opinion it has not. Supposing that the agents here had the same authority to bind their principals at the time the document of 25 May was signed, still there was no contract binding the plaintiffs, as there was nothing under the seal of the plaintiffs to give effect to it in the only way in which they could bind themselves. The agents had no authority under seal either original or retrospective. There was not therefore in my opinion any contract to be ratified. Then again there was no ratification under seal, which seems also a fatal objection . . .

CHAPTER 2.

RELATIONSHIP BETWEEN PRINCIPAL AND AGENT

An agent must exercise due care and diligence on behalf of his principal and *spondes peritiam artis*: a person professing a special skill must show an appropriate degree of skill, applies: *Kavanagh v Cuthbert* (Case 7) and *Chariot Inns Ltd v Assicurazioni Generali SPA* (Case 8).

Knowledge acquired by an agent is imputed to the principal but knowledge acquired before the agency arises, as a general rule, is not: *Taylor v Yorkshire Insurance Co. Ltd* (Case 9).

An agent stands in a fiduciary relationship with the principal. The agent must act in good faith and must not place himself or herself in a position where his or her duty to the principal conflicts with his or her personal interest: *Murphy v O'Shea* (Case 10).

The principal is never liable for the deceit of the agent: *United Dominions Trust (Ireland) Ltd v Shannon Caravans Ltd* (Case 11).

Case 7. Kavanagh v Cuthbert
Exchequer (1875) I.R. 9 C.L. 136

The facts are immaterial.

Dowse B.:

. . . In my opinion, it is sufficient to say that this count alleges that the plaintiff employed the defendant to conduct the sale, and that, having entered into the employment, he undertook to discharge all the duties incident to that employment; one of which was, if not to make a binding contract, to use proper care, skill, and diligence in procuring such a contract to be entered into by a purchaser. An auctioneer differs in no respect from any other person who holds himself out to the world as ready to undertake any work which he may be employed to do. He impliedly, by undertaking a work, undertakes to bring reasonable care, skill, and diligence to the doing of it. An important part of an auctioneer's work, when he sells real estate, on the very lowest estimate of his legal obligation to his employer, is to use reasonable care to have a binding contract, under the *Statute of Frauds*, entered into by the person who purchases the property at the auction. It may be he does not undertake without any qualification to make a binding contract. It cannot be seriously disputed that he undertakes to bring the same amount of care to this part of his work that he undertakes to bring to other parts of it. It is not necessary to put the case further than this to support the first count. In fact, it is on this view of the auctioneer's obligation to his employer that the plaintiff says his count is based . . .

Case 8. Chariot Inns Ltd v Assicurazioni Generali SPA
Supreme Court [1981] I.R. 199

The plaintiff sought fire insurance from the defendant and its director signed a proposal form which required the plaintiff to state its claims experience for loss over the previous five years. The plaintiff's director signed that form with the answer 'none' appearing thereon, having been advised so to do by a representative of an insurance broker who was advising the plaintiff on insurance matters and in particular, on the proper manner in which the proposal form should be completed. The defendant repudiated liability on the ground that, prior to the acceptance of the risk the plaintiff had failed to disclose material facts to the defendant. When the plaintiff unsuccessfully sued the defendant on the policy, it sought damages for breach of contract against the insurance broker.

Held that the insurance broker had been in breach of a contractual duty to exercise the skill and knowledge which the broker professed to have. The plaintiff was entitled to recover damages from the broker for that breach and for the negligence of the broker in failing to exercise reasonable care to protect the interests of the plaintiff.

Kenny J.:

. . . The defendant brokers were acting as insurance brokers for the plaintiff at the time when the proposal for material damage was completed, and H. was their employee. An insurance broker owes a contractual duty to his client to possess the skill and knowledge which he holds himself out to the public as having, and to exercise this in doing the client's business. He is also liable in tort if he fails to exercise that skill and knowledge. H. (whom the trial judge accepted to have been an experienced, competent, and completely honest broker) should have known that the fire . . . and the subsequent payment of £8,000 to the plaintiff were material to the risk which the defendant insurers were being requested to undertake. Therefore, the brokers are liable to the plaintiff in both contract and tort . . .

Henchy and Griffin JJ. concurred.

(See also Case 78, regarding disclosure in insurance.)

Case 9. Taylor v Yorkshire Insurance Co. Ltd
King's Bench [1913] 2 I.R. 1

The plaintiff through an agent insured a horse with an insurance company. On the expiry of the policy the company declined to reinsure the horse, a fact known to the agent. The plaintiff through the same agent insured the horse with the defendant. The agent filled out the proposal form. No answer was made to the question 'Have you had a proposal for livestock declined?' When the horse died and the plaintiff claimed under the policy the defendant repudiated the policy on the ground of non-disclosure. The plaintiff argued that the facts which the answer would have elicited were known to the agent and that this knowledge must be imputed to the defendant. Since the defendant was aware of the true position when the proposal was accepted the policy could not be repudiated for non-disclosure.

Held that as a general rule the knowledge acquired by an agent antecedently to becoming an agent ought not to be imputed to the principal so as to affect the principal's liability.

Palles C.B.:

... As to the first of these question, whether the agent's knowledge, acquired before the commencement of his agency for the defendant, binds it as principal, the general principle, subject to exceptions, to which I shall advert later on, upon which knowledge of an agent is deemed the knowledge of his principal, is the familiar one of *qui facit per alium facit per se* [he who does an act through another does it himself]. Every act of an agent, within the scope of his authority, is the act of the principal. Consequently, all knowledge acquired by the agent when acting within the scope of his authority, is the knowledge of the principal. In relation to the liability of the principal arising from the act of his agent, there is, in my opinion, no distinction between the act in or by which knowledge is acquired and any other act. It follows that knowledge acquired by the agent antecedently to the existence of the relation of principal and agent ought not to be imputed; and recollections or forgetfulness by the agent of matters known previous to the relation ought not to affect the liability of the principal, save in cases (of which many can be supposed, but of which this is not one) in which the principal purchases the previously obtained knowledge of the agent in relation to a particular subject-matter, or where the agent is—to use the emphatic words of Lord Halsbury—'an agent to know'. That is the conclusion which I should arrive at on principle irrespective of authority . . .

Gibson J. delivered a concurring judgment and Boyd J. concurred with both.

(See also Case 72, regarding disclosure in insurance, and Case 82, regarding the role of an agent in insurance.)

Case 10. Murphy v O'Shea
Chancery (1845) 1 Ir. Eq. Rep. 329

A wine merchant resident in Spain was the owner of some properties in Ireland which were managed by an agent. The agent proposed to his principal that the properties be sold and the principal agreed. The agent, with the connivance of others, gave the appearance to his principal that the properties were being sold to strangers whereas in fact the agent was the purchaser. After the deaths of both principal and agent, the heirs of the principal sought to have the transaction set aside.

Held that once it was proved some underhanded dealing had been performed by the agent the transaction would be set aside. To obtain relief it was unnecessary to prove that the properties had been sold at an undervalue.

Sugden L.C.:

. . . In a transaction between principal and agent, the moment there appears to be any underhand dealing—making use of the name of another person, for example—without the knowledge of the principal, however good the price or fair the transaction, in other respects, may be, from that instant the transaction has no validity in this court. Therefore, I am perfectly confident that I am doing what is right in making a decree for the plaintiff according to the prayer of the bill, directing all the costs to be paid by the defendant representing the estate . . .

Case 11. United Dominions Trust (Ireland) Ltd v Shannon Caravans Ltd
Supreme Court [1976] I.R. 225

A third party wished to obtain a sum of money to pay for a mobile home he had purchased. The third party approached a junior employee of the plaintiff and the employee suggested that the defendant, a dealer in caravans and mobile homes, should purport to sell the mobile home to the plaintiff and that the third party should then purport to purchase the caravan from the plaintiff under a hire-purchase agreement. The scheme was put into operation and the plaintiff paid the defendant and then executed the hire-purchase agreement with the third party. The defendant immediately paid the sum obtained from the plaintiff to the third party and did not benefit from the transaction in any way. When the third party had paid some of the instalments he became insolvent and the plaintiff on becoming aware of the true facts sued the defendant.

Held that the employee was privy to an act of deceit against the plaintiff and that this act of the employee could not be imputed to the plaintiff. Since there was a total failure of consideration the plaintiff was entitled to recover the amount paid.

Griffin J.:

. . . On the first question as to whether the knowledge of the plaintiff's employee is to be imputed to the defendant, counsel for the defendant submitted that, as this employee was employed to obtain business for the plaintiff and in the course of such employment became fully aware of all the facts and circumstances material thereto and of the true nature of the transaction, this employee had a duty to communicate such knowledge to his principals who are deemed to have notice thereof as from the time when they would have received such notice if the employee had performed his duty and taken such steps to communicate his knowledge as he ought reasonably to have taken; and that, therefore, the employee's knowledge must be imputed to the plaintiffs. In my opinion, this submission is not well founded. Whilst it is substantially what is stated as the general proposition in Bowstead on *Agency* (13th edn, art. 112 at p. 355), the learned author has a proviso that 'where an agent is party or privy to the commission of a fraud upon or misfeasance against his principal, his knowledge of such fraud or misfeasance, and of the facts and circumstances connected therewith, is not imputed to the principal'. This proviso is therefore, on the facts of this case, applicable.

However, the matter is put beyond doubt by the decision of this court in *Wall v New Ireland Assurance Co. Ltd* (1965) where the circumstances in which the knowledge of an agent is to be imputed to his principal were considered by this court. In that case Mr Justice Walsh in delivering the decision of the full court, said:

> In my view the case where an agent is a party or privy to the commission of a fraud or of an act of deceit upon his principal is different from the one where the agent, though being neither a party or privy to the commision of the fraud, is, nevertheless, aware of it but for the sake of his own interests does not reveal that situation to his principal. In the latter case the knowledge of the agent when he is under a duty to communicate such knowledge to his principal is deemed to be the knowledge of his principal even though in fact it has not been communicated to him. But in the former case I am of opinion that even when there is a similar duty on the part of the agent the fact that he is a party or privy to the commission of a fraud or misfeasance upon his principal precludes his knowledge from being imputed to his principal because his participation requires the suppression of his knowledge—a circumstance which is a negation of the basis of the general rule that the knowledge of the agent is to be imputed to the principal.

In the present case, not only was the employee privy to the commission of an act of deceit (to put it at its lowest) upon his principals but he it was who engineered and arranged it, and so his knowledge cannot be imputed to the plaintiff for the reason set out by Mr Justice Walsh in the passage cited . . .

O'Higgins C.J and Henchy J. concurred.

CHAPTER 3.

REMUNERATION

The agent is entitled to remuneration if there is an express or implied term to that effect in the contract. The amount of remuneration depends on the terms of the contract. In default of an agreed sum the courts will imply a reasonable remuneration where the relationship is commercial and payment is usual.

Frequently payment is by commission and whether it is payable depends on the precise terms of the contract. If the event contracted for has happened and if the agent was the cause of that happening then the agent is entitled to the commission: *Judd v Donegal Tweed Co. Ltd* (Case 12). This is so even where there is delay or indifference on the part of the agent, provided the relationship of principal and agent has not been broken: *North v Dinan* (Case 13).

Where the agent does not do what is required of him or her, the commission is not payable: *Stokes & Quirke Ltd v Clohessy* (Case 14) and *G.F. Galvin (Estates) Ltd v Hedigan* (Case 15).

Where the relationship of principal and agent is broken, or where the agent merely introduces the parties, a commission is not recoverable: *Brandon & Co. v Hanna* (Case 16). The description of the agency as a sole agency may not entitle the agent to a commission where the principal effects the transactions: *Murphy, Buckley & Keogh Ltd v Pye (Ireland) Ltd* (Case 17). Where the agent does everything that is demanded of him or her and the transaction is not completed due to some fault of the principal, commission is payable: *Rohan v Molony* (Case 18).

A commission cannot be paid if the result would be to breach a statute: *Somers v Nicholls* (Case 19).

Case 12. Judd v Donegal Tweed Co. Ltd
High Court (1935) 69 I.L.T.R. 117

The facts are immaterial.

Hanna J.:

Now, what is the law upon which the right to commission is based? In my opinion it is quite clear. In *Toulmin v Millar* (1887) before Lords Salisbury, Watson and FitzGerald, it was held that in order to found a legal claim for commission there must not only be a causal, but also a contractual, relation between the introduction of the purchaser and the ultimate transaction of sale. Lord Watson said:

It is impossible to affirm in general terms that A is entitled to a commission if he can prove that he introduced to B the person who afterwards purchased B's estate and that his introduction became the cause of the sale. In order to found a legal claim for commission there must not only be a causal, there must also be a contractual, relation between the introduction and the ultimate transaction of sale . . . If he was generally employed to sell and thereafter gave an introduction which resulted in a sale he must be held to have earned his commission although he did not make the contract of sale or adjust its terms; because in that case he had implemented his contract by giving the introduction and his employer could not defeat his right to his commission by determining his employment before the sale was effected.

In *Bow's Emporium Ltd v Brett & Co.*, though the case turned mainly on the finding of fact, Lord Haldane said: 'The question is whether the services of the agent were really instrumental in bringing about this transaction.' When we turn to the Irish cases we find in *Brandon & Co v Hanna* (Case 16) that the issue left by Kenny J. to the jury was, 'Did the sale really and substantially proceed from the plaintiff's acts?' Lord O'Brien L.C.J., approved of this question and Sir Samuel Walker L.C. enunciated again the well-settled principle that the agent is entitled 'to receive this commission if the sale had been effected (where the jury has so found and there is evidence fit to be submitted to them that the sale was really brought about by his act);' and Holmes L.J. said:

In every case where an agent employed to sell sues for commission on the purchase money he must, before he can succeed, establish that the sale was brought about by him. The mere introduction of the person who ultimately becomes the purchaser is not enough unless it appears that the introduction has led to the purchase.

In *North v Dinan* (Case 13) I followed the same principle.

Case 13. North v Dinan
High Court [1931] I.R. 468

The defendant owner of some property placed it on the books of the plaintiff auctioneer. Four years later the plaintiff received an inquiry for such a property and he sent particulars of the defendant's property. Later the plaintiff advertised for a type of property the subject of inquiry. When the defendant saw the advertisement he reminded the plaintiff that his property remained on the market. Subsequently the inquirer and the defendant negotiated a sale of the property without further assistance from the plaintiff. When the plaintiff discovered that a sale had been effected he sued for a commission.

Held that the relationship of principal and agent existed between the parties which had not been broken by the delay and inactivity of the plaintiff. The introduction of the purchaser by the plaintiff was the effective element in bringing about the sale and accordingly the plaintiff was entitled to be remunerated for his services.

Hanna J.:

. . . The question in this case is whether the plaintiff is entitled to any remuneration in respect of the negotiation of a sale of an estate the property of the defendant, which was subsequently purchased from him on behalf of the Carmelite community. The defendant purchased this estate in 1917. It contains 800 acres of land, an old castle, a mansion house, and several lodges. It is admitted that in 1925 it was put on the books of the plaintiff as well as of other estate agents for sale, the price for the whole estate being fixed at £30,000. It was a property difficult to sell by reason of its character, and it appears from the correspondence and the evidence that for some years past in this country the only possible purchasers for such properties have been religious communities. For three years the plaintiff had no inquiry in respect of such property, but in 1928 they offered it to the Jesuit Order through their representative in Dublin, but it was unsuitable.

In the end of July 1929, the plaintiff received a letter from a solicitor, inquiring for a large mansion house and estate, as appeared afterwards, on behalf of the Carmelite community, and the plaintiff submitted the particulars of it along with another property. The solicitor, by a letter of 1 August, kept the matter open until he got particulars of other properties. This correspondence or inquiry was not communicated by the plaintiff to the defendant, a fact which (together with the plaintiff's next step) has led to this dispute; for he, on the 7th, published an advertisement on his own account as wanting a large mansion house and grounds, such as the defendant had mentioned. The defendant seeing this advertisement, replied to it by letter to the plaintiff of 10 August reminding him that his property was still to be let or sold. The plaintiff replied that he had put the property before the intending purchaser, but it was too far from Dublin.

On 16 August there came an interview, which has caused a good deal of this trouble. The defendant's son came to Dublin and saw the plaintiff. He was told in a general way the position, and that the solicitor was acting for the intending purchaser. At his request the plaintiff gave him an introduction to the solicitor. I am of the opinion that from this time the defendant and his son were under the *bona fide* belief that the plaintiff had inserted the advertisement on behalf of the solicitor and were acting as his agents to obtain a suitable place. This belief was induced mainly by the plaintiff's advertisement, and I am satisfied that the attitude and conduct of the defendant after that date was due to his belief that he was acting on his own initiative and responsibility in the negotiations which he conducted, entirely by himself, without any assistance or advice from the plaintiff, who took no interest in the negotiations, which continued through September and October; nor did the plaintiff make any inquiry from the person supposed to be his client as to whether anything had been done.

On 11 October the solicitor asked the plaintiff for the telegraphic address of the defendant, and in consequence of this inquiry the plaintiff, on 12 October wrote to the solicitor asking was he still interested in the property. To this no reply was received. On 24 October the plaintiff wrote a letter marked 'Private', which confirmed the defendant in the opinion that he was acting for the solicitor. He had, in fact, seen the solicitor, but, without mentioning this fact, he wrote the letter recommending the defendant to moderate his price to between £8,000 and £9,000, and that business would result. I am satisfied on the evidence that at this time the defendant had, in fact, agreed with his purchasers that the value of the mansion house and the portion of the lands that they intended to buy was £14,000, a figure, for other reasons, subsequently reduced to £12,000. It is natural that both the defendant and his son should be now indignant that the person who claimed to be their agent, and is now seeking substantial commission, should have proffered them advice so favourable to the purchasers. If they had adopted it they would have lost between £3,000 and £4,000. They, of course, took no notice of the advice, and sold the mansion house and about one-third of the lands on 22 November 1929, for £12,000. The plaintiff, having heard of this, subsequently put in a claim for £232 10s. as commission, based on a sliding scale.

Now the question arises: Is he entitled to commission, and, if so, how much? The law is rather favourable to the agent, but it is quite clear. It is that, if an agent employed for that purpose brings parties together or into touch with one another in the relation of buyer and seller, and a contract ensues upon it, the agent is entitled to remuneration. Delays and postponement or indifference to the result on the part of the agent do not disentitle him to his commission so long as, in the opinion of the court, the relation of principal and agent has not, in fact, been broken, and the introduction was a vital element.

I find as a fact that, prior to the interview of 16 August, the relationship of principal and agent was not broken, notwithstanding the delay and inactivity of the plaintiff. I find this mainly upon the fact that the estate had not been taken off the plaintiff's books, and within a very short time prior to that date he had put the property before the solicitor.

The whole trouble in the case turns on the insertion of the plaintiff's advertisement of 7 August and the interview of 16 August. In my opinion, there was an honest misunderstanding of the position by the defendant and his son. I have no doubt they honestly believed that the plaintiff was acting for the solicitor, and the plaintiff did nothing to undeceive them; but, as a matter of fact, I am satisfied that the plaintiff was not acting for the solicitor, but in his own interests, when he put the advertisement in the press. I find also that the plaintiff still regarded himself as the defendant's agent, but, in my opinion, he thought nothing would ever come of the negotiations, and was rather casual about it, and willing to let the defendant do his best. This may affect the amount of remuneration to which he is entitled, but, in my opinion, it does not disentitle him to the appropriate recompense for the service of the introduction. If he had properly realised his position I am sure he would have given the defendant the benefit of his vast experience in the negotiation of such sales, and probably have obtained for him a larger sum.

As far as the defendant and his son are concerned I am satisfied that they acted honourably throughout, and had no desire to take the sale out of the plaintiff's hands, but honestly believed the latter was acting for the purchasers.

I find that the introduction was an effective element in bringing about the sale, and I must assess some compensation for the plaintiff's services . . .

Case 14. Stokes & Quirke Ltd v Clohessy
High Court [1957] I.R. 84

The defendant orally instructed the plaintiff auctioneers to sell his house. The plaintiff introduced a third party to the defendant who agreed to purchase the house, subject to an architect's report and to certain improvements being made by the defendant. Before a final agreement had been reached between the defendant and the third party, the defendant received a more advantageous offer from a party not introduced by the plaintiff and refused to complete the sale with the third party. The defendant withdrew his instructions from the plaintiff who was paid nothing in respect of the completed sale. The plaintiff claimed that the defendant expressly or impliedly agreed to remunerate the plaintiff at the rate of five per cent on the purchase price offered by the third party.

Held that as the contract between the parties was that the plaintiff should be entitled to commission only if a party was introduced who would actually complete the sale, or enter into a binding contract to do so. Since the plaintiff had failed to do this, he was not entitled to the commission as claimed.

McLoughlin J.:

. . . It is clear that there was no binding contract of sale, as between the defendant and the third party, either being free to withdraw from this bargain at any time. Further, there was no consensus between them as to the work to be finished. Whether, in these circumstances, the plaintiff is entitled to anything for the services it rendered in bringing a prospective purchaser so near to a binding contact depends on what the contract was between the plaintiff as agents and auctioneers and the defendant as a client. There was clearly no express contract that they were to be paid anything, and it remains to be decided as to what contract is to be implied from anything that was said and from the actions and circumstances of the parties.

The plaintiff, as auctioneers, and knowing the business better than the average property owner, could have made a contract express as to what it should be paid in any foreseeable eventuality, but did not do so. The client, the defendant, engaged them to sell the house and any services rendered short of that service were of no value to him. It cannot, to my mind, be implied from the circumstances in this case that he undertook to pay it a fee of any amount on an introduction of a possible purchaser whom he might be willing at the time to accept, or that he bound himself not to withdraw any acceptance of an offer made unless it were an acceptance which would be binding on him *vis-à-vis* a purchaser. Other than what did happen in this case, anything might have happened. The third party might have withdrawn from the bargain (if there was a final one) as he was quite entitled to do. Had he done so, any services rendered by the plaintiff to the defendant were of no value to him. The allegation in the claim of the civil bill that the defendant wrongfully and in breach of agreement refused to complete the sale to the third party is, in my opinion, entirely without foundation and it was not wrongful or in breach of agreement as regards either the third party or the plaintiff. In my view, the plaintiff's claim fails on all grounds submitted . . .

Case 15. G.F. Galvin (Estates) Ltd v Hedigan
High Court [1985] I.L.R.M. 295

The parties in 1980 entered into a written agreement which gave the plaintiff the 'sole selling agency' for the sale of the defendant's land. The plaintiff held itself out to be lobbyists and estate agents and the parties hoped that the land, which was then zoned as agricultural, would be rezoned for industrial purposes by the local authority. The written agreement stated that it was the defendant's intention to market the land at the earliest possible date after the hoped-for re-zoning. In 1982 the defendant sold the land to a neighbour without any assistance from the plaintiff. In 1983 the local authority passed a motion incorporating a provisional decision to re-zone the land. The plaintiff claimed a commission.

Held that the contract between the parties envisaged that the plaintiff's agency would arise only when the land was re-zoned, and not before. It would not be consistent with the expressed intention of the parties to imply into the agreement a term that the defendant would not sell the land without the plaintiff's consent prior to the land being re-zoned where, as happened, there was a two year delay in considering re-zoning. The claim was dismissed.

Costello J.:

. . . The plaintiff contends that the 'sole selling agency' granted to them commenced when the letter of 7 March 1980 was signed by the defendant. The defendant contests this and says that it was intended that it would only commence a good deal later. To construe this document I think it is relevant to bear in mind that the parties were carefully watching the review procedures which the elected members of the County Council were adopting and that they had come to the conclusion in March of 1980 that the Council would be in a position to consider a motion relating to the re-zoning of the defendants' lands in the very near future. So when the plaintiff acknowledged that it was the defendant's intention 'to market these lands at the earliest possible date after the hoped-for re-zoning' they had in contemplation that they would be put on the market in a short space of time after they wrote their letter, but not before the council considered the re-zoning motion. The matter is put beyond doubt by the terms of the defendant's acceptance. The plaintiff's request for a sole selling agency and a 3 per cent commission was 'confirmed and agreed' but with the following proviso: 'subject to the land of the principals above being and remaining re-zoned "Industrial" or a substantial portion thereof (say 90 per cent)'.

It seems clear to me that I must construe the express terms used by the parties as meaning that the plaintiff's sole selling agency would only arise if and when the lands were re-zoned, and as long as they remained so re-zoned—and not before that happened . . .

I conclude, therefore, that the parties agreed (a) that the plaintiff would be granted a sole selling agency if and when a motion was adopted that a proposal for their re-zoning be included in the draft variations which were to be made available for public inspection and (b) that the sole agency would cease if the re-zoning proposals were not included in the variations as finally adopted and (c) that the plaintiff would be entitled to commission at 3 per cent on any sale which took place after the first motion was passed provided the re-zoning proposals were later formally adopted.

There still remains for consideration the meaning of the phrase 'sole selling agency' employed in the contract, for it has been urged on the defendant's behalf that if and when the plaintiff's employment as sole selling agent arose this would not have precluded the defendant himself from selling the land without any obligation to pay the plaintiff 3 per cent or any, commission.

I was referred to *Murphy Buckley and Keogh Ltd v Pye (Ireland) Ltd* (Case 17) which was a case in which it was held the plaintiff's appointment as sole selling agent did not confer on them exclusive selling right so as to prohibit the landowner from selling themselves . . . I do not consider that this decision constrains me to find in the defendant's favour merely because the phrase 'sole selling agency' (and not 'exclusive selling rights') was used by the parties. I have to determine the parties' intention when using this phrase. I agree with counsel for the plaintiff's submission that this is by no means the ordinary case of an auctioneer being given exclusive rights to auction or sell his client's lands—here the auctioneers were employed to do different and additional work as lobbyists before their agency would arise. And it seems to me that the parties must have intended that if the plaintiff's efforts (along, of course with those of the defendant himself who was also active in canvassing support from local representatives) were successful to the extent of getting the first motion adopted, that then they would be entitled to commission even if they did not introduce the purchaser. I conclude, therefore, that if and when the plaintiff's sole agency arose by the adoption of the first motion by the council, the parties intended that the defendant could not defeat the plaintiff's claim to commission by himself selling the lands.

The conclusions which I have reached on the meaning of the express terms of the contract do not, of course, help the plaintiff, because the parties' expectations in March 1980 were not realised, and no motion in relation to the defendant's lands was considered by the council for over two years. Before that happened—that is, before the plaintiff's sole agency arose, the defendant himself sold the lands. The contract is silent as to what the parties rights were if a delay occurred in the adoption of the re-zoning motion and in particular whether in the event of such a delay the defendant was free to sell the lands without reference to the plaintiff's contingent rights. The plaintiff's contention (which I will now examine) is that the contract should be construed as containing an implied term protecting its interests.

Having concluded that the express terms of the contract meant that the sole agency was to arise when and if the first motion to which I have referred was adopted I cannot imply a term inconsistent with that to the effect that the sole agency was to commence immediately the letter of 7 March 1980 was signed. But the plaintiff suggests that I can imply a term to the effect that pending the adoption of the proposed re-zoning motion the defendant would not take any steps to prejudice the plaintiff's rights to earn commission under the contract—in effect, that the defendant was not free to sell their land in the interval between the contract and the consideration of the motion by the council without the plaintiff's consent.

Whether or not it would be proper to imply the suggested term depends on the intention of the parties to be collected from the words of the written agreement and the surrounding circumstances. This is a case in which the parties did not address their minds to the eventuality which in fact occurred but it is not one in which it is necessary to imply the suggested term in order to give business efficacy to the parties' agreement—the contract is a perfectly effective one (albeit one less favourable to the plaintiff in the absence of the suggested term) as it stands. Applying the officious bystander test and imagining an inquiry as to the parties' views on the possibility of a two year delay before consideration of the re-zoning issue by the council, I think it is extremely unlikely that the defendant would have agreed, either readily or at all, that during the intervening period he and his family would be precluded from selling without the plaintiff's consent . . .

In the light of the views I have just expressed on the parties contract I conclude that the defendant did not breach it. Some time after the contract a neighbouring landowner succeeded in having a motion adopted for the re-zoning of his lands in the proposals to be on public display. He then approached the defendant to buy the lands. He did so to increase the size of his holding and he paid more than the then market value of the defendant's land in the hope that they too would be re-zoned. The plaintiff was not in any way instrumental in bringing about this sale, which was embodied in contracts of 15 January 1982. A meeting took place between the plaintiff and the defendant just before Christmas 1981. I need not decide as to its exact date, nor need I decide what transpired at it beyond indicating that I do not think that the plaintiff referred to commission if a sale to [the neighbour] took place, or that the defendant agreed that commission would be payable. It is true that the plaintiff was extremely annoyed when he learnt of the deal . . . and an angry telephone conversation took place between the parties on 3 February 1982. All I need say about this conversation is that I think it highly unlikely the defendant made an admission of liability during it. So, before any motion relating to the re-zoning of the lands was adopted, the defendant's land had been sold. In April 1982 a motion was in fact adopted by the council proposing the re-zoning of these lands, but for reasons which were not explained in evidence, the variations as finally adopted contained no such proposal, so that the lands were never formally re-zoned by the council in accordance with the requirements of the statute . . .

Case 16. Brandon & Co. v Hanna
Court of Appeal [1907] 2 I.R. 212

The defendant was considering the sale of her business and requested the plaintiffs to find a purchaser. The plaintiffs introduced a party but at that time no sale took place because the defendant, with the concurrence of the plaintiffs, decided against selling. The defendant paid the plaintiffs their expenses. Subsequently, the defendant mentioned to a business acquaintance that she wished to retire and he passed this information on to the same party who had been introduced by the plaintiffs and who eventually purchased the business. The plaintiffs sued for a commission.

Held that the sale of the business had not resulted from any act of the plaintiffs and that the mere introduction of the eventual purchaser was not sufficient unless the introduction was responsible for the transaction.

Holmes L.J.:

In this case there is no controversy on material matters of fact. The defendant carried on a large drapery business in Newry; and the plaintiffs, through their representative, were employed to audit and adjust her accounts. In June 1904, she was thinking of retiring, and she asked this representative what his firm would charge for procuring a purchaser of the business and carrying out a sale. He replied that their payment would be by a certain percentage on the price, and it was distinctly agreed that if there was no sale there would be no charge. In the following October the representative informed the defendant that a particular firm might possibly purchase, and he brought one member of the firm to Newry to see the stock and the premises. Nothing definite came of this visit, inasmuch as the defendant had not finally resolved to sell, and the interested firm, though disposed to negotiate, would not make an offer while the matter was in this uncertain state. Between this time and February 1905, some communications passed between the defendant and the plaintiff's representative, on the one hand, and the representative and the interested firm on the other; but no further progress was made, in consequence of the defendant's mind being still in doubt. In February, the representative went to Newry to audit the defendant's accounts; and while he was there, she, apparently at his suggestion, determined not to sell, but to continue her business. Her returns, as the representative said, had been good, and her health was better. Hence her determination not to retire; and from that date no more was done by the plaintiff in relation to sale. On 19 May, the representative sent an account of his fees for the audit amounting to £7, and 'travelling expenses and cost of advertisement in *Drapers' Record* £1'. This sum was paid by cheque . . .

Shortly after the settlement of this account the defendant said to a commerical traveller with whom she had dealings, that she wanted to sell her business, as she had got into bad health, and asked him did he know any person likely to buy. The [firm who had expressed an interest] were customers of his, and, knowing that they were looking for additional premises, he mentioned their name to the defendant, and seeing one of the firm soon afterwards, he told him that the defendant wanted to sell her business, and strongly advised him to purchase it. In consequece of this, two of the firm went to Newry and examined the stock and premises. Negotiations between them and the defendant followed, and, at lenght, with the help of a bank manager, a price was fixed at which the sale was carried out. Kenny J. [the trial judge], reports that if he had been trying the case himself he would have found for the defendant; but being of opinion that there was evidence from which it might be inferred that the sale really and substantially proceeded from the plaintiffs' acts, he left this question to the jury, who answered in the affirmative.

In every case where an agent employed to sell sues for commission on the purchase-money, he must, before he can succeed, establish that the sale was brought about by him. The mere introduction of the person who ultimately becomes the purchaser is not enough, unless it appears that the introduction has led to the purchase. The judge's question was therefore necessary if there was evidence to support it; but I am of opinion that so far from this being the case, the admitted facts show clearly that what was done by the plaintiffs had no connection, direct or indirect, with the sale, and that therefore there was no evidence to support the finding. The introduction by the plaintiffs' representative of the eventual purchasers was wholly fruitless. No negotiations followed; and all hope of its leading to a sale was put an end to in February when the defendant, on the representative's recommendation, resolved to continue the business. After that date the plaintiffs took no further step; and the inclusion in their accounts of their expenses theretofore incurred shows that they regarded their contract with the defendant as no longer in existence. The actual sale originated in a casual conversation with the traveller when he was seeing the defendant on other business.

The traveller had not heard of any previous intention on her part to sell, of the employment of the plaintiffs, or of the communications with the eventual purchasers. From their being customers of his, he had become aware that they were looking for additional premises, and this led him to mention their name to the defendant. She then said that they had been down already to look at the place, and this may have suggested to the traveller that something relating to a sale had already passed between them; but it was certainly not this that caused him to speak to the eventual purchasers and to advise them strongly to purchase. It is impossible, consistently with our ordinary conception of cause and effect, to hold that there is any evidence that the sale resulted from the plaintiffs' acts, and, therefore I am of opinion that the case ought to have been withdrawn from the jury and a verdict directed for the defendant . . .

Sir Samuel Walker C. and FitzGibbon L.J. delivered concurring judgments.

Case 17. Murphy, Buckley & Keogh Ltd v Pye (Ireland) Ltd
High Court [1971] I.R. 57

The plaintiff was one of the several firms of auctioneers who were interested in acting for the defendant in the sale of its factory. While these negotiations were taking place the eventual purchaser of the factory made a first tentative enquiry directly to the defendant. The next day the defendant appointed the plaintiff to be its sole agent for the purpose of procuring a purchaser of the factory. It was agreed that a commission would be paid to the plaintiff if successful in effecting a sale. The defendant negotiated the factory's sale to the initial enquirer during the continuance of the plaintiff's agency and without informing it of such negotiations. The plaintiff sued for a commission.

Held that since the plaintiff's exertions as sole agents had not played any part in effecting the sale the action must be dismissed. The contract did not contain any express term forbidding the defendant to negotiate a sale during the continuance of the plaintiff's agency and no such term to that effect could be implied.

Henchy J.:

The plaintiff's case for commission, therefore, stands or falls on the submission that once it had been appointed sole selling agents, commission at the agreed rate became payable when the defendant . . . sold during the currency of the sole agency. In answer to this submission, the defendant relied primarily on the decision of McCardie J. in *Bentall, Horsley and Baldry v Vicary* (1931). The head-note of that case reads as follows:

The defendant, the owner of property, appointed the plaintiffs, who were estate agents, his sole agents for the sale of the property for a stipulated period, it being agreed that, if the plaintiffs introduced a purchaser, they should receive a commission of 5 per cent. on the purchase price. During the period of the agency the defendant negotiated personally and quite apart from the plaintiffs with a purchaser who had never had any communication with the plaintiffs and whom the plaintiffs did not know. The result of the negotiations was that the property was sold to this purchaser. The plaintiffs thereupon claimed from the defendant damages for breach of contract on the ground that, in selling the property direct to the purchaser, he had acted in breach of his contract with them and had thereby deprived them of their commission: *Held*, that the plaintiffs were not entitled to damages, as the contact contained no express prohibition against a sale by the defendant himself, and the implication of such a prohibition was not necessary to give business efficacy to the transaction. *Held* further, on the terms of the contract, that the plaintiffs could not recover commission at the agreed rate on the purchase price received by the defendant, as they had failed to introduce the purchaser, nor could they recover on a *quantum meruit*.

The terms for the agency in that case were orally agreed and later confirmed in a letter from the agents to the principals as follows: ' . . . we are to be appointed sole agents for the sale of the property for a period of six months to 1 October and that, if we introduce a purchaser, we are to receive a special commission of 5 per cent on the price realised.'

Commenting on the form of the contact, McCardie J. said:

> In the contract now before me I see nothing to prevent the business efficacy of the document by reason of the circumstances that the defendant was himself entitled to sell. If the plaintiffs had got a purchaser within the six months and before the defendant had himself sold, then they would have gained their full commission together with their right to advertisement expenses. It is to be noted that the contract contains no express words at all indicating a prohibition against a sale by the defendant himself. If the parties intended such a prohibition nothing would have been easier than to insert the appropriate words. It is also to be noted that the defendant does not say by the contract: 'I give you the sole right to sell.' He says only: 'I appoint you sole agents for the sale', which is, in my opinion, quite a different thing.

It seems to me that these observations are fully applicable to the present case. In so far as I have been able to ascertain the terms of the contract from the conversations that led up to it, and from the correspondence and the conduct of the parties, there was nothing in the contract which gave the plaintiff the sole right to sell: it was merely appointed sole agents to find a purchaser who would be ready to complete at a price acceptable to the defendant, and the defendant was to have the right to revoke the agency. It is clear that the contract precluded the defendant from selling through another agent during the currency of the plaintiff's agency; it is equally clear that the contract contained no express terms which precluded the defendant itself from selling. If I am correct in thinking that, in this respect, the contract in the present case is indistinguishable from that in the *Bentall Case*, then under authority of the latter case it is not possible to read into the contract in the present case an implied term precluding the defendants from selling.

In *Luxor (Eastbourne) Ltd v Cooper* (1941) it was held in the House of Lords, according to the head-note, that 'where an agent is promised a commission only if he brings about the sale which he is endeavouring to effect there is no room for an implied term that the principal will not dispose of the property himself or through other channels or otherwise act so as to prevent the agent earning his commission.' Viscount Simon L.C., having stressed the dangers of formulating general propositions as to contracts with agents for commission which depend in each case on the precise terms of the contract under consideration, said:

> . . . in contracts made with commission agents there is no justification for introducing an implied term unless it is necessary to do so for the purpose of giving to the contract the business effect which both parties to it intended it should have . . . It may be useful to point out that contracts under which an agent may be occupied in endeavouring to dispose of the property of a principal fall into several obvious classes. There is the class in which the agent is promised a commission by his principal if he succeeds in introducing to his principal a person who

makes an adequate offer, usually an offer of not less than the stipulated amount. If that is all that is needed in order to earn his reward, it is obvious that he is entitled to be paid when this has been done, whether his principal accepts the offer and carries through the bargain or not. No implied term is needed to secure this result. There is another class of case in which the property is put into the hands of the agent to dispose of for the owner, and the agent accepts the employment and, it may be, expends money and time in endeavouring to carry it out. Such a form of contract may well imply the term that the principal will not withdraw the authority he has given after the agent has incurred substantial outlay, or, at any rate, after he has succeeded in finding a possible purchaser . . . But there is a third class of case (to which the present instance belongs) where, by the express language of the contract, the agent is promised his commission only upon completion of the transaction which he is endeavouring to bring about between the offeror and his principal. As I have already said, there seems to me to be no room for the suggested implied term in such a case. The agent is promised a reward in return for an event, and the event has not happened. He runs the risk of disappointment, but if he is not willing to run the risk he should introduce into the express terms of the contract the clause which protects him.

It seems to me that the contract in the present case falls into the third category of cases outlined by Viscount Simon in that passage. The contract made between the plaintiff and the defendant was one under which the owner of the property appointed an estate agent to be the owner's sole agent for the purpose of finding a purchaser, and agreed that, if the agent through its activities was instrumental in bringing about an actual sale, the agent would be remunerated at a fixed percentage of the purchase money. In such a case it was held by McCardie J. in the *Bentall Case* that there was no room for an implied term that the owner will not himself sell and thereby deprive the agent of commission; and that decision was expressly approved in the Court of Appeal in *George Trollope & Sons v Martyn Bros.* (1934) by Scrutton, Greer and Maughan L.JJ., and in the House of Lords in the *Luxor Case* by Viscount Simon L.C. and by Lord Wright.

Counsel for the plaintiff, faced with the decisions in the *Bentall Case* and in the *Luxor Case* and having to abandon the case for an implied term, sought to distinguish the present case by submitting that the contract gave the plaintiff more extensive rights than those of a sole agent, in fact that it gave it the full right to sell so long as the agency lasted, subject to an exception in the case of the completion of pending negotiations with American or Italian companies. The veil of secrecy with which the defendant concealed from the plaintiff its negotiations with the eventual purchasers is pointed to as showing that the defendant knew that it was acting in breach of the contract.

I am unable to construe the contract as having given the plaintiff anything more than a right to commission on the purchase money at an agreed rate on a sale to a purchaser who had been introduced by the plaintiff during the currency of a sole agency which was terminable at the option of the defendant. In other words, there was no express term that the plaintiff would have a sole and exclusive right to sell during the currency of the agency; and counsel for the plaintiff has abandoned (quite rightly in my view) any claim that such a term arose by necessary implication . . .

Case 18. Rohan v Molony
High Court (1905) 39 I.L.T.R. 207

The plaintiff auctioneer sold land for the defendant on the terms that the purchasers would pay five per cent commission. The plaintiff did all that lay upon him to do but the defendant wrongfully refused to complete the sale. The plaintiff sued the defendant for his commission. The plaintiff also sought a sum to cover advertising expenses.

Held that the plaintiff was entitled to recover his commission despite the position that the defendant would require the purchasers to do so. Having regard to the previous dealings between the parties, and in the absence of express agreement, the claim for advertising expenses was dismissed.

Andews J.:

. . . When the defendant refused to complete, the plaintiff repaid to the purchasers the sums they had paid to him, and under the circumstances stated he, in my opinion, became clearly entitled to his commission on the sales or to compensation in the nature of a *quantum meruit* for his services. The provision in the case of each of the sales—that the purchaser was to pay 5 per cent commission—did not enable the plaintiff to sue the purchasers: *Cherry v Anderson* (1876).

The parties to the contracts of sale were the defendant (the vendor) and the purchasers. Under the contracts the defendant was entitled to require the purchasers to pay the commission, but the plaintiff was entitled, as between him and the defendant, to look to the defendant who employed him for his commission, and, having done all that it lay upon him to do in order to earn his commission, he was entitled to be paid it or a *quantum meruit*, notwithstanding that the sales were not completed, their noncompletion having been through the wrongful act and default of the defendant in breaking off and refusing to complete. Authority would scarcely seem to be required for this, but there are a number of authorities on the subject, amongst which I may refer to *Pickett v Badger* in which it was held that an agent employed on commission, who succeeded in finding a proper purchaser, was entitled to reasonable remuneration for his services when the vendor afterwards declined to sell, and the principle—

that the owner of the property to be sold cannot, by wrongfully refusing to complete the sale, deprive the auctioneer or agent, whom he has employed to sell it, of his commission or a due remuneration for his services when he has done all that it lay upon him to do—is recognised in many cases and is obvious justice. The commission payable by the defendant to the plaintiff in the present case must, in my opinion, be taken to have been at the rate of 5 per cent., mentioned in the condition of sale, and the plaintiff is therefore entitled to be paid by the defendant the sums . . . which were justly earned by him, whether these are to be called commission or remuneration. The only remaining sum in dispute is the sum for advertisements. The plaintiff paid this amount for advertisements, and he stated in his evidence that the defendant told him to advertise, but it appears that there is no invariable practice that in such a case as this the vendor pays the auctioneer for the advertisements in the absence of any express agreement to do so. The defendant stated in his evidence that on previous similar occasions the plaintiff had paid for the advertisements of sales by him for the defendant and had never applied for repayment, but treated the payment as covered by the commission, and, having regard to this previous course of dealing between them and to the absence of any express agreement by the defendant to pay seperately for the advertisements, I am of opinion that the plaintiff is not entitled to the sum for advertisements.

Case 19. Somers v Nicholls
High Court [1955] I.R. 83

The defendant was the owner of a hotel which he wished to sell. The plaintiff introduced a buyer to the defendant and claimed commission by virtue of an alleged agreement that commission would be paid should the plaintiff introduce a purchaser to the defendant. The defendant claimed that commission could only be paid to a house agent licensed under the *Auctioneers and House Agents Act 1947*, which the plaintiff was not.

Held that during the transaction the plaintiff had acted as a house agent within the meaning of the statute and being unlicensed could not legally contract with the defendant to recover commission.

Ó Dálaigh J.:

Section 7 sub-s. 1 of the *Auctioneers and House Agents Act 1947*, enjoins, subject to exceptions which are not relevant, that no person shall on or after the operative date carry on, or hold himself out as carrying on, the business of house agent, except under and in accordance with a house agent's licence issued under the Act. Sub-s. 3 reinforces sub-s. 1 by making it an offence, punishable by excise penalty, to contravene the prohibition. The expression 'house agent', is defined earlier in the Act at s. 2. The definition is: 'a person who, as agent for another person and for or in expectation of reward, purchases, sells, lets or offers for sale or letting, or invites offers to purchase or take a letting of, or negotiates for the purchase, sale or letting of a house otherwise than by auction or attempts to effect such purchase, sale or letting.'

Counsel for the defendant submits that even if the plaintiff's evidence be accepted, the action must, nevertheless, fail because it seeks to enforce a money claim which would be enforceable only if the plaintiff were a duly licensed house agent. It is admitted that the plaintiff has not at any time held a house agent's licence. In acting in this transaction for reward, the plaintiff was, it is submitted, contravening the statute; and *ex turpi causa non oritur actio* (no right of action arises from a base cause).

Counsel for the plaintiff in his resourceful argument submits that the plaintiff is not caught by the statute, because in using his good offices to persuade M. to a purchase he was not 'agent for' the defendant; and that, as he points out, is an essential limb in the definition of the expression, 'house agent'. The plaintiff was not agent for the defendant, he argues, because the plaintiff could not bind him contractually; and an agent, he says, must be in a position to bind his principal. Counsel also adds that his client was at large as to the means he would employ to persuade M. to a purchase, and (as I follow his submission) that the plaintiff is, therefore, to be regarded as an independent contractor rather than as an agent. I do not understand counsel to contest that in all other respects the plaintiff satisfies the definition of the expression, 'house agent'; nor, indeed, do I think he could do so . . .

I accept it that the plaintiff was not subject to the control of the defendant as to the manner in which he would carry out his engagement, and, moreover, that he was not in a position to bind the defendant contractually in the sense that he could conclude a contract or, indeed, do more by the terms of his engagement than assist in promoting a sale. The agent of the definition may clearly, in some cases, do no more than invite offers of purchase.

What the plaintiff says he did in promoting the sale, he did on the authority of the defendant: it is essential to his own case that that be so. He did it 'for' the defendant—on his behalf. So acting on his authority and on his behalf, can it be said he is not his 'agent' as the term is used in the definition of the expression, 'house agent'?

What in its ordinary meaning is an 'agent' except one who acts for or on behalf of another? I do not see that the plaintiff was any the less agent for the defendant because he was necessarily at large as to the modes of persuasion he might employ or because he had not authority enough to conclude a sale. In my opinion 'agent' in the context of the definition has no greater meaning. It is not used as a term of art, but is synonymous with 'one who acts . . . ' So construing it, I reject the plaintiff's argument and I must give effect to the defendant's plea of the statute and dismiss the plaintiff's action.

CHAPTER 4.

RELATIONSHIP BETWEEN PRINCIPAL AND THIRD PARTY

Generally, once an agent enters into a contractual obligation on behalf of the principal the agent drops out of the transaction and privity of contract exists between the principal and third party.

An undisclosed principal is one of whose existence the third party is unaware at the time of contracting. Under the doctrine of undisclosed principal the third party can either sue the agent or the principal, when the principal's identity becomes known, but he cannot sue both: *Jordie & Co. v Gibson* (Case 20).

Case 20. Jordie & Co. v Gibson
County Court (1894) 28 I.L.T.R. 83

The plaintiffs sold goods on credit to the defendant's son and when these remained unpaid for, sued and obtained judgment against the son. At that time the plaintiffs were unaware that the son was acting as his father's agent. When the plaintiffs unsuccessfully attempted to enforce the judgment against the son, because of his lack of goods, they then sued the father.

Held that where an agent having made a contract in his own name has been sued on it and judgment obtained against him an action will not lie against the principal on the same contract, although satisfaction has not been obtained on the judgment against the agent and although the plaintiff was not until after the legal proceedings aware of the existence of the principal. The right of election to sue either the agent or principal is determined where either is sued to judgment though the the fact of the agency was not discovered until after the date of judgment.

Judge Colquhoun:

The facts in this case are clear, and I would give the plaintiffs a decree for the sum sued for, but that a serious question of law arises. The defendant carried on the business of a public house through his son and the defendant, who did not appear in the transaction at all, was unknown to the plaintiffs until after they had supplied the goods and sued the son, to judgment. The question now is—Does this judgment, recovered against the son, bar the plaintiffs (although they have not received satisfaction) from now proceeding against the defendant, who at the time the judgment was recovered filled the position of an undisclosed principal? I think on the authorities it does. In the case of *Priestly v Fernie*, the owner of a ship was sued on a bill of lading which was signed by the master in his own name; the defendant pleaded that the plaintiff had already obtained judgment against the master for the same cause of action; the plaintiff replied that the judgment was unsatisfied, and that he had not before the recovery of the judgment any notice or knowledge that the bill of lading was made by or on behalf of the defendant. Bramwell B. delivered the judgment of the court, and, no doubt, treated the case as one of *election*, but he clearly lays it down that if the agent be sued to judgment no action can afterwards be brought against the principal, and he does not suggest any difference even if the plaintiff at the time of recovering the judgment does not know that there is a principal. It might be forcibly contended that until the plaintiff becomes aware of the existence of a principal he cannot have exercised any election, because the existence of an election would imply that the fact of two courses being open was known to him. The result of the authorities, however, appears to me to be, that election exists up to the time of judgment, but after judgment has been recovered against the agent it is not possible to sue an undisclosed principal, and have two judgments against different persons in different capacities (i.e., one against the agent and another against the principal) for the same cause of action. In *Calder v Dobell* (1871), Kelly C.B. says: 'I think the plaintiffs had a right to sue either the agent or principal at their election. No doubt the election being once determined there is an end of the matter, as where the agent has been sued to judgment.' And in another case of *Ex parte Williamson* the case of *Priestly v Fernie* was adopted as a binding authority. There is one other case of *Kendall v Hamilton* (1879) in which the point was not actually decided, but the judgment of Lord Cairns is very valuable; the defendant in that case was a sleeping partner, and the plaintiffs had sued to judgment . . ., the ostensible partners. Lord Cairns deals with the case as if it were one of undisclosed principal and agent, and says:

In the present case I think that when the plaintiffs sued Wilson and M'Lay, and obtained judgment against them, they adopted a course which was clearly within their power, and to which Wilson and M'Lay could have made no opposition, and that, having taken this course, they exhausted their right of action, not necessarily by reason of any election between two courses open to them, which would imply that in order to make an election, the fact of both courses being open was known, but because the right of action which they pursued could not, after judgment obtained, co-exist with a right of action on the same facts against another person. If Wilson and M'Lay had been the agents, and Hamilton (the defendant in this action) alone the undisclosed principal, the case could hardly have admitted to a doubt; and I think it makes no difference that Wilson and M'Lay were the agents, and the undisclosed principals were Wilson, M'Lay, and Hamilton.

I am, therefore, coerced to decide, though I would rather decide otherwise, that the action is not maintainable against the defendant, and I must dismiss the present civil bill.

PART TWO

SALE OF GOODS

A contract for the sale of goods can be defined as 'a contract whereby the seller transfers, or agrees to transfer, the property in the goods to the buyer for a money consideration called the price'. While the general principals of contract law apply to contracts for the sales of goods, statute has modified these rules. The *Sale of Goods Act 1893* and the *Sale of Goods and Supply of Services Act 1980* are the relevant statute law.

CHAPTER 5.

FORMATION OF THE CONTRACT

Formation of a sale of goods contract is largely governed by the general rules of contract law: there must be agreement, intention to create legal relations and consideration. The consideration in a contract for the sale of goods must be money. The contract may be made by deed, in writing, verbally, by the conduct of the parties, or a mixture of these.

A contract for the sale of goods of the value of ten pounds or upwards is not enforceable unless the buyer accepts and actually receives part of the goods, or gives something in earnest to bind the contract, or unless some note or memorandum in writing of the contract has been made and signed by the party to be charged.

The note or memorandum may be contained in a number of documents but these must contain all the agreed material terms. Where there is not complete agreement between the parties, the written documents are insufficient: *Haughton v Morton* (Case 21). The absence of a material term from the document is also fatal: *Mahalen v Dublin & Chapellizod Distillery Co. Ltd* (Case 22).

A tendered but rejected cheque is neither something given in earnest to bind the contract nor part payment: *Kirwan v Price* (Case 23).

Whether or not there is an acceptance of the goods which negatives the statutory requirements as to writing is a question of fact in each case: *Hopton v McCarthy* (Case 57) and *Jennings v C.E. Macaulay & Co. Ltd* (Case 58).

Case 21. Haughton v Morton
Queen's Bench (1855) Ir.C.L.Rep. 329

The plaintiff verbally ordered a quantity of grain from the defendant which was to be delivered at a future date. The grain could not be delivered because the ship carrying the grain was lost. The plaintiff sued for damages for the non-delivery of the grain. In support of the cliam he proved an entry in a memorandum book which was not signed by the defendant and a letter written by the defendant which admitted the sale but stating it was subject to certain conditions agreed on by the plaintiff.

Held that neither the entry nor letter was a sufficient memorandum as was required by the statute.

Crampton J:

. . . The entry, not being signed by the defendant, does not satisfy the requirements of the statute. The only other document is the letter of 7 November, which was signed by the defendant; and no doubt if that letter admitted the statement in the entry to be a correct statement of the contract, it would be a case within the statute. The question therefore is, whether that letter does admit the unsigned agreement as contained in the entry? . . . Neither document alone can contain a binding contract; and the authorities show that want of signature to the original document can only be supplied by an admission in writing, signed by the party, that such was the contract. But the defendant here, in referring to the original document, does not admit that the entry contained the whole contract; on the contrary, it alleges that its agreement with the plaintiff was subject to conditions, which were not contained in the entry. The effect of the defendant's letter is this—We did enter into an agreement with you; but a different contract from that upon which you rely, and which omits an essential term of the contract made between us. The *Statute of Frauds* [now s.4(1) of the *Sale of Goods Act 1893*] can only be satisfied by a signature acknowledging the very contract; and where there is a different one, there is no such agreement signed as will take the case out of the statute.

Moore and Perrin JJ. concurred while Lefroy C.J. dissented.

Case 22. Mahalen v Dublin & Chapelizod Distillery Co. Ltd
Queen's Bench (1877) I.R. 11 C.L. 83

The parties agreed on the sale of a quantity of whiskey. The method of payment verbally agreed was that the goods should be paid for in cash within one month or by a bill of exchange at four months with interest. The plaintiff sued for non-delivery of the whiskey.

Held that an invoice which represented the sale solely for cash did not satisfy the statute.

Fitzgerald J.:

The agreement then being within s.13 of the *Statute of Frauds* [now s.4(1) of the *Sale of Goods Act 1893*] requires that there should be part payment or acceptance or 'some note or memorandum in writing of the said bargain.' The plaintiff relied on the invoices. There are three invoices and a summary which require examination . . .

The defendants contend that these invoices do not contain a memorandum of the final bargain, inasmuch as, first, they represent a sale for net cash, which means cash on delivery or transfer, whereas the bargain which the plaintiff relies on in proof and pleading gives the plaintiff a right to substitute for net cash his own bill at four months, adding the interest . . .

Thus it was contended that the invoices differed from the agreement in an important particular, and could not therefore constitute a memorandum in writing of the bargain.

As to the option to turn the transaction into one of four months' credit in place of 'cash', the plaintiff contended that this did not vary the agreement, but was a mere stipulation as to the mode of payment, and need not be noticed in the memorandum. We are, however, of opinion that the option of the plaintiff to pay by a bill at four months became and was a very material portion of the bargain, and that an invoice which omits that and states an agreement to pay net cash is not a memorandum of that bargain sufficient to satisfy the *Statute of Frauds* . . .

We are all of opinion that the invoices do not contain the substantial and material terms of the sale, and do not amount to a memorandum of the bargain within the meaning of the statute . . .

O'Brien and Barry JJ. concurred.

Case 23. Kirwan v Price
Circuit Court [1958] Ir.Jur.Rep. 56

The parties agreed to the sale of a horse but later disputed the price. The plaintiff buyer tendered a cheque for £300 which was refused by the defendant seller who wrote a letter claiming the proper price was £350. The plaintiff sought specific performance of the contract.

Held that the contract was not enforceable because there was no note or memorandum in writing. The plaintiff could not rely on the defendant's letter because he disputed the facts contained in it. The cheque which was tendered but rejected was not something in earnest to bind the contract nor part payment.

Judge Deale:

I am of opinion that this action fails. It is brought to enforce an oral contract for the sale of a horse, and it is clear that the parties were not *ad idem* on the price. The plaintiff thought that the price was £300 and he sent his messenger with a cheque for this sum, to be given in exchange for the horse. The defendant refused to accept the cheque because she thought the price she had agreed to accept was £350, and she wrote a letter to the plaintiff, saying so, and calling off the deal.

Upon this letter the plaintiff relies as the note or memorandum in writing required by s.4 of the *Sale of Goods Act 1893*, but he cannot do so. He claims to enforce a contract at a price of £300; the letter does not refer to this contract, but to one for £350, which is either a different contract altogether, or a contract which he mistakenly believed to be one for £300. The goods never passed nor was any part payment made by the plaintiff. It was argued by his counsel that the offering of the cheque was the giving of an earnest within the meaning of s.4, but this submission must be rejected. The cheque was not accepted but was returned immediately so that nothing was 'given' by the plaintiff. To give implies an acceptance.

Accordingly, if there was a contract at all, which is doubtful, having regard to the difference between the parties on the price, it is unenforceable by reason of the failure to bring the transaction within s.4 of the Act, and the action must therefore be dismissed with costs.

CHAPTER 6.

PASSING OF THE PROPERTY IN GOODS

A contract of sale exists where the seller transfers, or agrees to transfer, the property in the goods to the buyer for the price. Property, in this context, means ownership and is distinct from mere physical possession. The passing of the property is central to a contract for the sale of goods. A number of consequences flow from the passing of the property. The parties may expressly determine when the property is to pass. Failure to agree on this vital term activates statutory provisions.

The primary general rule is that the property passes when the contract is made: *Clarke v Michael Reilly & Sons* (Case 24). The property also passes when the goods are appropriated to the contract: *Spicer-Cowan (Ireland) Ltd v Play Print Ltd* (Case 25).

Case 24. Clarke v Michael Reilly & Sons
Circuit Court (1962) 96 I.L.T.R. 96

The parties entered into a contract of the supply of a new car to the plaintiff and agreed that the plaintiff should 'trade in' his old car and pay the balance of the purchase price in cash to the defendants for the new car. Before the new car was delivered and before the old one was 'traded in' the old car was involved in an accident and the defendants purported to repudiate the contract.

Held that when the contract was concluded between the parties the plaintiff had parted with the property in the old car to the defendants and that accordingly the plaintiff was entitled to specific performance of the contract notwithstanding that his 'trade in' car had been damaged.

Judge Deale:

This case raises a novel point under the *Sale of Goods Act 1893*, which is of importance to the motor trade.

There is no real conflict as to the terms of the contract entered into between the plaintiff and the sales representative of the defendants, on 1 March 1961. The defendants agreed to sell to the plaintiff a new Volkswagen car in consideration of the payment by the plaintiff of the sum of £192 cash and the 'trade-in', as it is called, of his 1958 model Volkswagen car. The plaintiff thereupon wrote his cheque for £192 which the sales representative accepted. The time of delivery of the new car was discussed, and the sales representative estimated it would take from about fourteen to twenty-one days. The plaintiff asked the sales representative what he would do for a car until then as he needed the daily use of a car in his business, and the sales representative replied that he could use the old car until delivery of the new one.

The discussion about the permission to use the old car is, in my opinion, of critical importance in determining the legal effect of the contract upon the ownership of the 1958 car, as I shall call it, pending the delivery of the new one. The plaintiff would never have asked this question if he had not had some doubt as to who was the owner of the 1958 car after the contract was made. The sales representative could not have given permission to the plaintiff to use the 1958 car if the property in it had been unaffected by the contract, although he said in evidence that he thought the car was still the plaintiff's property. In my opinion the ownership of the 1958 car passed to the defendants as soon as the contract was made, and the plaintiff was given the right to use the car until delivery of the new one. It is important to realise that the transfer of ownership did not take place by reason of a sale of the 1958 car, to the defendant. He agreed to give it—to transfer the ownership in it—along with the cash of £192 in return for the promise of the new car.

So from the time to the contract the plaintiff was no longer the owner of the 1958 car. He had the custody of it as bailee. This position was indeed recognised by the sales representative in evidence when I asked him what would he think if the plaintiff had sold the 1958 car to someone else before delivery of the new car, and he said that the plaintiff would have committed a breach of contract. This in my opinion is a correct statement of the legal position, except that, it would have been legally impossible for the plaintiff to sell a car which he no longer owned.

The question therefore upon which this action turns is: At whose risk was the 1958 car from the date of the contract? Nothing was said about this when the plaintiff was given permission to use the car, and so the ordinary rule applied as between bailor and bailee, that the bailee must take reasonable care of the chattel entrusted to him. There is nothing in the evidence to show that the plaintiff failed to take such care and so he is not liable to make good the damage caused to the defendant's car whilst it was in his custody. This damage must be borne by the defendants. I understand that in fact the insurers of the car have made some offer to cover this damage or part of it, but that is irrelevant.

Accordingly, the defendants cannot require the plaintiff, as they have sought to do, to pay an additional sum to compensate them for the loss represented by the damage to the 1958 car. The contract of 1 March 1961 stands and the defendants must perform it even though that performance may involve them in some loss which they did not contemplate or expect. The plaintiff is therefore entitled to an order for specific performance.

Case 25. Spicer-Cowan (Ireland) Ltd v Play Print Ltd
High Court, unreported, 13 March 1980

The plaintiff contracted with the defendant to supply paper, payment to be made by bills of exchange. Part of the order was delivered and payment was made. When the balance of the order arrived in Dublin the defendant, because of storage problems, was unable to take immediate delivery of it. Consequently, the paper was stored with a third party. A fire took place at the third party's premises in which the paper was destroyed. When the plaintiff presented the bill of exchange for payment it was dishonoured and the plaintiff sued. The defendant claimed that since the property in the paper never passed to it, it was not liable for the amount claimed.

Held that the property in the paper had passed to the defendant and that therefore the plaintiff's action succeeded.

Doyle J.:

. . . An employee in authority at the plaintiff's stated in the course of her evidence that there had been a phone call from the defendant at the relevant time indicating why the 30 tonnes of paper which had sought to be delivered could not be received by it. The representative of the defendant informed her that the company in whose premises the defendant carried on business was accustomed to allow it space to store goods from time to time but that, at the critical time, space was not available and so the goods could not be received. This witness also confirmed that the first delivery of 20 tonnnes had been delivered direct to the defendant and had not been put into storage. A storeman employed by the third party, gave evidence that he remembered the second part of the consignment, that is to say the 30 tonnes, being received at his employer's warehouse. He recollected the arrival of this consignment because of the particular circumstance that the pallets had to be sorted out in such a way that all the different colours could be dealt with as required. He recollected that they were put into a special bay which was large enough to accommodate the 30 tonnes. It had been planned to store them, he recollected, in such a manner that the fork-lift driver who was moving them would place them as to be readily accessible for delivery in such parcels or quantities as might be necessary. He recollected the 22 pallets, part of this consignment, being loaded on a trailer for despatch to the defendants. An invoice clerk employed by the third party gave evidence that he had partly completed a warehouse despatch note and had written the words 'refused back to store' in respect of the 22 pallets of paper which it had been sought to deliver to the defendant. The driver and helper respectively on the lorry which had carried the 22 pallets to the defendants' premises gave evidence in support of the claim that the goods had had to be returned because the defendant had no room to store them. Evidence was also given of discussions between the parties after the fire and when the dispute arose as to payment, but the particular circumstances which I have previously related lead me to believe that there was, at the critical time, no doubt in the minds of either side that the ordinary consequences of acceptance of a bill of exchange were intended to operate and did operate. The evidence that the first consignment was delivered direct persuades me that the delay in attempted delivery of the second consignment was because of the defendant's storage space difficulties and at its request. It seems to me to have been demonstrated as a probability that the goods were appropriated by it both in their disposal at the third party's warehouse in the particular way in which that was done so as to afford ready access for the defendant's purposes and also because of the fact that the goods were taken from the store at request and sent back it was unable temporarily to accommodate them.

In all of these circumstances I am of the opinion that the plaintiff has made out its case that the defendant was in breach of its contract and that the plaintiff therefore its entitled to damages in the amount claimed.

CHAPTER 7.

RESERVATION OF TITLE

The property in goods passes from the seller to the buyer when the parties intend it to pass. Failing agreement on the matter, the property passes when the contract is made. Since the matter lies primarily with the parties, it is possible to defer or reserve the passing of the property until some conditions are met. It is now common practice where goods are sold on credit for the seller to include a reservation of title clause in the contract. Invariably the express terms provide that the property in the goods is not to pass until payment in full is received by the seller. The reservation of title clause offers some security to the seller.

Before such a reservation of title clause can be considered to have achieved its purpose, it must, like all terms of a contract, be proved to have been incorporated into the contract which the agreement made. Should this be proved by the party relying on the clause, it is incorporated: *Sugar Distributors Ltd v Monaghan Cash & Carry Ltd* (Case 26) and should that party fail in this task the clause is not incorporated: *Union Paper Co. Ltd v Sunday Tribune Ltd (In Liquidation)* (Case 27).

A simply drafted reservation of title clause is sufficient to effect its objective where the goods in question remain in the same state in which they were supplied: *In re Stokes & McKiernan Ltd* (Case 28), *Frigoscandia (Contracting) Ltd v Continental Irish Meat Ltd* (Case 29) and *Sugar Distributors Ltd v Monaghan Cash & Carry Ltd* (Case 30). This rule equally applies where the goods have been attached to the premises provided they remain a tenant fixture: *In re Galway Concrete Ltd (In Liquidation)* (Case 31).

Where the original goods supplied have been transformed by a manufacturing process, the reservation of title clause will not suffice of itself to retain for the seller title to the goods: *Kruppstahl AG v Quitmann Products Ltd* (Case 32) and *Somers v James Allen (Ireland) Ltd* (Case 33).

It is possible for the seller to waive a retention of title clause which was incorporated into the contract for the seller's protection: *S.A.*

Foundries du Lion MV v International Factors (Ireland) Ltd (Case 34), though in that case the evidence did not support the buyer's claim that the seller had waived the reservation of title clause.

Case 26. Sugar Distributors Ltd v Monaghan Cash & Carry Ltd
High Court [1982] I.L.R.M. 399

Four years after the parties first did business the plaintiff printed on the front of its invoices a reservation of title clause. When the defendant went into liquidation and the plaintiff sought the return of unsold sugar in the defendant's possession the question arose whether the reservation of title clause had been incorporated into the contract between the parties.

Held that despite the fact that the plaintiff had failed to prove that the reservation of title clause had been specifically drawn to the defendant's attention the clause had been incorporated into the contract because reasonable notice of it had been given by the plaintiff in that the invoices received by the defendant for a period of fifteen months contained the clause which was not intimidatory in complexity and which was printed on the front of these documents.

Carroll J.:

The first issue is whether the clause shown on the face of the invoices is a binding condition.

The evidence was that the plaintiff and the defendant first did business in 1974 when the defendant approached the plaintiff for sugar during a sugar shortage. The condition in question was introduced about fifteen months before June 1978, the first relevant date. An employee who took up duty with the plaintiff company as secretary in 1977 could not himself say that a letter drawing the attention of customers to this clause was sent out, though he believed it had been.

The managing director of the defendant company, said that his attention was not drawn to any retention of title clause, by phone or letter. He also said that in relation to invoices he was only concerned to check each one for quantity and price and that he could not carry on business if he read all the small print on the invoices. He did, however, notice a change in the form or size of the invoices. In answer to a question whether it could have made any difference if he had read it, and would he have stopped buying, he said he did not think so.

The manager of the defendant company, in answer to a question whether anyone had told him about the retention of title clause, said not that he could remember.

I therefore hold that the plaintiff has failed to prove that the special attention of the defendant was drawn to the retention of title clause which was introduced by the plaintiff approximately 2 to $2\frac{1}{2}$ years after the parties had first commenced trading with each other. Therefore I must proceed on the basis that the invoices alone provided the information. The question arises whether there was a duty on the plaintiff to draw the defendant's attention to the clause specifically or whether the defendant ought to have known of the existence of the clause because it was on all invoices for a period of about 15 months before the relevant dates.

I have been urged by counsel for the defendant to hold as Barrington J. held in *Western Meats Ltd v National Ice & Cold Storage Ltd* that the plaintiff had not given the defendant reasonable notice of the contents of its standard condition.

But the circumstances of that case are not similar to the present one. There was a businessman offering a specialist service (i.e. cold storage) but accepting no responsibility for it. There the business relationship was commenced by a meeting followed by a letter, in the text of which there is no mention of standard conditions. Here there is a supplier of goods, the plaintiff, incorporating a condition of sale via its invoices which according to the cases cited has apparently become quite common. The managing director of the defendant company said he did not read it and that he never read the small print on invoices but apparently if he had it it would not have made any difference to him. The invoice itself is a simple enough document. Three conditions appear on its face and they are not intimidating in complexity.

I consider that the defendant, having received these invoices for fifteen months, ought reasonably to have known the terms on which the goods were supplied. In my opinion the plaintiff gave reasonable notice of the conditions applicable to these transactions by putting them on the face of the invoices and there was no special duty on the plaintiff to draw the defendant's attention specifically to the retention of title clause. I therefore hold that the condition was a valid and binding condition . . .

Case 27. Union Paper Co. Ltd v Sunday Tribune Ltd (In Liquidation)
High Court, unreported, 27 April 1983

The plaintiff manufacturer of newsprint claimed ownership and immediate possession of unpaid newspaper originally delivered to the defendant. The claim rested on the existence of a reservation of title clause in the general trade rules which it was argued formed part of the contract of sale.

Held that the plaintiff had not established that the general trade rules, which contained the reservation of title clause, had formed part of the contract between the parties and that therefore property in the paper had passed to the defendant.

Barron J.:

In this action the plaintiff claims to be the owner and entitled to immediate immediate possession of certain newsprint originally sold by it to the defendant and now in the possession of a third party. The plaintiff's claim rests on the existence of a reservation of title clause in the Contract of Sale between it and the defendant. If such contract did not contain such a clause, then its claim fails . . .

The plaintiff is a manufacturer of newsprint and a member of the Norwegian Papermakers Association. It carries on its business in this country through selling agents . . . The manner in which this business was carried out with the defendant was that orders were placed verbally by the sub-agent in Ireland with Scottish agents, who in turn passed on these orders in writing to the plaintiff in Norway. On receipt of such orders, the plaintiff issued confirmation notes in writing which it sent to the Scottish agents. These confirmation notes were in turn sent . . . to the sub-agent in Ireland with a copy for the customer. Each of these confirmation notes contained on its face the following reference: 'This order is booked subject to general trade rules adopted by Norwegian, Swedish and Finnish Papermakers Associations.' Reference to such trade rules was not set out on any other document arising in the course of dealings between the parties nor were the rules themselves ever furnished to the defendant.

When the goods were ready for delivery, they were dispatched by sea under a bill of lading and were accompanied by an invoice. The goods were paid for by acceptance of a bill of exchange and it was at that stage that a copy invoice was received by the defendant.

The general trade rules adopted by Norwegian, Swedish and Finish Papermakers Association were established in 1925 and were revised in 1929. A further revision took place in 1980. Neither the 1925 rules nor the 1929 rules contained any provision for reservation of title to the property in the goods supplied. The rules of 1980 introduced such a provision for the first time.

Both the 1925 rules and the 1929 rules showed clearly that they were general trade rules adopted by the Norwegian, Swedish and Finnish Papermakers Associations. The 1980 rules were printed without any such acknowledgment. This was apparently in the belief that such rules might have contravened provisions of the EEC as to cartels. In any event, the only copies circulated in this country were circulated on behalf of members of the Finnish Papermakers Association and made no reference to such rules having been adopted by any other association.

For the terms of these 1980 rules to apply to the Contracts of Sale between the plaintiff and the defendant, it is necessary for the plaintiff to establish that the parties contracted with knowledge of the existence of these rules and of their provisions. The plaintiff submits that it has discharged the onus of proof in relation to this issue of fact by showing that the confirmation notes came to the notice of the defendant and that this company continued to trade with the plaintiff thereafter. The defendant contends that the fact that its dealings were subject to general rules was never brought to its notice . . .

The evidence upon which the plaintiff relies is essentially that of its sub-agent in Ireland. His evidence is that in most cases he left the confirmation note personally at the reception desk in the defendant's offices, in an envelope marked for the accounts department. His explanation for using the expression 'in most cases' was that he did not know if he got these documents in all cases. If his evidence is correct, then most of these documents should have come to the actual notice of the accounts department and should have been filed with the other documents relating to the same transactions.

The evidence on behalf of the defendant is that these documents never reached the company. The financial controller of the company and also its secretary gave evidence that he had never seen a confirmation note relating to the orders of newsprint from the plaintiff. Any document left at the reception desk addressed to the accounts department would have been passed to him. The chief executive of the defendant also gave evidence to the effect that he had never seen a confirmation note relating to these orders. The liquidator gave evidence that he had not personally inspected the files of the company, but had directed his assistant to seek the documentation to the relevant transactions from the financial controller. The documents furnished included the relevant invoices but no confirmation notes. The liquidator subsequently directed his assistant to make a further search and his assistant gave evidence that he had searched but had found no further documents and specifically had not found any confirmation notes. The only other evidence relevant to this issue of fact was that of the Scottish agent who confirmed the procedural steps taken in relation to the making of orders.

The evidence of the Irish sub-agent suggest that the Scottish agent may have been mistaken in stating that the confirmation notes together with the copy were sent to him in relation to each order. This seems unlikely, though there did seem to be some doubt from the documents produced by the Irish sub-agent as to whether he always sent on the original confirmation note rather than a copy of it.

I found the financial controller to be a truthful witness and I accept his evidence that he never saw a confirmation note. I also accept the evidence of the chief executive to the same effect and that of the liquidator's assistant that no such documents were to be found in the records of the company. I do not accept the evidence of the Irish sub-agent that he left these documents at the reception desk of the company as he said. In particular, I found his explanation of the reason why these documents were not left with the company in all cases unconvincing. It seems to me also that as the arrangement between the sub-agent and the defendant was that he would ensure a four-to-six weeks supply of newsprint it is probable that he did not consider it necessary for the company to be given details of the orders he was placing.

It follows from this view of the facts that I find that the plaintiff has not established that the contractual arrangements between it and the defendant included the general trade rules . . .

Case 28. In re Stokes & McKiernan Ltd
High Court, unreported, 12 December 1978

When a receiver was appointed to the company it was in possession of unpaid goods supplied by four suppliers and the question arose concerning the ownership of these goods. The four suppliers claimed ownership and possession on foot of reservation of title clauses and claimed a right to trace the purchase price of goods which had been resold. Two suppliers claimed the return of goods which had been paid for.

Held that each of the four suppliers was entitled to the return of the goods in the possession of the company at the time of the receiver's appointment. The company was bound to account to the four suppliers for monies obtained from the resale of goods sold in the course of business. The claim by the two suppliers for the return of paid goods was dismissed in that the reservation of title clauses were not effective to retain ownership in such goods.

McWilliam J.:

. . . The company at all material times carried on the business of wholesale distributors of electrical and motor factoring goods. Each of four companies which supplied goods to the company has claimed to be the owner of certain goods supplied by it to the company and in the possession of the company on 14 April 1978, and to be entitled to trace the proceeds of their goods sold by the company and to recover such money as was held by the company on their behalf. These four companies are Oerlikon Electrodes (Ireland) Ltd (hereinafter called Oerlikon), Thor Appliances Ltd (hereinafter called Thor), A.E.T. Ltd (hereinafter called AET) and Tecalemit Garage Equipment Company Ltd (hereinafter called Tecalemit).

In the case of Oerlikon, new conditions of sale were introduced in April 1977. At this time its account with the company was clear. The new conditions included the following: '12. *Ownership:* (a) The risk in the goods passes to the buyer upon delivery but equitable and beneficial shall remain with the seller until full payment has been received (each order being considered as a whole), or until prior re-sale in which case the seller's beneficial entitlement shall attach to the proceeds of re-sale or to the claim for such proceeds: (b) Should the goods become constituents of or be converted into other products whilst subject to the seller's equitable and beneficial ownership, they shall have the equitable and beneficial ownership in such other products as if they were solely and simply the goods and accordingly sub-clause (a) shall as far as possible apply to such other products.'

Evidence has been given on behalf of Oerlikon that notice of this new condition was sent to each of its customers, including the company, in April 1977, but that the acknowledgment note sent with it was not returned by the company, as was the case with many other customers. Evidence was given by the general manager of the company that he had never seen the notice and by the receiver that he did not find any such notice amongst the papers of the company. The probabilities are that the notice was received by the company but that no particular consideration was given to it. After the introduction of the new conditions an order . . . was placed with Oerlikon by the company and the goods were delivered. Part of this order . . . was in the possession of the company when the receiver was appointed and the remainder had been sold.

In the case of Thor, all invoices and receipts contained the following condition subject to which all goods supplied by them were sold, that is to say: 'The title of goods sold shall not pass to the buyer until the full purchase price and any sums due have been paid by the buyer to the seller, but the risk in the goods passes to the buyer on delivery of the goods.' Thor claims to be entitled to a sum of which some is the value of goods sold prior to the appointment of the receiver and the remainder is the value of goods in the possession of the company at the time of his appointment. There were also, at the time of the appointment of the receiver, goods supplied by Thor in the possession of the company . . . which had been paid for by the company. Thor also claims to be entitled to these goods under the conditions of sale. It has not been disputed that the goods were sold by Thor subject to the condition, and the goods in the possession of the company at the time of the appointment of the receiver, which had not been paid for, have been returned to Thor.

In the case of AET it is claimed that the goods were sold subject to the following conditions: '10. *Passing Of Property*. The property in the goods shall not pass to the customer until the full purchase price (less any agreed discount or other deductions) has been paid.' Each consignment of goods was delivered with a despatch note which contained the following statement at the bottom of it, i.e., 'All goods are sold subject to the company's General Conditions of Sale, a copy of which is available on request.' Following delivery of the goods an invoice was sent which contained the same statement. It is claimed that the company was not aware of these conditions and was not bound by them. A large number of copy statements and invoices from 1976 onwards which contain the statement mentioned above has been produced. At least one despatch note signed on behalf of the company has also been produced but the date on the copy furnished to me is not legible. I am satisfied that the company purchased the goods with notice of the condition and is bound by it . . .

In the case of Tecalemit, new conditons of sale were introduced in

February 1977, when the following condition was included for the first time, that is to say: '5. *Property in Goods*. Notwithstanding any agreed terms of payment, no consignment or installation shall be deemed completed so as to vest the same in the purchaser until fully paid for, and all materials, plant and machinery, whether erected or not, shall remain the company's property until the whole purchase price has been paid, and the company shall, in addition to any other remedy, have the right to cancel the contract and to remove them or any part thereof if the price be not paid in accordance with the contract, so as to recoup itself to or for any sum or damage owing or due to itself.' Although the receiver only found a copy of the previous conditions of sale, I am satisfied that the new conditions were brought to the notice of the company when they were introduced. Tecalecmit claims a sum of which an amount is due in respect of goods sold by the company prior to the appointment of the receiver and . . . the remainder is in respect of goods still in the possession of the company at the time of his appointment. In addition, there were, at the time of the appointment of the receiver, goods . . . in the possession of the company which had been paid for by the company. All the goods were supplied between the months of December 1977 and April 1978.

The condition relied upon by each claimant is different, but each condition, in one form of words or another, contains the provision that the property in the goods shall not pass until the full price has been paid for them. It has not been suggested that, where such a clause applies, it is not effective to retain the property in the goods in the vendor while the goods remain in the possession of the purchaser, and I do not think it could now be so argued (see *Aluminium Industrie Vaassen BV v Romalpa Aluminium Ltd (1976)*). Accordingly, each of the claimants is entitled to the return of the goods in the possession of the company at the time of the appointment of the receiver which had not been paid for or the price for which he may have sold them.

In the case of Oerlikon the condition provided that, in the case of re-sale, Oerlikon's beneficial entitlement should attach to the proceeds of the re-sale or to the claim to such proceeds. This is a perfectly clear condition and the company was bound to hold the proceeds of the re-sale of the goods on trust for Oerlikon and Oerlikon is entitled to follow the proceeds of this sale in accordance with the decision in the *Romalpa Case*.

The conditions of the sales by the other three claimants do not inlcude any express condition that the claimants' rights should attach to the purchase money on a re-sale by the company. Although there were references in the judgments to an additional clause in the condition in the *Romalpa Case*, which clause is not included in the conditions before me, it seems to me that the decision in that case is based on the ground that the goods remained the property of the vendor and, although the purchaser was entitled to re-sell them in the course of his business, the purchaser was selling on behalf of the vendor to the extent to which money was still owing to the vendor in respect of the goods and that the purchaser was, therefore, bound to account to the vendor for this money. I accept that this is the position and that the claimants in this case are entitled to trace the purchase price of their goods in the hands of the receiver.

A further point arises in the claims by Thor and Tecalcemit with regard to the goods in the hands of the receiver which had been fully paid for. This is a question of the construction of the two conditions. In the *Romalpa Case* the condition was that 'ownership . . . will only be transferred to the purchaser when he has met all that is owing to A.I.V. no matter on what grounds.' The two conditions in the present case are not so strong as this or so clear and it appears to me that, where two interpretations are equally applicable, I should construe a condition most strongly against the party who has prepared it for his own advantage. It seems to me that the phrase 'any sums due' in the Thor condition is equally referable to sums due in respect of the goods sold as to all sums due on any contract and it would have been perfectly easy to make the condition clear in this respect if it was so desired. The clause in the Tecalemit contract is quite different and it seems to me that this clause on its ordinary meaning did only refer to the purchase price of the goods sold on the particular contract in which the condition was included.

Accordingly, I will refuse the claims of these two companies in this respect.

Case 29. Frigoscandia (Contracting) Ltd v Continental Irish Meat Ltd

High Court [1982] I.L.R.M. 396

The plaintiff sold machinery to the defendant on terms which allowed payment to be made by instalments. The conditions of sale included a retention of title clause. When the defendant went into liquidation there were sums outstanding and the plaintiff sought the return of the machinery.

Held that the retention of title clause clearly established that the entire property in the machinery was to be retained by the plaintiff until all the sums that were owing had been paid.

McWilliam J.:

This case concerns the construction and effect of a clause which, in one form or another, is becoming increasingly common in contracts for the sale of goods. Here, the goods consist of refrigerating equipment for a factory producing meat products of a hamburger or similar nature . . .

The machine was sold by the plaintiff subject to conditions which included the following: (1) Until all sums due to the seller have been fully paid to it, the plant, machinery and materials supplied by the seller herein shall remain the seller's personal property and retain its character as such no matter in what manner affixed or attached to any structure. (2) If the buyer fails fully to perform this contract, the unpaid portion of the purchase price shall, at the option of the seller, become immediately due and payable without notice, together with all reasonable legal or collection agency fees incurred in the collection thereof. (3) In the case of default, the seller reserves the right to enter upon the premises where the materials are located and take possession of and remove the same, if the seller so elects. In the event of such removal the seller may retain all payments made therefor as compensation for the use of the materials.

Essentially, there is no dispute about the facts. The machine was supplied and installed and put into operation but only a comparatively small quantity of samples had been produced before the bank appointed the second-named defendant as receiver of the property of the first-named defendant. At this time there was, and there still is, a sum . . . due to the plaintiff in respect of the contract.

On behalf of the plaintiff it is claimed that the machine is still the property of the plaintiff and a claim is made for its return, but I understand that the plaintiff, in fact, agreed to a sale of the factory with the machine without prejudice to its claim and will be agreeable to accept the money still outstanding in satisfaction of its claim.

On behalf of the defendant it is argued that the property in the goods passed either on delivery or once use commenced, that the terms of the contract were only effective to create a charge on the machine or some other form of security for the purchase price, that this was not registered in accordance with the provisions of s.99 of the *Companies Act 1963*, and is, therefore, void as against the receiver and the creditors of the defendant company.

I had occasion to consider the effect of a number of these clauses last December in a case of *In re Stokes & McKiernan Ltd* (Case 28). I was then referred to the case *Aluminium Industrie Vaassen BV v Romalpa Aluminium Ltd (1976)* which held . . . that a clause such as condition (1) in the present case was effective to retain the property in the goods in the vendor even though the goods were in the possession of the purchaser. Unfortunately, the very full judgment of Slade J. in the case of *Bond Worth Ltd (1979)* had not then been delivered and I did not advert to the considerations which influenced Slade J. in coming to the conclusion that the clause in the contract he was construing (which was similar to the clause in one of the four contracts in the *McKiernan Case)* created equitable charges only on the property sold and was not effective to retain the property in the goods in the vendor.

As pointed out by Slade J. the clauses in the *Bond Worth Case* and the *Romalpa Case* were very different. The clause in the *Bond Worth Case* was as follows: 'The risk in the goods passess to the buyer upon delivery, but equitable and beneficial ownership shall remain with us until full payment

has been received (each order being considered as a whole) or until prior
resale, in which case our beneficial entitlement shall attach to the proceeds
of resale or to the claim for such proceeds.'

The clause in the *Romalpa Case* was similar to that in the present case in
that the entire property in the goods was expressed, although in a different
form, to be retained by the vendor until all that was owing had been paid.
The clause was as follows: 'The ownership of the material to be delivered
by AIV will only be transferred to purchaser when he has met all that is
owing to AIV, no matter on what grounds.'

A difficulty which arises with regard to clauses of this nature is that they
are included in the contracts to secure the payment to the vendor of the
price of the goods and therefore it may be said, as has been argued, that
the goods, once delivered, are intended to be held by the purchaser as
security for such payment and that the transaction is in the category of a
mortgage in that the vendor, although retaining ownership or an interest in
the goods, cannot take possession of them provided that the specified
instalments are paid, and that this leads to the conclusion that such a
clause must be treated as creating a mortgage or a charge over the goods.

In my opinion such a conclusion can have no general application to these
clauses and each case must depend on its own facts. The parties to a
contract can agree to any terms they wish and, amongst others, they can
agree that the property in the goods shall not pass to the purchaser until
all the instalments of the purchase price have been paid; see s. 17 of the
Sale of Goods Act 1893. The court has to decide what was the intention of
the parties as shown by the provisions of the whole agreement. When
expressions such as 'equitable and beneficial ownership remaining with the
vendor' are used or the nature or circumstances of the transaction make it
unlikely that there could have been an intention that the property in the
goods should not pass immediately to the purchaser, the ascertainment of
the intention of the parties may present difficulty and require an earnest
consideration of all the facts of the case. In the present case no such
difficulty arises. The clause itself is clear, there was only one article sold,
this article was intended to be kept in the factory of the purchaser and it
was of such a nature that its re-sale could not have been reasonably
contemplated by the parties.

Accordingly, I am of opinion that the plaintiff is entitled to succeed in
its claim.

Case 30. Sugar Distributors Ltd v Monaghan Cash & Carry Ltd
High Court [1982] I.L.R.M. 399

The plaintiff sold a consignment of sugar to the defendant. There was
a reservation of title clause printed on the face of each of the plaintiff's
invoices. When the defendant went into liquidation the plaintiff sought

the return of the unsold sugar which remained in the defendant's possession.

Held that the plaintiff was entitled to the return of the unsold sugar.

Carroll J.:

This case concerns a retention of title contained on the front of the plaintiff's invoices sent out to customers and marked 'Conditions of Sale'.

This form of clause is as follows:

1. The ownership of the sugar to be delivered as per invoice shall only be transferred to the purchaser when the full amount of the purchase price has been discharged. In default of payment title shall remain with Sugar Disbributors Ltd and it shall have the right to repossess the sugar without notice or other formality.

There are two other clauses also shown on the face of the invoice which are not relevant to the issues here . . .

The . . . question for consideration is the legal effect of such a condition. Counsel for the plaintiff opened to me two Irish cases, the first of these, *In Re Stokes and McKiernan Ltd* (Case 28), McWilliam J. considered four different retention of title clauses. In the 'Oerlikon' clause, the relevant provision was that *equitable and beneficial ownership should remain*. In the 'Thor' clause, the relevant provision was that *title of the goods sold should not pass*. In the 'AET' clause the relevant provision was that the *property in the goods should not pass*. In the 'Tecalamit' clause, the provision was that *all materials (etc.) should remain the company's property*.

In this case, the retention clause refers to *'ownership' only being transferred when* payment made and in default *title should remain*.

In the second case, *Frigoscandia v Continental Irish Meat Ltd* (Case 29), the relevant clause provides that *until payment, plant etc. should remain the seller's personal property*.

Counsel also cited two English cases. In *Aluminium Industrie Vaassen BV v Romalpa Aluminium Ltd* (1976) the relevant clause provided that the *ownership of the material etc. would only be transferred to the purchaser when, etc.* In *In re Bond Worth Ltd* (1979) the relevant clause provided that the *equitable and beneficial ownership of the goods was to remain* with the sellers until full payment.

In deciding the *Stokes and McKiernan Case* in favour of all four claimants under the retention of title clauses, McWilliam J. adopted the views expressed in the *Romalpa Case*. When he came to deliver judgment in the *Frigoscandia Case,* he adverted to the fact that the judgment of Slade J. in the case of *Bond Worth Ltd* had not then been delivered and that the clause in that case was similar to one of the four contracts in the *McKiernan Case*, (i.e. the 'Oerlikon' clause). But he still held that the claimant in the *Frigoscandia Case* was entitled to succeed.

In the *Bond Worth Case*, Slade J. held that the legal title or property in the goods passed to the buyer on delivery.

In my opinion the clause in this case is not similar to the *Bond Worth Case*. It is similar to the one in the *Romalpa Case* and to three of the clauses considered in the *Stokes and McKiernan Case*. The entire property in the goods (i.e. ownership/title) is expressed to remain in the vendor until payment. In my opinion the retention of title clause departs from the usual debtor/creditor relationship and shows an intention to create a fiduciary relationship. I adopt the views of McWilliam J. in *Stokes and McKiernan Ltd* as follows:

> Although there were references in the judgments to an additional clause in the condition in the *Romalpa Case*, which clause is not included in the conditions before me, it seems to me that the decision in that case is based on the ground that the goods remained the property of the vendor and although the purchaser was entitled to resell them in the course of his business, the purchaser was selling on behalf of the vendor to the extent to which money was still owing to the vendor in respect of the goods and that the purchaser was therefore bound to account to the vendor for his money. I accept that this is the position and that the claimants in this case are entitled to trace the purchase price of their goods in the hands of the receiver.

Case 31. In re Galway Concrete Ltd (In Liquidation)
High Court [1983] I.L.R.M. 402

The company ordered a piece of machinery and installed it as plant in its premises. Payment was to be made by instalments. It was provided that the goods were to remain the property of the suppliers until the purchase price had been paid in full. On the company's liquidation before the full price was paid the question arose as to the ownership of the machinery. The liquidator argued that the machinery had been substantially incorporated into the premises and that the retention of title clause was of no effect. The suppliers contended that whilst the machinery had been affixed to the premises it was in the nature of a tenant fixture removable at any time and that the right to remove it remained vested in the suppliers.

Held that the machinery had become so affixed to the premises as to become part of it but since this was for the purpose of the company's trade it was in the nature of a tenant fixture which could be removed by the tenant. Accordingly, the suppliers were entitled to regain possession of the machinery.

Keane J.:

. . . An oral agreement as to the method of payment for the plant was entered into between the company and the suppliers and a written memorandum of that agreement was signed on behalf of both parties in September 1979. That agreement provided *inter alia* as follows:

General Conditions: The complete plant with all attachments remain our our property Malachy Quinn (Machinery) Ltd, until paid for in full.

The plant to be insured fully for all risks and damage. Certificate of Insurance to be sent to us for confirmation annually. The plant to be maintained to our satisfaction with all spares replaced by Galway Concrete Ltd, when required. Our personnell (*sic*) allowed free access to the site and plant at all times.

Written agreement from Galway Concrete confirming the goods are the property of Malachy Quinn (Machinery) Ltd, until paid for in full.

. . . It is submitted on behalf of the liquidator that the plant, upon becoming affixed to the land in the manner just described, became part thereof, that is components thereupon lost the character of chattels and that the property in them became vested in the owner of the land under the maxim *quid quid plantatur solo, solo cedit*. It is further submitted on his behalf that, as a necessary consequence, the clauses in the agreement under which the title to the plant was purportedly retained by the suppliers are of no effect.

It is submitted on behalf of the suppliers . . . that the component parts of the plant, while admittedly affixed to the land, were so affixed for the purpose of carrying on the company's trade and were, accordingly, 'tenant's fixtures' which were removable at any time. It is submitted on behalf of the suppliers that the right to remove them remained vested in the suppliers by virtue of the memorandum of agreement . . .

In an affidavit dated 22 March 1982, the secretary of the company, owners of the land, stated that they had no interest in the plant and claimed no title to it.

It was accepted that the plant had become so affixed to the land as to become part of it. It is also clear, and again this matter was not seriously in dispute, that it was so attached to the land for the purpose of carrying on the company's trade. It follows that, *quoad* the owner of the land, the plant was in the nature of a 'tenant's fixture' which could be severed and removed by the tenant at any time before the expiration of his tenancy. It is conceded on behalf of the liquidator that the company in the present case could avail of that right at any time during their occupation of the land, notwithstanding the fact that they were in occupation under a caretaker's agreement and not under any contract of tenancy. It is also clear that the owner of chattels let to a tenant under a hire purchase agreement containing a clause entitling the owner to re-possess the chattels in the event of a default in payment is entitled at common law to require the tenant to sever the chattels (where they have become tenant's fixtures) or to avail himself of the right of the tenant to enter and sever them.

In this case, the agreement did not contain any clause empowering the supplier to re-possess the goods in the event of a default in payment by the company. I have no doubt, however, that it was intended that the suppliers should have that right. This was essentially a conditional sale agreement, a form of agreement which has an important feature in common with hire purchase agreements, viz. a common intention that the property in the chattels should not pass from the owner to the hirer or purchaser until, at the earliest, the entire purchase price has been paid. As with hire purchase agreements, the reason for this is obviously to secure the owner against the possibility of a default in payment by the hirer or purchaser. Its objects would be wholly frustrated if the owner was not entitled to re-possess the chattels in the event of a default in payment on the part of the buyer or, at the very least, in the event of a repudiation on the part of the buyer of the agreement. Such authority as I have been able to discover supports the view that the right of the owner of the chattels to require the tenant to sever the chattels which have become tenant's fixtures or to avail himself of the right of the tenant to enter and sever them does not depend upon the existence of a clause expressly conferring on the owner a right to re-possess the chattels.

In the present case, there has been a default in payments by the company; and it is obvious that the liquidator does not intend to perform the company's obligation under the agreement by paying the arrears and meeting the further instalments as they become due. The company having thus clearly repudiated the agreement, although there has been no formal disclaimer of it by the liquidator, the suppliers, as between themselves and the company, are entitled to enter the site and remove the plant . . .

Case 32. Kruppstahl AG v Quitmann Products Ltd
High Court [1982] I.L.R.M. 551

The plaintiffs claimed against the defendant a sum for steel sold and delivered. The defendant was in receivership and the plaintiffs, relying on a retention of title clause in the contract, sought the return of (a) unworked steel and (b) worked steel in the defendant's possession.

Held that unworked steel in the defendant's possession remained the plaintiffs' property and could be reclaimed. In so far as the steel had been put to use in the manufacturing process, the defendant was constituted a trustee for the plaintiffs to the extent of its indebtedness, and its accountability operated as a charge upon the property for the discharge of such sums due. The realisation of any such security granted by way of charge created by the defendant, a registered company, was not permitted unless the particulars of the charged had been registered under the provisions of the *Companies Act 1963*. No such charge having been registered, the plaintiffs had no priority and the charge was void as against the claims of the other creditors.

Gannon J.:

It follows therefore that as between the defendant and other parties, including a debenture holder or other creditor, the unworked steel in the possession of the defendant which was delivered there by the plaintiffs pursuant to the German contract in respect of which payment was more than one month overdue is, according to Irish law, not the property of the defendant.

The next stage is to consider what are the requirements of Irish law in relation to any of the steel the property of the plaintiffs in the possession of the defendant which was put to use by the defendant with the agreement of the plaintiff in accordance with the German conditions and law in a manufacturing process notwithstanding the defendant's liability for overdue payments to the plaintiffs in respect thereof. This involves also a consideration of what effect, if any, can be given in Irish law to the agreement between the plaintiffs and the defendant in their conditions in relation to manufacturing goods incorporating the plaintiffs steel (that is for which payments were overdue) which were sold by the defendant to other parties. As paragraphs 2 to 7 inclusive of Clause A.III, as construed in accordance with German law, constitute an immediate assignment of future interests and an agreement for security for whatever indebtedness on the part of the defendant to the plaintiffs might later arise, paragraph 9 gives recognition to the applicability of Irish law relative to the enforcement of the security. In so far as the steel (the subject of overdue payment account) is put to use by the defendant in the manufacturing process, although the property of the plaintiffs, such use is with the consent of the plaintiffs as limited by the conditions. To that extent therefore the defendant is constituted trustees of property of the plaintiffs for which the defendant is accountable to the plaintiffs in the manner prescribed by the contract. The accountability is limited to the extent only of the indebtedness, and the manner of securing payment is a form of 'tracing' conforming to equitable principles . . . As such it is in the nature of a charge upon the property as a means of security for the discharge of an indebtedness which is the primary factor in that agreement. But the agreement goes beyond the scope of mere tracing goods for their value. On the basis that German law permits the possessor of goods which are not his own property to sell and recover the value of his workmanship in converting them to other marketable articles the plaintiffs and the defendant have agreed that the property and the interest therein so conferred by German law upon the defendant in processed goods incorporating the plaintiffs steel (the subject of overdue payment account) are by this contract assigned in anticipation to the plaintiffs. Such agreement relates in part to an existing quantity of steel delivered by the plaintiffs but to the extent only that it may later be incorporated in a finished manufactured article not then in existence nor identifiable and only if and when such article should have been manufactured. Any such assignment can be construed only as an equitable interest in the nature of a floating charge manifestly created only as a means of security for a potential indebtedness . . .

The realisation or enforcement of any such security granted by way of charge created by a company will not be permitted in Ireland unless the particluars of the charge have been registered with the registrar of companies pursuant to s. 100 of the *Companies Act 1963* . . .

Case 33. Somers v James Allen (Ireland) Ltd
High Court [1984] I.L.R.M. 437

The defendant supplied animal feed to a company. The contract contained a retention of title clause. When the plaintiff was appointed receiver over the company's assets the goods supplied were identifiable and had not been used in a manufacturing process. The plaintiff sought the assistance of the court with regard to the effect of the retention of title clause and argued, *inter alia*, that the supplier of goods to a manufacturer who knows that the goods are to be used in manufacturing cannot rely on a simple reservation of title clause.

Held that the simplicity of retention of title clause did not prevent it from being an effective reservation of title of the goods still existing in the supplied state. The title had not been extinguished by manufacture. The clause was not sufficiently complex to create a charge over manufactured goods and had the goods been manufactured the defendant's title to the goods would have disappeared.

Carroll J.:

The defendant supplied the goods subject to conditions of sale set out on the back of its invoice. It includes the following clause: '9. The transfer of title to you of the goods as detailed in this contract shall not occur until the invoice covering same has been paid in full, and accordingly, the goods wherever situtated shall be thereupon at your risk.' It is not denied that the conditions formed part of the contractual relations between the company and the defendant.

Counsel for the plaintiff's second proposition is based on a *dictum* of Bridge L.J. in *Borden UK Ltd v Scottish Timber Products* (1979) to the effect that if a seller of goods to a manufacturer who knows his goods are to be used in the manufacturing process before they are paid for, wishes to reserve to himself an effective security for the payment of the price, he cannot rely on a simple reservation of title clause. Counsel submits that the reservation of title clause in this case is simple, the goods were intended to be used in a manufacturing process and therefore the clause was ineffectual to reserve a security . . .

The second proposition is based on a misinterpretation of the *dictum* of Bridge L.J. in the *Borden Case*. The learned judge was referring to an attempt to acquire rights over the manufactured article. He goes on to say in the next sentence: 'If he (i.e. the seller) wishes to acquire rights over the finished product, he can only do so by express contractual stipulation.' In this case I am not concerned with whether the reservation of title clause was effective to create or preserve an interest in the goods to be manufactured. I am concerned only with goods which still exist in the same state as they were supplied by the defendant. They have not been mixed with similar goods or transmuted into a manufactured product. The question therefore is whether a simple reservation of title clause is effective to reserve title in the goods in the same state as they were supplied.

In the *Borden Case* Bridge L.J. was prepared to admit this. While he says that he is attracted by the view that the beneficial interest in the resin passed to the buyers, and the sellers retained bare legal title, he goes on to say:

> But I am quite content to assume that this is wrong and to suppose that up to the moment when the resin was used in manufacture it was held by the buyers in trust for the sellers in the same sense in which a bailee or a factor or an agent holds goods in trust for his bailor or his principal. If that was the position then there is 'no doubt that as soon as the resin was used in the manufacturing process it ceased to exist as resin, and accordingly the title to the resin simply disappeared.'

In the same case, Templeman L.J. said:

> They (the buyers) could not sell and make title to the resin because the title had been retained by the sellers. But the buyers were free to employ the resin in the manufacture of chipboard.
>
> When the resin was incorporated in the chipboard, the resin ceased to exist, the sellers' title to the resin became meaningless and the sellers' security vanished. There was no provision in the contract for the buyers to provide substituted or additional security. The chipboard belonged to the buyers.

In my opinion, the simplicity of the provision in the contract does not *per se* prevent its being an effective reservation of title of the goods as supplied to the company and still existing in that state. *Prima facie* title is not to be transferred until payment in full. That title has not been extinguished by manufacture. It still exists, and because payment has not been made, that title has not been transferred . . .

In *Kruppstahl AG v Quitmann Products Ltd* (Case 32) . . . a detailed retention of title clause [was in issue] which dealt with *inter alia* handling, processing, blending and mixing the goods which were steel. The contract was to be construed according to German law but that does not affect the basic issue at stake here.

Gannon J. held that as between the defendant (the buyer) and other parties, including a debenture holder or other creditors, the unworked steel in the possession of the defendant in respect of which payment was more than one month overdue was not the property of the defendant.

In considering the position regarding the steel used in the manufacturing process, he held that the interest created was in the nature of a floating charge. The realisation of such security granted by way of charge was not permitted unless the particulars were registered pursuant to s. 100 of the *Companies Act 1963*. Therefore any claims by the plaintiffs against the defendant for overdue payments for any steel used in the manufacturing process were deferred to the claims of the debenture holder and receiver.

This case therefore illustrates that a seller can make an effective reservation of title to goods prior to manufacture but if he requires security over the manufactured goods the buyer will have to grant him this and this would require registration . . .

In this case the clause in question is not complex enough to create a charge over future manufactured goods, the title to which cannot exist at the date of the contract. The contract deals only with the present title to the goods sold and not with future title of goods to be manufactured.

The *Sale of Goods Act 1893* allows the parties to decide when the property in the goods is to be transferred to the buyer (s. 17). Here the parties have agreed by a simple condition to reserve title and risk to the seller until payment. The goods were to be used in manufacture. It follows therefore that the unpaid seller intended to retain title as long as those goods existed, as supplied. When those goods were manufactured into another product, the seller's title disappeared . . .

Case 34. S.A. Foundries du Lion MV v International Factors (Ireland) Ltd
High Court [1985] I.L.R.M. 66

The plaintiff manufactured goods which were imported into Ireland by a third party. The defendant was a company which had obtained possession of the plaintiff's goods as factors* for the third party. The plaintiff supplied the goods under conditions of sale which included a retention of title clause. The defendant argued that the plaintiff in a telex message waived the retention of title clause.

Held that the plaintiff had not waived its retention of title clause and that the defendant was liable to account to the plaintiff for the goods.

*A *factor* is an agent remunerated by a commission, who is entrusted with the possession of goods to sell in his or her own name, as apparent owner.

Barrington J.:

Condition 14 of the printed conditions on the back of this invoice, contained two sentences, and was in the following terms: 'Unless there is stipulation to the contrary, the goods sold and delivered remain our property until the moment we receive complete settlement. The goods may be re-sold or used by the customer through normal trade channels, but may not be given as security.' The condition quoted is succinctly worded but I am satisfied it is a retention of title clause, and was accepted by the defendant as being a retention of title clause, of the kind discussed in *Aluminium Industrie Vaassen BV v Romalpa Aluminium Ltd* (1976) and in *Frigoscandia v Continental Irish Meat Ltd* (Case 29) but, as McWilliam J. pointed out in the latter case, each of these clauses arises in a particular contract and must be interpreted in accordance with its own terms and the other terms of the contract in which it arises.

There has been no serious controversy about the meaning of clause 14. It consists of two sentences. The first sentence provides that the goods are to remain the property of the manufacturers until the manufacturers receive complete settlement. The second sentence permits the importer to deal with the goods in the normal course of trade but forbids him to give them as security. There can be no doubt that the goods, as long as they remain in the importer's warehouse, remain the property of the manufacturer. The exporter is merely a bailee of the goods. There can be no doubt either that the importer may not give the goods as security. Again there can be no doubt that the importer can sell the goods in the normal course of trade. The real difficulty is concerning the proceeds of such sales. It appears to me that such proceeds are proceeds of sales of goods which were, at the time of the sale, the property of the manufacturer. It would therefore appear, on the principles of the *Romalpa Case*, that the importer must account to the manufacturer for the proceeds of the sale until all monies owing from the importer to the manufacturer in respect of the goods have been paid. If therefore the proceeds can be traced in the hands of the importer or in the hands of any person who took them with notice of the retention of title clause it would appear that the manufacturer is entitled to trace them.

The real controversy in the present case turns upon the question of whether the plaintiff, as manufacturers, in fact waived the retention of title clause.

The background to this dispute is as follows: The sales manager of the plaintiff has been doing business with the importers, the third party, for some time and regarded them as good customers who always paid their accounts on time. He was on good personal terms with . . . the managing director of the third party.

Unknown to the sales manager however, the third party were experiencing cash shortages in December 1982 and for that reason on 20 December 1982 they entered into a factoring agreement with the defendant for the discounting of debts due to them in respect of the sale of the plaintiff's stoves to their customers. In the course of these negotiations the defendant was made aware of the retention of title clause and of condition 14 of the terms on which the plaintiff had supplied the stoves to the third party.

On 6 December 1982 the defendant sent a telex to the sales manager of the plaintiff in the following terms:

Taylor Factor, their debts with International Factors (Ireland) Ltd. It is noted that you retain title to the goods until paid. Please confirm that goods sold onwards by Taylors and factored will be excluded from Clause 14 of your conditions of sale.

This was the first the sales manager heard of any factoring agreement, and he was puzzled by it. On 15 December 1982 he telexed the third party quoting the telex he had received from the defendant and adding the query—'Could you tell us what it means and what they want from us.'

The managing director of the third party subsequently spoke with the sales manager on the telephone and they discussed these telexes. I am satisfied, on the evidence of both of them that the sales manager's attitude at this stage was that he was prepared to consider the problem which was put to him but that he had not yet reached a conclusion as to what he should do. He regarded the third party as a good customer; he was on good terms with its managing director and he was prepared to discuss the problem of the retention of title clause further. He was planning to visit Ireland on business and hoped to discuss the matter further with the managing director then. Unfortunately when he visited Ireland the managing director was engaged at the Labour Court and was unable to see him.

On 22 December 1982 the managing director wrote to the sales manager in the following terms: Sorry I could not meet you at Dublin Airport but as Leo explained I was engaged at a Labour Court hearing. However I trust we will meet in the near future.

With regard to the telex you received from F.P. Crowley and your subsequent telex to me on 15 December I would explain that what we require from you is a telex granting exclusion from clause 14 of your conditions of sale goods sold onwards by John R. Taylor Ltd and factored. Because of the very extended credit we must give in this market together with the imposition of VAT at point of entry I have decided to factor a proportion of our debts with the Bank of Ireland and this in turn will give a much healthier cash flow to the company. In order to do this the bank want this exclusion which in fact means that cookers sold by John R. Taylor to a client and installed in that person's house are excluded from your clause 14. Really it shouldn't present you with a problem as I don't think we could get these cookers back anyhow.

Our principal suppliers have deleted such clause . . .

On 23 December 1982—and presumably before he had received the letter . . . the sales manager telexed the defendant in the following terms: 'We could accept to cancel the second sentence concerning the goods resold by Taylor to his customers. But we confirm that we maintain the first sentence concerning our property on the goods being in the inventory by Taylor.'

Most of the controversy at the hearing has turned upon the meaning of this telex. The sales manager gave evidence at the hearing before me and he is a man with considerable command of the English language. Nevertheless the telex is clearly the composition of a person whose first language is not English.

Meanwhile the defendant had, on 20 December 1982, entered into a factoring agreement with the third party. This related both to accounts concerning goods supplied by the plaintiff and to other accounts. The fact that this agreement was entered into before the alleged waiver was received by the defendant is not material as the general manager of the defendant told me, and I accept, that the defendant would not have factored any invoices relating to goods supplied by the plaintiff until they had received a waiver from the plaintiff.

When, however, the general manager of the defendant received the telex of 23 December 1983 he proceeded to discount invoices in respect of goods supplied by the plaintiff, feeling that he had a sufficient waiver from the plaintiff to justify him in doing this. He did not go back to the plaintiff to clarify the telex as he did not consider this necessary.

The sales manager was however surprised that no one came back to him concerning the matter.

The general manager took the telex to mean that the plaintiff was waiving its rights in respect of goods which had been sold on by the third party and that they might be prepared even to waive their rights in respect of goods still retained in the third party's warehouses.

The sales manager, on the other hand says that what he intended to convey was that he might be prepared to waive the second sentence in condition 14 but that he would not under any circumstances waive the first sentence.

I am satisfied that the sales manager's interpretation of his telex is the correct one. It appears to me that the telex is no more than an expression of interest and goodwill which at the same time, indicates what is negotiable and what is not. It appears to me that the sales manager is saying that his rights under the second sentence are negotiable but that his rights under the first sentence are not. Or, possibly that he might waive his rights concerning goods which have been sold on but that he will not waive his rights concerning goods still retained in the third party's warehouse.

In any event it appears to me that while the telex is an indication that the plaintiff might, in certain circumstances, be prepared to waive some of its rights it does not itself waive any of its rights.

It therefore appears to me that the telex referred to did not waive any of the plaintiff's rights. No other alleged waiver is suggested and it is accepted that the defendant had notice of the retention of title clause in clause 14. Under these circumstances it appears to me that so far as the defendant is concerned the plaintiff retains all rights under clause 14 of its invoice.

CHAPTER 8.

TERMS OF A CONTRACT OF SALE

A statement becomes a contractual term if the maker of it, expressly or by implication, warrants it to be true. Contractual terms may be express or implied. The courts have implied terms into a contract for the sale of goods on the reasoning that the parties would have agreed to such terms if they had expressly considered them.

Statute, namely the *Sale of Goods and Supply of Services Act 1980* (which replaced the *Sale of Goods Act 1893* in this regard), has implied a number of terms into contracts of the sales of goods with stated consequences for the breach.

a. Implied Term as to Description

Section 13 of the combined Acts of 1893 and 1980 provides that where there is a contract for the sale of goods by description, there is an implied condition that the goods shall correspond with the description: *American Can Co. v Stewart* (Case 35), *O'Connor v Donnelly* (Case 36), *Egan v McSweeney* (Case 37), *McDowell v E.P. Sholedice & Co. Ltd* (Case 38), *T. O'Regan & Sons Ltd v Micro-Bio (Ireland) Ltd and Intervet Laboratories Ltd* (Case 40), *Webster Hardware (International) Ltd v Enfield Mills Ltd* (Case 39), *McCullough Sales Ltd v Chetham Timber Co. (Ireland) Ltd* (Case 41) and *Tokn Grass Products Ltd v Sexton & Co. Ltd* (Case 46).

Case 35. American Can Co. v Stewart
King's Bench (1915) 50 I.L.T.R. 132

The defendant in writing ordered a number of American adding machines from the plaintiffs, relying on statements made by their agent and on a book of instructions supplied which represented that the machines would add together sums of money and would reduce or convert the total obtained from pence to shillings and from shillings to pounds in one operation simultaneously. The process of reduction or conversion was carried out with the assistance of a 'conversion table' which was contained in the book of instructions. It was necessary in certain combinations of figures to adopt a particular process which has not pointed out either by the plaintiff's agent or in the book of instruction. After the delivery of the machines the defendant made his discovery that each machine would not accurately reduce the total to shillings and pence in one operation. He refused to accept or pay for the machines. The plaintiffs sued for the price.

Held that the plaintiffs had not supplied the articles contracted for. Therefore no property in the machines had passed to the defendant and he was not liable to accept or pay for them.

Kenny J.;

The great merit claimed for the instrument is its simplicity in operation. Counsel have worked the machine in our presence, and, while simplicity may be its leading characteristic in dealing with a decimal system, where no conversion is necessary, the moment one attempts to work it in connection with British currency I think it must occur to the operator that he is dealing with a very complicated design, and, as is admitted in the case, a design that does not ensure accuracy in every case where the conversion tables are applied. And it must be remembered that without the conversion tables no attempt can be made to use the machine for the purpose of addition of British currency so as to bring out a result showing pounds and shillings and pence under 20s. and 12 pence respectively—a state of things that has induced the argument that when the machine or instrument is spoken of it must be taken as the physical thing *plus* the conversion tables. The defendant's case is that while in a vast number of cases the figures are appropriate, there are many cases—his counsel said he could point out at least 1,340—in which they are not, and, consequently, that he did not get what he contracted for, namely, a machine which would in all cases add correctly, and in a single operation convert into British currency. The plaintiffs' agent called on the defendant at his office . . . on 25 March 1914, and having brought a sample machine with him, gave the defendant a demonstration in the working of it, showed him the advertisement of it, a book of instructions, and a conversion table, and told him that although it was a decimal machine it could be and was used for British currency by means of the conversion table, and that the conversion could be effected in one operation. The agent went away for a couple of hours, leaving the machine, book of instructions and conversion table with the defendant, and on his return found the defendant working at it. An agreement, in writing, for the purchase by the defendant of 30 of the machines was then come to, and four further agreements were signed appointing the defendant agent for the sale of the machines for the whole of Ireland except Ulster. The agent deposed that conversion could be carried out in one operation in nearly every case, but that in one or two cases a second small operation was necessary; but he admitted that he could not remember having told the defendant that there were any exceptions. The plaintiffs' manager gave a demonstration of the working of the machine. He took some combination of figures, such as the following: 39s. 15d., and while showing that the proper figure in the conversion table for 15d. was 88, admitted that the figure 80 in the table applicable to 39s. would not produce a correct result and that the next figure in the table, namely, 160, would have to be used. Again, with the figures £88 79s. 80d., admitted that if the figure 240, shown in the table for 79s., be used, a wrong answer would be the result. Three other combinations of figures were submitted to him, and he was obliged to admit that in those cases also a second operation was necessary. The defendant received the 30 machines some time between 30 April and 4 May, and on testing them seems to have discovered that they were not universally accurate; and on 4 May wrote to the plaintiffs explaining his position, and offering to return the instrument. On 7 May he wrote refusing to accept the machines. Now assuming, as I must, that the machine in several cases produces inaccurate results, is the defendant entitled to repudiate his contract and decline to accept or pay for the machines on the ground that they do not answer the description on which he bought? What he wanted and what was sold to him was a machine that would add currency figures swiftly and accurately, and would in a single operation convert the sum of that addition into its proper component parts of pounds, shillings and pence, and to effect that end he was furnished with an instrument and a cardboard conversion table. No result in conversion could be obtained without a combination of both, and I, therefore, think that when the 'machine' is referred to in connection with the process of conversion it must be taken as meaning the instrument *plus* the conversion table. Accuracy in the working of the machine thus constituted was essential to the defendant, not only in the user in his own establishment but as the plaintiffs' agent for sale. And the accuracy contracted for was accuracy that would be obtained with the tables on the conversion card. That seems to me to have been the subject-matter of the contract. A machine that in some instances involved more than a single operation for conversion would not have been a very marketable one—I do not think it matters whether that further operation was a mental or a manual one. It is sufficient to say that no such additional operation was contemplated by the plaintiffs or defendant at the date of the contract. The book of instructions and conversion table make no reference whatever to the necessity of any process save and except the use of the figures shown in the latter, and which figures have been demonstrated as not being effective in all combinations. The defendant bought on the description of the machine in the book of instruction, and in my opinion he did not get what he bargained for. It was argued before us that if there was any cause of action under the circumstances it was one for damages for breach of warranty, inasmuch as the property in the machines passed, it was said, to the defendant. Whether the property passed must depend on whether the plaintiffs supplied the thing contracted for. If they did not, no property passed, and the case seems to be almost as strong as that put by . . . Martin B. in *Azémar v Casella* (1867) where he says that if one offers to buy peas of another and the latter sells him beans it is not a case of warranty, but of non-performance of his contract . . .

Case 36. O'Connor v Donnelly
Circuit Court and High Cout [1944] Ir.Jur.Rep. 1

The plaintiff purchased a tin of 'John West Middle Cut' salmon in the defendant's shop which was for the purpose of human consumption. After eating some of the fish the plaintiff and his family suffered illness. He sued the defendant for damages under the *Sale of Goods Act 1893* alleging that he had made known the purpose for which the goods were being purchased and that he had relied on the seller's skill and judgment and that the goods did not correspond with the description and were not of merchantable quality.

Held that while the plaintiff had made known to the defendant the purpose for which the goods were required he had not relied on the defendant's skill and judgment. On the other hand, the sale was one by description and the goods supplied did not correspond with the description and were not of merchantable quality. The plaintiff was awarded damages.

Judge Davitt:

I find the facts to be as follows: The plaintiff is a farmer who resides on his farm of sixty acres . . . He has two daughters. Previous to taking up farming the plaintiff had kept a little shop in which, amongst other commodities, he sold tins of salmon and sardines. He did not often deal in salmon, but when he did buy it he preferred John West Middle Cut which he considered the best brand. The defendant has a grocery and provision shop and in the course of his business sells tinned salmon, including John West Middle Cut. The plaintiff did not deal exclusively with the defendant for his provisions, but made frequent purchases from him. On 6 December 1940 the plaintiff went into the defendant's shop and asked the assistant for a tin of salmon and a box of cheese. What he intended to buy was John West Middle Cut, and the assistant, possibly knowing his taste from previous experience, said 'John West Middle Cut?' and placed a tin of same, easily recognisable from the label, on the counter in front of the plaintiff, together with the box of cheese. The plaintiff paid for the goods, put them in his pocket, and went home. He and his two daughters had the salmon for their tea and, after an interval, all three were ill, the plaintiff alarmingly so, and his daughters to a lesser degree. I am satisfied, on the evidence, that the illness was the result of eating the salmon. These are the facts. They are all the facts necessary to determine the issue of liability in this case.

The next stage is to determine what interferences should be drawn from these facts. Did the plaintiff make known to the defendant, through his assistant, the particular purpose for which the goods were required? The answer is, of course, 'yes'. It was clearly understood that they were to be used as human food. Was this purpose made known to the defendant in such a way as to show that the plaintiff was relying on the defendant's skill and judgment? That is a question not so easy to answer. I am, however, reasonably free from doubt in answering in the negative. It is true, as was pointed out by Lord Wright in *Grant v Australian Knitting Mills* (1936), that the mere fact of purchase itself may raise the implication of reliance. He says:

> The reliance will seldom be express: it will usually arise by implication from the circumstances: thus to take a case like that in question, of a purchase from a retailer, the reliance will be in general inferred from the fact that a buyer goes to the shop in the confidence that the tradesman has selected his stock with skill and judgment: the retailer need know nothing about the process of manufacture: it is immaterial whether he be the manufacturer or not: the main inducement to deal with a good retail shop is the expectation that the tradesman will have bought the right goods of a good make.

The goods in question in *Grant's case* were woollen underwear, and the learned Law Lord's remarks should in reason be read as mainly applicable to goods of that general nature. It is worthy of note that in *Wren v Holt (1903)*, *Morelli v Fitch and Gibbons (1928)* and *Daniels v White & Sons and Tarbard (1938)*—all cases in which proprietary articles were sold over the counter—it was not found as a fact that the buyer relied upon the seller's skill and judgment. Quite apart from such considerations and from the circumstance that the plaintiff in this case was, in all probability (having regard to his previous experience of shop-keeping), possessed of just as much skill and judgment in relation to tinned salmon as the defendant or his assistant, I do not consider that the evidence in this case raises the implication of reliance. The plaintiff, in reality though not in words, asked for and received a tin of John West Middle Cut. In my opinion the proper, because on all the evidence the far more probable, implication is that he was relying, not on any skill or judgment of the defendant or his assistant, but on the reputation of a widely advertised, well known, and popular brand of tinned salmon with which he in fact was familiar and which he esteemed as the best on the market.

This inference of fact which I have drawn is quite sufficient to exclude the plaintiff from the benefit and operation of sub-sect. (1) of s. 14 (now s. 14 (4) of the Combined Acts). I think it right, however, to dispose of all

issues of fact relevant to this sub-section. It seems clear to me on the
evidence that the sale in this case was the sale of a specified article under
its trade name. Accepting the opinion of Farwell L.J., in *Bristol Tramways
& Carriage Co. v Fiat Motors Ltd* (1910), that a trade name has to be
acquired by user, I am satisfied to hold on the evidence in this case that
the name 'John West Middle Cut' is a trade name well established by user.
I am satisfied so to hold quite irrespective of the circumstance, not
established in evidence but impossible entirely to exclude from judicial
cognisance, that the merits and superiority of that brand have for ten years
past been proclaimed from almost every advertisement hoarding. I
therefore hold that the sale in this case was the sale of a specified article
under its trade name, and that on this ground also the plaintiff fails to
bring himself within, or rather is by the terms of the proviso excluded
from, the operation and benefit of the first sub-section of s. 14 of the Act.

Counsel for the plaintiff was not much disposed to base his case upon
this first sub-section, and preferred to rely more upon the second (also s.
14(2) of the Combined Acts). Was the sale in this case a 'sale by
description' with the consequence of an implied condition that the goods
were of merchantable quality? The answer to this question involves two
stages. We have first to be clear as to what constitutes a sale by description
within the meaning of the sub-section; and have then to determine whether
the facts of this case bring the sale within such meaning. The question as
to what constitutes a sale by description is not a particularly simple one.
The Act provides no definition, and it is clear from the authorities that
prior to the Act the expression was not one which had been defined
judicially. A review of the cases cited in argument, and of other cases
which appear to be relevant, leads to two conclusions: first, that the matter
is one which is not specifically covered by any authority binding upon this
court; and second, that it is not free from conflict of judicial opinion.

The relevant authorities in chronological order appear to be the
following: *Varley v Whipp*, *Wren v Holt*, *Wallis v Russell* (Case 42),
Bristol Tramways v Fiat Motors, *Thornett and Fehr v Beers & Sons*,
Morelli v Fitch and Gibbons, and *Daniels and Daniels v White & Sons and
Tarbard*. *The Sale of Goods Act* was adopted in New Zealand by the Sale
of Goods Act 1899, and a case of *Boys v Rice (1908)* would appear [to be
relevant].

I do not think it is necessary to review these cases in detail. It will be
sufficient for me to state their general effect. The only Irish authority is
Wallis v Russell (Case 42), which was decided after, though reported
before, *Wren v Holt*. The facts of the case are too familiar to require any
mention. The case was decided under the first sub-section, but FitzGibbon
and Holmes L.JJ., expressed opinions as to whether the sale of the crabs
in that case was a sale by description within the meaning of the second
sub-section, and the opinions were opposite. In no judgment in any of the
subsequent cases is their difference of opinion referred to. In *Morelli's
Case* and *Daniels' Case* the facts closely resembled the facts of the present

case. In all three there was a sale over the counter of a proprietary article of food or drink in a sealed container. *Wren's Case* differs in as much as the beer in that case was most probably draught beer. In each of these cases it was held that the sale was a sale by description, and the decision was for the plaintiff under the second sub-section. The decisions in *Morelli's Case* and *Daniels' Case* were based either mediately or immediately upon the authority of *Wren's Case* and the *Bristol Tramways Case*. In *Wren's Case* Vaughan Williams L.J. expressed a doubt as to whether the sale could properly be termed a sale by description, and his observation was dissented from by one member of the court, the other expressing no opinion. In the *Bristol Tramways Case* the remarks in the judgments relative to sales by description must, I think, be considered *obiter*, since there was no finding by the trial judge that the goods were not of merchantable quality, nor was such an inference clearly to be drawn from the facts. In none of the judgments in the cases mentioned was there any very close examination of what constitutes a sale by description within the meaning of the sub-section, and in none was there any consideration of *Varley v Whipp* and the observations made upon this point by Channel J. The only cases in which an approach was made towards attempting to define a sale by description are *Varely v Whipp (1901)* and *Thornett and Fehr v Beers & Sons (1919)*. The effect of these two cases is to indicate that there is a sale by description when the buyer relies in whole or in part on the description given.

   In these circumstances it is, I think, advisable to approach the construction of the Act with as open a mind as the circumstances permit. Section 13 of the Act (now s. 13(1) of the Combined Acts) relates to one aspect of a contract for the sale of goods by description, s. 14 (2) to another. What is meant by a contract for the sale of goods by description, or by saying that goods are bought by description? What is meant first and most obviously is that at some time a description has been attached to the goods, in effect, by one or other of the parties or both, and that this has been done during the formation of the contract. It is to be noted that ss. 13 and 14 occur in part 1 of the Act which relates to the formation of the contract of sale. The word 'description' in its ordinary sense includes shades or degrees of meaning varying from mere praise or commendation, through warranty in law, to something going to the very root and essence of the contract. For instance, on the sale of a horse the animal might be described by the vendor as a splendid animal, with beautiful action and so forth, without creating any legal obligations; or it might be described as sound in wind and limb, resulting in a warranty; or it might be described as a thoroughbred yearling colt X out of Y, which would be of the essence of the contract. Impressing a sale with the stamp or character of a sale by description differentiates it from other contracts of sale and involves important legal consequences. It is not, therefore, reasonable to assume that the statute could intend to invest with such importance words used by the parties in the formation of their contract, but used merely incidentally. A warranty is an agreement with reference to the goods but collateral to the main purpose of the contract, and involves its own particular legal consequences. Such a collateral agreement may accompany any contract, but a description which has the effect of introducing a condition into the contract itself must be something different. It is reasonable therefore to conclude that the description with which we are concerned is something more than a mere commendation, something above a warranty, something going to the very essence of the contract. This essential character of the description must originate with the parties themselves. Such a description, whether it originates with the buyer or the seller, will be of more immediate importance to the buyer, as he will be using it, or depending upon it, to ensure that his requirements whether for use or for resale will be fulfilled. If he wants the description to fulfil such a function he must by words or conduct make his wants known to the vendor. In every case of a sale of goods the buyer must make his requirements known to the seller, in some way or another, otherwise there would be no contract. We have come therefore to the crux of the matter, and to the difficulties mentioned by Holmes L.J. in his judgment in *Wallis v Russell* (quoted at page 93). Is every sale of goods a sale by description?

It is pointed out in *Benjamin on Sale* that while in the case of a contract for the sale of unascertained or future goods the goods can at the time of the making of the contract have no description save that given by the contract itself, it is otherwise in the case of a sale of specific goods. In such a case two descriptions of the goods may be in question. There is a description given by the buyer when indicating his requirements to the seller, and there is also the actual physical identity or appearance of the goods themselves. In the case of a sale of such specific goods over the counter there may be a question as to which of these descriptions is operative. The answer to that question must depend on the circumstances. If a man goes into a fruit shop and asks to buy an orange, and the shopkeeper tenders him an apple which he accepts and pays for, is that a sale by description? It is clear that the buyer attached no importance or reliance to his description. Suppose he asked for an apple in the first instance, is that a sale by description? Again I think not. Though the goods receive a description which goes to the root of the contract, as soon as the apple is produced to the sight of the buyer and seller alike the verbal description ceases to have any significance by reason of the evidence of identity presented by its visual appearance. Now let us return to the case of the horse. In that case, however satisfactory to the buyer the appearance of the animal may be, it will not serve to prove its exact breeding. If it were the fact that instead of being by X out of Y it was of a very much more plebian origin, delivery of the horse shown would not be a performance of the contract. The distinction it obvious. In one case no real, or ultimate, reliance is placed by the buyer on the description; in the

other case every reliance is so placed. If I am so far right in my reasoning
then the key to the matter appears to be the reliance placed by the buyer
on the description.

We may now, I think, attempt some definition of our conception of what
constitutes a sale by description. Where two parties contract for the sale of
goods, and in the formation of the contract a description is attached to the
goods whether by buyer or seller or both, and the description relates to
some essential characteristic of the goods as distinct from quality, and it is
apparent from the words used by the parties in contracting or is to be
implied from the circumstances that the buyer, to the knowledge of the
seller, really and ultimately relies upon the description to ensure that the
goods will meet his requirements, and the parties contract on that basis,
then the description is of the essence of the contract and the sale is a sale
by description.

This definition has at least the merit of appearing fully to justify the
consequences attached to a sale by description by s. 13 of the Act. It also
appears to justify the findings in *Wren's Case*, *Morelli's Case*, and *Daniels'
Case*, that the goods were sold by description. It is manifestly clear, I
think, that the contracts in these cases would not have been fulfilled by the
supply, respectively, of any beer other than Holden's, any ginger wine
other than Stone's, or any lemonade other than White's. It also appears to
meet the difficulties expressed by Holmes L.J. in his judgment in *Wallis v
Russell*, since it excludes from the operation of s. 14 a very numerous class
of sales, namely sales over the counter of specific goods described by name
only, where the correspondence of the goods with such description is
apparent to the buyer. I think the definition also serves to justify the
consequences attached to a sale by description by s. 14 (2). At common
law, where the buyer had no opportunity of inspecting the goods there was
a condition implied that the goods should answer the description. There
was also implied what was often in text books and judgments referred to as
a warranty, but which was, as pointed out in *Randall v Newson* (1877) by
Lord Esher, in reality a condition, that the goods should be saleable or
merchantable. This was first clearly stated by Lord Ellenborough in
Gardiner v Gray (1815). In the case of a sale of specific goods where the
buyer had an opportunity of inspecting the goods no such condition was
implied, the reason being as stated by Meller J. in *Jones v Just* (1868), that
in such a case the buyer was in a position to rely on his own judgment. If
an inspection was likely to prove inconclusive, or if he distrusted his own
judgment, then he could require an express warranty or else buy at his risk
or refuse to deal. The distinction between the two classes of sales was that
in one case the buyer had perforce to rely entirely on the description,
while in the other it was considered that he had not.

If our definition is correct then what s. 14 (2) did was to abolish this
distinction where the buyer, though he had the opportunity of examining
the goods, by his failure or refusal to examine them showed that he was in

fact relying on the description. For these reasons I am of opinion that our definition is a reasonably workable one. Applying it to the facts of the present case I am of opinion that the sale of the tinned salmon was a sale by description. In the formation of the contract a description was attached to the goods, namely a tin of John West Middle Cut Salmon. This description related to an essential characteristic as distinct from quality, since it is clear that the contract would not have been fulfilled by the supply of any other brand of tinned salmon no matter how good the quality. It was apparent to the seller that the buyer was relying really and ultimately on the description, since, though the tin bore the well known label of John West, the correspondence of the goods supplied, i.e., a sealed tin with the said label, with the description, i.e., a tin containing salmon of the desired brand, was not and could not be apparent to the buyer. For all that the buyer could see the tin might not have contained salmon at all, much less the particular description of salmon he desired, and this must have been apparent to the seller. The contract was made on that basis, and in my opinion, it was a sale by description within the meaning of the section.

Were the goods merchantable? As regards the meaning to be attached to the words 'merchantable quality' I am well satisfied to adopt the interpretation of Lord Wright in *Grant v Australian Knitting Mills*. He says 'Whatever else merchantable quality may mean, it does mean that the article sold, if only meant for one particular use in ordinary course, is fit for that use; merchantable does not mean that the thing is saleable in the market merely because it looks all right.' In this case the salmon was meant for only one particular use in ordinary course, namely for human food as I have already found. It was not fit for that use, and I am of opinion therefore that it was not merchantable. There was accordingly a breach of the conditions implied in the contract by s. 14 (2) for which the plaintiff is entitled to damages.

The defendant appealed to the High Court.

Gavan Duffy J.:

I have carefully considered the able arguments I have heard, but I do not think there is any need to review the cases. I find that the goods were sold by description and were not merchantable. I accept the view of the Judicial Committee in *Grant v Australian Knitting Mills Ltd*, that 'merchantable', as applied to an article meant in the ordinary course for one particular use, means that the article sold is fit for that use, and that there is a sale by description even though the buyer is buying something displayed before him on the counter, provided the article is sold as a thing corresponding to a description. The appeal must be dismissed.

Case 37. Egan v McSweeney
High Court (1956) 90 I.L.T.R. 40

The plaintiff purchased coal from the defendant. Some of this coal was placed on a fire and an explosion occured which caused serious injury to the plaintiff. It was probable that there was some explosive matter in the coal which had been supplied to the plaintiff. The plaintiff claimed that the coal was not reasonably fit for the purpose for which it was purchased, namely to burn in a domestic fire, that the coal did not correspond with the description by which it was purchased and that it was not of merchantable quality.

Held that the implied conditions as to description, quality and fitness had been breached and the plaintiff was entitled to damages for personal injuries.

Davitt P.:

The plaintiff in this case, either by word of mouth or by means of a postcard, ordered from the defendant two one cwt. bags of coal. The order was taken by the defendant's daughter who attended to that part of his business as a coal merchant. The order was fulfilled and the two bags of coal delivered to the plaintiff on 4 March 1953. For some considerable time previous to this the plaintiff had been getting her coal from the defendant and nobody else. On 15 March, the plaintiff set a fire in the grate of her diningroom in the usual way, with paper, kindling wood and coal, and lighted it with a match. Some minutes later, while she was sitting in front of the fire on a stool, bending forward to clean the hearth, there was a loud explosion which scattered portion of contents of the grate around the room. It also had the following effects. Portions of the tiled surround were chipped or broken off. A flying fragment of something struck the plaintiff's son, on the leg, drawing blood. The plaintiff was thrown backwards off her stool on to the floor. She was dazed. She was also struck by flying fragments upon the hands, arms and face and, particularly, some fragments struck and penetrated her left eye. Eventually the eye had to removed.

All the probabilities indicate that there was some explosive matter in the coal which had been supplied by the defendant and I am satisfied so to hold. Microscopical examination and chemical analysis of fragments extracted from the plaintiff's hands disclosed the presence of pure copper in minute quantities. This is, I think, consistent with the presence of a copper detonator in the coal. It is also, I think, consistent with its absence. What is quite clear, however, is that there was some explosive substance in or among the pieces of coal, which should not have been there and which one would not normally expect to find there.

I take the view that the contract in this case was a contract of sale by description. Whether it was made by word of mouth or by means of a postcard, the plaintiff must have made known her requirements by describing them and by ordering two bags of coal. I think it is reasonably clear that what she wanted was coal and not coke, or turf, or anthracite or any other form of fuel; and that she relied upon her description to ensure that she got what she wanted. I also take the view, though not so clearly, that the implication arises that the plaintiff was relying upon the defendant's skill and judgment. Having regard to the course of dealing between the parties, it is quite clear that the defendant knew the purpose for which the coal was required, namely, for domestic use. The plaintiff had been dealing with the defendant for some twenty years and must have placed considerable reliance upon him as a coal merchant who would supply her with coal of a satisfactory nature and quality. As in the case of *Grant v Australian Knitting Mills* (1936), I think the mere fact of purchase raises the implication of reliance. In these circumstances, both sub-sections of s. 14 of the *Sale of Goods Act 1893* (now the 1980 Act), apply and there was an implied warranty that the coal was fit for domestic use and was of a merchantable quality. I am quite satisfied that it was neither the one or the other. The plaintiff is therefore entitled to damages, which must, of course, be considerable.

It is an unfortunate case. No blame whatever that I can see attaches to the defendant. There is no suggestion that he was in any way negligent. He is, however, liable in contract to recompense his customer . . .

Case 38. McDowell v E.P. Sholedice & Co. Ltd
Supreme Court, unreported, 31 July 1969

The plaintiff farmer had for some years been engaged in onion growing and began a new venture of growing onion sets from seeds. The onion seed selected by the plaintiff was 'Stuttgarter', which produced an onion best suited to the Irish market. The plaintiff purchased his requirement from the defendant seed merchant. The plaintiff ordered a ton of 'Stuttgarter' seed which the defendant was unable to supply. The defendant offered instead 'Lyaskovaki' seed which the plaintiff did not know and asked for a description of it which was given. On receipt of this description the plaintiff did not immediately confirm an order. Instead he consulted a number of advisers, none of whom were familiar with the 'Lyaskovski' seed. The plaintiff gave his order. The seed cropped well but as it matured it produced an onion unsuited for the Irish market. After several attempts to dispose of the crop failed, the onions were ploughed back into the ground. The plaintiff sued the defendant for damages.

Held that the sale was one by description and that the goods supplied did not correspond with the description and that the goods were not of merchantable quality.

Ó Dálaigh C.J.:

... The plaintiff, on this appeal, has challenged both of the grounds upon which the President [of the High Court] rejected his claim. These grounds are summarised by the President in his judgment in the following passage:

I have so little information as to what the 'Lyaskovski' seed is expected to produce that I cannot find that the plaintiff has established that the seed which was given him was anything other than Lyaskovski Bulgarian onion seed, which he appears to have accepted right through his evidence, although he complained that it did not produce the type of onion set which he required for the Irish market, and since the onus is on the plaintiff, in my view, to establish that what he got did not correspond with what his contract entitled him to get, it appears to me that he has failed to establish that the goods [did not so correspond]. I believe this was a sale by description—and I think he has failed to establish that they did not correspond with the description or were otherwise not of merchantable quality. In other words, in my view, he had delivered to him what he contracted to buy and his complaint really is that he was not pleased with the result.

The plaintiff's account of his negotiations for the purchase from the defendant of the onion seed was not challenged at the trial. This account establishes that he was unwilling to buy 'Lyaskovski' as such because, as he told the defendant, he 'knew nothing of this stuff'. It was then the defendant said it would get him a description of it. Now it is true that on receipt of this description the plaintiff did not immediately place his order, but delayed while he sent the catalogue page containing it to a number of horticultural specialists. None of these specialists had previously heard of 'Lyaskovski', but they obviously considered it suitable by reference to its stated characteristics. It was only then the plaintiff placed his order, and the defendant's acceptance note of 9 January 1964 is for the supply of 'up to 1 ton of Lyaskovski Bulgarian onion seed'.

The President's first ground for rejecting this part of the plaintiff's claim is that the plaintiff had failed to establish that the goods supplied did not correspond with what his contract entitled him to get.

What was the plaintiff entitled to get? The President's view was that all the plaintiff was entitled to get was 'Lyaskovski Bulgarian onion seed', and that he did not establish that the defendant had failed to deliver what he had ordered. In my judgment this is not a correct view of this transaction. The plaintiff's contract with the defendant was for the sale of goods by description. This is unquestionably the effect of the dealings between the parties. The plaintiff wanted *Stuttgarter*; he wanted Stuttgarter, because its characteristics suited the Irish market for which he was catering. The defendant offered to provide Lyaskovski as a substitute—in good faith and on the recommendation of his English suppliers. But the plaintiff was still not satisfied. He required a description of Lyaskovski. This the defendant furnished, doubtless as supplied to the defendant by his English supplier.

This description satisfied the plaintiff that the seed offered had the characteristics of 'Stuttgarter'. Then and then only did he give his order. All this in my judgment amounts, and amounts uncontrovertibly, to one thing only, a sale by description, that is to say, by reference to the description furnished to the plaintiff of the characteristics of 'Lyaskovski'.

But the goods supplied (described by reference to the crop they would produce) did not correspond with the goods ordered. The *Sale of Goods Act 1893* (now the 1980 Act) in effect makes the defendant's failure to supply goods of the description ordered a breach of condition. Section 13 provides that 'where there is a contract for the sale of goods by description there is an implied condition that the goods shall correspond with the description.' Section 14 further provides that where goods are bought by description that there is an implied condition that the goods are of merchantable quality if the defendant seller dealt in goods of the description in question. That the defendant dealt in such goods is unquestionable. The only question then outstanding is whether or not the goods were merchantable. The evidence need not be repeated. The defendant agreed that there was nothing to be done with the crop except to plough it back into the soil. This is what was done. The crop was, by admission of the defendant, of no value whatsoever; it was saleable in no market that the parties were aware of. One need not therefore waste time in examining the decisions of the precise meaning of 'merchantable'. On no construction of the term can it be said these goods were merchantable.

. . . The goods not being merchantable, there was on the defendant's part a clear breach of the condition implied under s. 14 of the Act; and it is equally clear that the defendant must pay the plaintiff's damage in respect of this breach. Unless the parties can agree on the amount of the damages to which the plaintiff is entitled, an inquiry as to damages should be directed.

Walsh and FitzGerald JJ. concurred.

Case 39. Webster Hardware (International) Ltd v Enfield Rolling Mills Ltd
High Court, unreported, 16 January 1981

The plaintiff manufactured chromium-plated door and window fittings by a process of electrolytic deposition using copper. The plaintiff purchased a quantity of electrolytic copper chippings which contained phosphorus from the defendant, the purpose of the purchase being known to the defendant. The plaintiff was not aware of the different grades of electrolytic copper and that such copper containing phosphorus would not be suitable for its machinery. The plaintiff sued for damages on the grounds that the goods were not fit for the purpose for which they were supplied and were not of merchantable quality.

Held that the goods supplied corresponded with the description of the goods ordered and that they were of merchantable quality.

McMahon J.:

. . . Up to 1974 the plaintiff used solid copper anodes supplied by the company which had supplied the plaintiff's plant. The operating instructions for the plant stated that: 'It is essential to use anodes manufactured from copper which has been electrolytically refined. The alternative grade of copper available in this country, described as fire refined, contains appreciable quantities of harmful impurities and the use of this type of copper anode will result in the formation of dull and unsatisfactory deposits'.

In 1974 the plaintiff's production manager learnt that a cheaper form of electrolytic copper than solid anodes could be used. This was electrolytic copper chippings. These are pieces of copper made from process waste in factories producing electrolytic copper extrusions for the electrical trades. The defendant carries on a business of that kind and in that year its Irish representative canvassed the plaintiff for an order for extruded copper anodes. The production manager asked if the defendant could supply copper chippings and said it must be electrolytic copper. After enquiring from the defendant, the representative informed the plaintiff that it could supply electrolytic copper chippings and he got an order for 500 kilos by letter dated 22 October 1974. In that order the goods are described as 'electrolytic copper chippings'. The same description was used in the plaintiff's next order placed in December 1975 and in the order after that which is the order giving rise to the present action and which is contained in a letter dated 27 July 1976.

I am satisfied that the plaintiff did not make known to the defendant anything about its requirements other than what is conveyed by the terms of the order, namely that it required electrolytic copper. The defendant's representative knew that it was required for copper plating but he did not know and was not told that the plaintiff was using a cyanide solution in their tank. If the plaintiff was using a different kind of solution, referred to by the expert witnesses as an acid solution phosphorus deoxidized copper, which the plaintiff claims to have been the cause of its difficulties, it would have been perfectly suitable. The plaintiff was not aware of the different grades of electrolytic copper but placed its order relying on the operating instructions it received with plant which required merely that the copper should have been electrolytically refined. In my view the plaintiff relied only on the description 'electrolytic copper' to obtain the material it required.

I am also satisfied that the material supplied by the defendant was electrolytic copper, that is copper which had been electrolytically refined. The plaintiff does not now say that any of the material supplied was fire refined copper but it contends that a portion of the copper supplied which was admittedly phosporus deoxidized copper (hereinafter referred to as PDO copper) does not comply with the description in the plaintiff's order for electrolytic copper because of the presence of phosphorus. The British Standards Institution specifications for raw copper show that phosphorus deoxidized copper is one grade of a number of types of electrolytic copper. The evidence establishes that cathode copper (BS 1035/1964) is the cheapest grade and for that reason is usually supplied where solid anodes are used. Use of the other grades—that is electrolytic tough pitch HC copper, oxygen free HC copper and phosphorus deoxidised copper—is only economic when these are available as process scrap or waste.

I accept the evidence of the defendant's technical manager that PDO copper is obtained by melting electrolytic tough pitch copper and adding phosphorus which removes the oxygen leaving only a trace of the phosphorus behind. The defendant supplies the copper plating trade with chips which are a mixture of all grades of electrolytic copper including PDO copper. There was no evidence that other suppliers of copper chippings exclude those of PDO material in supplies to the plating trade. In my view the copper supplied fell within the description, electrolytic copper, and it follows that it was of merchantable quality as electrolytic copper . . .

---

b. Implied Term as to Quality or Fitness

Section 14 (2) of the combined Acts provides that where the seller sells goods in the course of a business there is an implied condition that the goods supplied under the contract are of merchantable quality, except that there is no such condition (a) as regards defects specifically drawn to the buyer's attention before the contract is made, or (b) if the buyer examines the goods before the contact is made, as regards defects which that examination ought to have revealed: *O'Connor v Donnelly* (Case 36), *Egan v McSweeney* (Case 37), *McDowell v E.P. Sholedice & Co. Ltd* (Case 38), *T. O'Regan & Sons Ltd v Micro-Bio (Ireland) Ltd and Intervet Laboratories Ltd* (Case 40) and *McCullough Sales Ltd v Chetham Timber Co. (Ireland) Ltd* (Case 41).

Section 14 (4) provides that where the seller sells goods in the course of a business and the buyer, expressly or by implication, makes known to the seller any particular purpose for which the goods are being brought, there is an implied condition that the goods supplied under the contract are reasonably fit for that purpose: *Wallis v Russell* (Case 42). But this condition is not implied where the buyer does not rely, or where it is unreasonable for him to rely, on the seller's skill or judgment: *E.P. Sholedice & Co. Ltd v Hurst Gunson Cooper Taber Ltd* (Case 43) and *Draper v Rubenstein* (Case 44).

Case 40. T. O'Regan & Sons Ltd v Micro-Bio (Ireland) Ltd and Intervet Laboratories Ltd
High Court, unreported, 26 February 1980

The plaintiff carried on the business of rearing broiler chickens and required a vaccine to prevent infectious bronchitis. A vaccine, sold under a brand name and manufactured by the second defendant, was recommended by an employee of the first defendant. The plaintiff used the vaccine and the chickens suffered a high mortality rate. The first defendant was sued for damages for the misdescription and unfitness of the vaccine. The defect alleged in the vaccine was that it was more potent than it should have been. The first defendant sought an indemnity from the second defendant.

Held there was a breach of the implied condition as to description in that the vaccine sold did not correspond with that description because of its greater potency. There was also a breach of the implied condition as to merchantable quality and fitness in that the plaintiff relied on the seller's skill and judgment to supply a vaccine for use against infectious bronchitis in broiler chickens under the conditions normally obtaining where such fowl are reared in this country. The first defendant was liable to the plaintiff but the manufacturer was bound to indemnify the supplier against such loss.

McMahon J.:

O'R. is the principal of the plaintiff firm and has over twenty-five years experience of intensive poultry raising. He got the idea of vaccinating against infectious bronchitis because his chickens had suffered some respiratory troubles which resulted in loss of condition and he had heard that other growers had good results by vaccinating against infectious bronchitis. In December 1975, O'R. consulted . . . a veterinary surgeon about the project. This veterinary surgeon has had considerable practical and professional experience of intensive poultry rearing and is employed as a whole-time consultant by the poultry industry. In a letter to O'R. on 2 January 1976 explaining the nature of infectious bronchitis and the methods of vaccinating against it and recommending vaccination, the veterinary surgeon explained the method of vaccination which for all practical purposes is identical with that recommended by the second-named defendant. Chicks can be vaccinated at one day old by a water spray which contains one seventh the dose required for older chickens. Chickens can be vaccinated at the age of about 18 days by putting an amount of vaccine constituting a full dose for each chicken in their drinking water. The veterinary surgeon's letter recommended over protection of the chickens by the use of both methods where there had been previous infectious bronchitis.

O'R. was accustomed to purchase animal pharmaceuticals from the first named defendant and he contracted its manager . . . by telephone and enquired about a vaccine for infectious bronchitis. I am satisfied that the veterinary surgeon had not given the name 'Intervet H–120' to O'R. and that the manager recommended 'Intervet' by name as a very reliable vaccine produced by a multinational corporation, which he said was used with good results by large producers. As a result of what the manager said O'R. ordered forty vials of the vaccine, each containing sufficient for 7,000 doses for adult chickens. The vaccine, together with a leaflet explaining the method of using it, was received by the plaintiffs early in January 1976 from the first-named defendant. I am satisfied that O'R. and his employee carefully studied the 'Intervet' instructions and that the vaccine was administered in accordance with those instructions. The instructions contained advice on antibiotic medication. They stated that where stock are known to be infected with mycoplasma or there was a history of other infections, e.g. E. Coli, it was recommended that antibiotics be administered to reduce the level of infection. I am satisfied that at the time when the plaintiff's chickens, both day-old and 18-day-old, were vaccinated they were not showing any sign of infection by these diseases . . .

I accept O'R.'s evidence as to the apparent results of administering the vaccine. The 'Intervet' instructions stated that the reaction after primary vaccination is mild and takes the form of slight respiratory symptoms four to seven days later. The witnesses referred to these symptoms as 'a slight sniffle'. O'R. could detect no reaction after seven days and he telephoned the manager who told him not to worry—that the matter would sort itself out. At four weeks old the birds vaccinated using 'Intervet' vaccine showed a severe reaction with respiratory trouble and coughing. The reaction took place in all the houses after the same time interval almost to a day. The birds appeared to lose health and they fed less and began to die at five weeks and there was a heavy mortality rate at five weeks and three days.

The contrast between the mortality experienced in the different houses was striking. Where a single dose of 'Intervet' vaccine was used there was a mortality rate between 20 and 25 per cent. Where a double dose was used the mortality rate was around 60 per cent. Where Smith-Kline vaccine was used the mortality rate did not exceed 8 per cent and where no vaccine was used the mortality rate was about 5 per cent. The veterinary surgeon investigated the mortality in the plaintiff's houses on 22 March and he reported that mycoplasma organisms were infecting the birds and prolonging and complicating the vaccine reaction and resulting in chronic respiratory disorder. He said that the main problem was gangrenous dermatitis which he said is a culminating disease rather than an entity on its own.

The major controversy in the case has been as to whether the birds contracted these diseases because of the effect of being vaccinated with a defective vaccine or whether the birds were already infected with these diseases before they were vaccinated and died as a result of the natural progression of their diseased condition . . .

An expert's conclusions were that the plaintiff's supply of the vaccine H–120 was untypical in its effect. It had a potency or virulence which was intermediate between other samples of H–120 vaccine tested and H–52. The expert concluded that there was increased mortality associated with the plaintiff's vaccine and in farm conditions it would stress birds more than would be anticipated and the birds would be made liable to develop those endemic diseases present on every farm. I accept the expert's conclusions. The defendants gave evidence that H–120 vaccine of the same batch as that supplied to the plaintiff was distributed to many different growers in Ireland and England. There was no complaint about the results except possibly in one case which I disregard, as no evidence was given to identify the nature of the complaint. Notwithstanding this evidence I am satisfied on the evidence of O'R. and the expert that the particular supply of vaccine sold by the first-named defendant to the plaintiff was untypical and defective, that it over-stressed birds and rendered them liable to contract diseases endemic in poultry rearing farms. There is no evidence to determine whether the apparent increased potency in the plaintiff's vaccine was caused by a less attenuated virus than should be contained in H–120 or was due to some other unknown element in the vaccine.

The second-named defendant produced the production protocol relevant to this particular batch of H–120 virus. This is a document which must be furnished by the manufacturers to the appropriate government department in nearly every European country which permits the importation and use of this vaccine. It is a record of the way in which the vaccine was produced and the quality control and tests which were applied to it to ensure that it is safe for use. The plaintiff did not question the accuracy of the protocol or the sufficiency in the present state of scientific knowledge of the production method quality controls and tests employed. While the evidence of the effect of the vaccine supplied to the plaintiff on chickens in my view establishes a *prima facie* case of negligence in the preparation of the product I am satisfied that the second-named defendant has discharged the onus of proof on it by showing that it has taken all reasonable care in the manufacture of the vaccine. In the result any liability of the first-named defendant to the plaintiff and the second-named defendant to the first-named defendant rests in contract only.

The result of my findings is that as between the plaintiff and the first-named defendant there was a breach of the condition implied by s. 13 of the *Sale of Goods Act 1893* (now the 1980 Act) because the vaccine was sold under the description H–120 but did not correspond with that description because of its greater potency. There was also a breach of the implied condition as to quality or fitness under section 14 of the Act because I am satisfied that the circumstances of the sale show that the plaintiff relied on the seller's skill and judgment to supply a vaccine suitable for use against infectious bronchitis in broiler chickens under the conditions normally obtaining where such fowl are reared in Ireland. The goods were described in the contact by their trade name but the contract was not for the sale of the goods under their trade name but was for the sale of a vaccine which the sellers recommended to the buyer. There was also a breach of the condition of merchantable quality contained in s. 14 sub-sect. (2) of the Act (now s. 14 (4) of the 1980 Act).

As between the first- and second-named defendants there was no suggestion by the second-named defendant that the first-named defendant had interfered with the vaccine in any way while it had possession of it and I am satisfied that it passed the vaccine on to the plaintiff in the same condition in which it received it from the second-named defendant. The first-named defendant ordered the vaccine from the second-named defendant by its brand name but I am satisfied that the sale was a sale by description and that the first-named defendant relied on the skill and judgment of the second-named defendant to supply vaccine suitable for use by persons such as the plaintiff and that on that sale the same condition would be implied by the *Sale of Goods Act 1893* as are implied in the sale from the first-named defendant to the plaintiff. There was therefore, as between the first- and second-named defendants, a breach of the same implied conditions as in the case of the sale to the plaintiff, and the first-named defendant is entitled to an indemnity against the second-named defendant for damages and costs . . .

Case 41. McCullough Sales Ltd v Chetham Timber Co. (Ireland) Ltd
High Court, unreported, 1 February 1983.

The plaintiff builders providers in Northern Ireland, supplied a special type of building material known as 'Celuform'. The defendant timber importer in the Republic purchased quantities of 'Celuform' from the plaintiff. When the defendant sued for the price of the goods, it claimed that the goods supplied were in breach of contract, defective, unusable for the purpose for which they were required, and not of merchantable quality.

Held that the goods as supplied did not correspond with the description of the goods when the contract was made, that the defendant knew the purpose for which the goods were required, that the goods were not reasonably fit for that purpose and were not of merchantable quality. The action for the price of the goods was dismissed.

Doyle J.:

. . . I have come to the following conclusions of fact. 'Celuform', to the extent that it comprised sections or lengths of an inert plastic substance, could in particular circumstances be an acceptable or even superior alternative to timber in certain building operations. The nails produced by the plaintiff to the defendant as the proper method of affixing the plastic lengths of material I find to have been defective and in many cases completely inefficient. Moreover, these nails, together with the punches with which they were intended to be applied, were in short supply and not delivered with the lengths of plastic, sometimes a considerable time afterwards. I find that the initial transactions between the parties amounted to this: the defendant was offered 'celuform' by the plaintiff as an improved and more efficient method of constructing architraves, skirtings and suchlike fittings associated with the building industry. 'Celuform' as offered, in my view, comprised not only the man-made inert substance produced to a high finish, enabling painting to be dispensed with, but also the accompanying distinctive feature that it was supplied with special nails and a nailing system which would obviate the necessity to 'fill' and 'paint over' after the material had been affixed by these hidden or 'secret' nails. Moreover, I consider that it was clearly known to the plaintiff, as shown by its franchising arrangements with the defendant, that the system would be sold for use in the building conditions and practice customary in the Republic: it was stated by the managing director of the plaintiff that the density of concrete in use here was higher than that used in Northern Ireland. I find as a fact that the managing director on behalf of the defendant agreed with the managing director on behalf of the plaintiff to buy, as he said, a system: 'Celuform', affixed by the special nails and nail method. Unless it could be affixed to concrete blocks it would not be of any use, in the managing director of the defendant's stated view. I find therefore that, in the manner which I have indicated, the plaintiff was in breach of its agreement to supply the 'Celuform' system to the extent that I have mentioned, and that the defendant has thereby suffered damage . . . I accept that the managing director of the defendant was truthful when he stated, 'we were never in a position to market this product because there was never an effective method of fixing it'. He also stated, 'we still have all the architraves and skirtings except about £50 worth which we sold to various people as samples'. It seems at least likely that the £50 received for these samples was outweighed as a benefit to the defendant's business by the loss of goodwill on the part of those who paid for the samples. Making a rough approach, I am disposed to ignore the evidence relating to these transactions in relation to the samples.

As previously indicated I am satisfied that what the defendant intended to buy was a system, which system was described to them by the managing director of the plaintiff at their first meeting in Dublin; a description, partly oral and partly demonstrated by the yellow brochure which he produced to the defendant, and also, I think, the sample nails which he also had at that time. The description centred around the provision of architraves, skirtings and comparable members for house building by the use of this new plastic-type substitute for timber and the process also, apparently novel, of the fixing of the plasterboard with secret nails by means of the punch which has been described in the review of the evidence. I have no doubt that the managing director of the plaintiff was a persuasive salesman and I am satisfied that the managing director of the defendant was entitled to place reliance upon and did rely upon what was shown and spoken about and generally described orally and with reference to the brochure. Having regard to the business interests of both parties, it goes without saying that the plaintiff knew the purpose for which the defendant required the goods and it is not contested that it was an important part of the plaintiff's business and so regarded by them to supply the 'Celuform' method of building construction.

The course of the evidence makes it clear that the goods in question were not reasonably fit for the said purpose, at least when adopted for use under Irish building conditions and when sought to be applied to Irish concrete walls—that is to say, concrete walls of the consistency common in building practice in the Republic of Ireland. For the same reason, it is clear that they were not of merchantable quality or capable of being readily sold by the defendant to its building customers. The managing director of the plaintiff, in the course of his persuasive and what proved to be successful, initial sales talk, clearly represented that the 'Celuform' system would be highly advantageous to the defendant's customers for the building purposes for which it had been devised and also perhaps for the defendant itself if it should use it in building operations on its own account. I accept the managing director of the defendant's statement that he was persuaded and that he did rely upon these representations and bought on foot of them. Since the initial contract was entered into after this discussion, which was accompanied only by the production of the brochure as well as the persuasive descriptions already referred to and, perhaps, the three sample nails, and since a firm order was thereafter placed, it seems clear that the defendant was not afforded an opportunity of examining the actual system itself and bought entirely upon the managing director of the plaintiff's description. The managing director of the defendant could not reasonably have anticipated the defects which subsequently appeared when the 'Celuform' scheme was delivered and put into operation in the various places described in the course of the evidence.

It seems to be the case that the provisions of s. 14 of the *Sale of Goods Act 1893* are intended to modify, restrict or otherwise eat into the legal implications covered by the phrase *caveat emptor*. The maxim has been in no sense abrogated by the provisions of the section, as has been explained by many learned judges; it has merely been modified in its application. In the famous Irish authority of *Wallis v Russell* (Case 42) familiar to practitioners for many reasons, some not directly related to the scope of the law of contract, Lord Justice FitzGibbon had this to say:

the maxim, *caveat emptor*, applies to the purchase of specific things upon which the buyer can and usually does exercise his own judgment . . . it applies also where, by usage or otherwise, it is a term of the contract express or implied that the buyer shall not rely on the skill or judgment of the seller, but is has no application to any case in which the seller has undertaken and the buyer has left it to the seller to supply goods to be used for a purpose known to both parties at the time of the sale.

In my view this last example given by FitzGibbon L.J. is apposite and should be applied in the present circumstances . . .

Case 42. Wallis v Russell
Court of Appeal [1902] 2 I.R. 585

The plaintiff sent her granddaughter to the defendant's shop, a fishmonger, for two crabs. The granddaughter told the defendant's manager that the plaintiff wanted two nice fresh crabs for her tea. The manager stated that he had no live crabs, but that he could give her boiled ones. The manager went to the window and took up two crabs. The granddaughter pointed to another crab, and asked if he did not think it better. The manager took it up and felt it, and said it was by the weight one should judge and not by the size and put it away. The granddaughter asked were they nice and fresh and the manager replied that they were. The granddaughter paid for the crabs and took them away. The defendant honestly believed the crabs to be fresh and fit for human food. The plaintiff and her granddaughter ate portions of the crabs that evening and both became seriously ill. In an action for damages the trial court found that it was made known to the defendant that the crabs were required for use as human food, that the plaintiff relied on the defendant's manager to select fresh crabs and reasonably fit for that purpose, that the crabs were goods which it was in the course of the defendant's business to supply, and that those supplied were not fresh and reasonably fit for human food. The defendant appealed.

Held that the crabs were bought for a particular purpose, made known to the seller, within s. 14 (1) of the *Sale of Goods Act 1983* (now s. 14 (4) of the combined Acts) so as to show that the buyer relied on the seller's skill and judgment, and that the defendant was liable for damages.

Holmes L.J.:

The question which the court is asked to decide in this case is whether a fishmonger, who sells over his counter two boiled crabs to a customer, gives an implied warranty that they are fit for use as human food. This question is raised by a state of facts free from complication. Although the issue as to the quality of the goods left to the jury combined the element of freshness with fitness for food, there was not only no evidence to show that the crabs had become tainted or decomposed by reason of their having been kept an undue time after they were caught; but there was a strong body of testimony the other way. The crabs purchased by the defendant formed part of a consignment received by the fishmonger the day before the sale. When delivered they were all alive, and thirty of them were killed with a view to, and immediately before, their being boiled. Twenty-six of them, that have been traced, were proved to have been eaten without injurious consequences; and although one, or both, of those sold to the defendant was or were unfit for food, it is impossible to say with certainty what was the cause of such unfitness. Whatever it arose from, it was not discovered by either vendor or purchaser. Not only did the defendant, according to the finding of the jury, honestly believe the crabs to be fit for food, but there seems to have been no way except perhaps by opening them, and thus rendering them unmerchantable, by which it was possible for anyone, however skilful, to find out their condition. The three persons who partook of them noticed nothing unusual in their taste or smell; and at the time of sale they undoubtedly presented the appearance of good wholesome crabs.

There was nothing peculiar in the circumstances attending the purchase. The jury negatived the only express warranty suggested by the evidence, and the transaction was the ordinary one of a person buying in a shop specific goods then and there delivered, paid for, and carried away.

The degree of inspection which a purchaser gives to what is thus bought varies greatly. It depends to a certain extent on the thing itself. Articles of dress or ornamaent, the selection of which is largely governed by individual taste, receive for the most part careful examination. It also depends upon the buyer, whether he is keen or easy-going, in haste or at leisure, possessed of, or without, special knowledge. But whether he avails himself of it or not, he is given the opportunity of forming his own opinion of the quality of the goods before the sale is completed.

In the purchase of boiled crabs which appear outwardly sound and good, there is little room for skill or judgment. They are probably chosen by size or weight; and the buyer in this case pointed out one that seemed larger than those offered to her, but on the shopman saying that it was lighter she did not take it. We have thus the question of implied warranty on the sale of specific goods, which there was an opportunity of inspecting at the time of sale, raised in the simplest and most elementary shape.

A young lawyer might think it was a case for applying the rule of *caveat emptor*; but with more experience he would know that a Latin maxim goes but a short way towards solving legal difficulties. The case was treated in the King's Bench Division, and in the argument here, as turning entirely upon the construction of s. 14 of the *Sale of Goods Act 1893* (now the 1980 Act); and although at one time I entertained doubt on this point, I am now satisfied that this is the true mode of dealing with it.

It might be expected that a statute, the object of which, as declared by its extended title, was to codify the law relating to the sale of goods, would provide exhaustively for implied warranties or conditions arising from or incorporated with the contract of sale; and I am of opinion that everything needed for the purpose of determining this appeal is to be found within it. The 14th section enacts that, subject to the provisions of that and other Acts, there is no implied warranty or condition as to the quality or fitness for any particular purpose of goods supplied under a contract of sale, except as therein specified. The jury having negatived an express warranty, it is necessary for the plaintiff to show that there was some implied warranty or condition; and the only implied warranty or condition that would entitle the plaintiff to a verdict must be either as to the quality of the goods, or as to their fitness for a particular purpose. A warranty that the crabs were merchantable, or that they were fit for food, would or *might* sustain the action; but these would be warranties as to their quality, and therefore covered by the negative portion of the 14th section. The plaintiff is therefore obliged to show that her cause of action arises under the provisions of the Act of 1893, or of some other statute in that behalf.

There are specific provisions in sections 13, 14 and 15 relating to two kinds of contract of sale—one called a sale by sample; the other called a contract for the sale of goods by description; and it is to be noted that in the first class there is implied condition that the goods shall be free from any defect rendering them unmerchantable, which would not be apparent on reasonable examination of the sample; while in the second class there is in a certain state of circumstances an implied condition that the goods shall be of merchantable quality. As the sale in this case was certainly not a sale by sample, there is no need to refer further to the provisions that deal therewith; but counsel for the plaintiff, after arguing at length upon sub-sect. 1 of s. 14, concluded by saying that sub-sect. 2, quite independently of the preceding clause, gave him a cause of action upon which, if necessary, he was prepared to reply. I can find no reference to such a proposition in the judgment of Palles C.B. [in the Kings Bench Division]; but although it was not presented to this court with much conviction, it ought not to be passed over in silence. I am of opinion that, having regard to the evidence and findings of the jury, there was in this case no sale by description within the meaning of s. 13 or of s. 14, sub-sect 2. Before the passing of the Act of 1893, sale of goods by description was often referred to by judges in contradistinction to a sale of specific goods, shown and delivered to the buyer at the time of purchase. I do not suggest that this is conclusive as to the meaning of the same words when used in the statute. Indeed, the language of s. 14, sub-sect. 2, appears to show that goods *in esse*, and examined at the time of sale, may be brought within its meaning. But where a customer buying an article in a shop gives no description of it beyond asking for it by its usual name, and the article thus asked for is delivered and carried away, such a purchase in ordinary parlance would not be a purchase of goods by description. If the crabs in this case were sold by description, no sale otherwise than by description would be possible. The 13th, 14th, and 15th sections of the Act may doubtless be construed as dividing all sales of goods into sales by sample, or sales by description, the result of which would be that in every sale there would be an implied warranty against latent defects undiscoverable by examination. But this would in my opinion be a forced and unnatural interpretation of the language. It would, moreover, have the effect of making a fundamental change in the law as it existed previous to the Act. I think I am justified in saying that under the common law the purchaser of a specific chattel delivered to him at the time of sale takes the risk of a latent defect, at least where the seller is neither the grower nor the manufacturer . . .

I come now, to s. 14 sub-section 1 (now s. 14 (2)), upon which Palles C.B. rested his judgment. This provision has been read more than once; and I can state my view of its construction with comparative brevity. An argument that the sub-section only refers to manufactured goods, which was considered in great detail by the Lord Chief Baron, has not been used in this court. It has, however, been argued that the provision does not apply to goods *in esse* passing by delivery at the time of sale; but the only answer that need be given to this proposition is to read the clause which *prima facie* refers to all sales of goods, and which contains nothing to suggest a limitation that would be in my opinion arbitrary and artificial. The true question is, what is meant by 'a particular purpose'? and here, again, there is, I think, no necessity to go beyond the language of the legislature. There are many classes of goods which are sold and used for different purposes, and the selection of an article out of the class depends upon the special purpose for which it is needed. Horses, for example, are purchased to be used as beasts of draught, or burden; and this might be described as the general purpose for which they are required. But one man is looking for a racehorse, another for a hunter, a third for a polo pony, a fourth that it may be used in a brougham or a plough. Each of these may be described as the particular purpose for which the horse is bought. Or let me take an illustration from articles of food. I ask a vendor of fruit to show me some apples, and I tell him that they are for a special purpose. If I say that they are to make up a dessert dish for that day's dinner, or to be stored during the winter, or to be converted into cider, or to be cooked in a pie or pudding, he understands me, and he produces apples which he believes to be suited for the purpose indicated. These cases suggest one construction of sub-section 1—a construction which emphasises 'particular'

as contrasted with 'general', much in the same way as *species* is
distinguished from *genus*. The language is capable of this interpretation,
and some reasons can be offered for adopting it . . .

I have stated the arguments urged on behalf of the defendant that seem
to me most deserving of consideration, and I willingly admit their force. It
has been after great fluctuaton of mind that I have decided to reject them,
and even now I am not sure that I have not misunderstood the intention
and misinterpreted the language of the legislature. The construction of the
sub-section must be gathered from all its parts; and I think that the key
that unlocks the meaning of 'particular purpose' may be found in the
words 'so as to show that the buyer relies on the seller's skill and
judgment'. I have already said that, according to our law as it stood
previous to 1893, when there was a sale of a specific chattel produced at
the time of sale, and then and there handed over to the purchaser, there
was in the absence of comment or observation on either side no implied
warranty against either patent or latent defects. There were no doubt
exceptions to this rule founded on special circumstances, but I think I have
stated the general principle correctly; and I have no reason to believe that
it has been altered by the *Sale of Goods Act*. But it rarely happens that
articles are thus sold in silence. There is generally some conversation
accompanying the sale, which may either amount to an express warranty,
or, if it falls short of that, supplies grounds from which a warranty may be
implied. Section 14, sub-sect. 1, (now s. 14 (4)) enacts that this implication
will arise when the buyer directs the attention of the seller to the purpose
for which the goods are required in such a way as to convey that he is
relying on the seller's skill and judgment to select a suitable article.

I am unable to conceive any intelligible reason for drawing, in such a
case, a distinction between the sale of an article which may be used for
several purposes and of an article which can only be used for one. The
skill and judgment of a person whose business is to deal in the goods is as
likely to be appealed to in the one case as in the other. If a purchaser of
apples, by calling attention to the fact that they are wanted for dessert,
secures a warranty that the fruit supplied is fit therefor, the warranty is
broken whether they prove to be rotten dessert apples or good baking
apples. Why should there be a warranty implied in this case if there is not
also a warranty in favour of the buyer of a razor who, without looking at
the article offered him, tells the vendor pointedly that the razor is to
shave? The only way of avoiding this and kindred anomalies is to adopt
the view of the Lord Chief Baron, and to read 'particular purpose' as
meaning any purpose made known by the buyer to the seller. Although
this has the effect of making the word 'particular' surplusage, statutes are
scarcely more free from this defect than general literature, in which a loose
or redundant use of this adjective is very common.

There can, I think, be no doubt that the present case comes within the
terms of the sub-section thus construed. The granddaughter's request for

two nice fresh crabs, wanted by the plaintiff for tea, followed by the selection of both the crabs by the shop assistant on his own judgment, notwithstanding her preference of another, proves that she made known the purpose for which the crabs were required in such a way as to convey to the seller that she was relying on him to make a suitable choice.

In stating my reasons for arriving at the foregoing conclusion, I have not thought it necessary to form an opinion as to what would have been the state of the law in a case like this previous to the passing of the Act of 1893. An examination of numerous authorities referred to during the agrument has revealed no decision precisely in point, and it is difficult to extract a general rule from the *obiter dicta* of judges directed to, or called forth by, the special facts before them. Little guidance is to be expected from an investigation that has led Palles C.B. and FitzGibbon L.J. to opposite conclusions. The value of a codifying statute consists in the removal of doubts and difficulties caused by the ambiguous and sometimes inconsistent utterances of judges and comments of text-writers. Occasionally the draftsman of such an Act regards his duty as more mechanical than intellectual; but the *Sale of Goods Act 1893*, is drawn clearly and carefully. It deserves praise for having swept away by unequivocal language all implied warranties or conditions as to the quality or fitness for any particular purpose of goods supplied under a contract of sale save as provided therein, or in some other statute. I have, therefore, tried to solve the questions in this action by the language of the sections that deal with conditions and warranties; and if I have fallen into error I fear that I should not have been saved therefrom by a fuller study of the antecedent law.

Lord Ashbourne C., FitzGibbon and Walker L.JJ. delivered concurring judgments.

Case 43. E.P. Sholedice & Co. Ltd v Hurst Gunson Cooper Taber Ltd
High Court, unreported, 28 July 1972

The plaintiff seed merchants sued the defendant seed merchants for damages in relation to a contract under which the plaintiff purchased from the defendant a quantity of onion seed for resale to a third party. The third party had recovered damages from the plaintiff on the ground that the seed supplied did not correspond with the description and was not of merchantable quality (see case 38). During the course of negotiations the defendant stated that if the plaintiff agreed that the seed was suitable for the Irish market it would be ordered but that the defendant would not recommend it in any way. The defendant sought to exclude liability on foot of exemption clauses contained both in its catalogue and on its invoice sent with the seed.

Held that the effect of the discussions prior to the sale was that the plaintiff could not rely on the seller's skill and judgment to gain protection of s. 14 (1) of the Sale of Goods Act 1893 (now s. 14 (4) of the combined Acts) but that the goods were sold by description and accordingly, unless otherwise excluded, it was a condition, under s. 14 (2) of that Act (also s. 14 (2) of the combined Acts) that the goods should be of merchantable quality. The defendant could not rely on the exemption clause in the catalogue in that the negotiations between the parties negatived its effect, that the clause was vague and further that the exemption clause on the invoice sent with the goods could not be invoked to regulate a contract which had been concluded some time previously. The plaintiff was entitled to damages.

O'Keeffe P.:

. . . The real dispute in this case is whether, the seed not being of merchantable quality, the defendant is liable to the plaintiff in breach of contract. The defendant claims that the terms on which it was sold were such as to protect it against any liability. This, it says, is for two reasons.

In the first place it says that in the discussions between the plaintiff and defendant it was made clear that no liability should attach to it, and secondly it says that it is protected by a clause exempting it from liability, which was contained in their 1963 seed catalogue, and on the invoices for the seed in question.

The defendant had undoubtedly got this seed specially for the plaintiff, and was not familiar with its merits or defects. This he made clear to the plaintiff. The director of the plaintiff in cross-examination said that he did not understand that the defendant was accepting any responsibility for the performance of the seed. Indeed he said that he would accept that the defendant was not accepting any responsibility. He said: 'I knew that the defendant was taking no responsibility for the performance of this seed, and that is what I would expect them to do.' Later he said that he agreed that an employee of the defendant told him that he knew nothing about this seed.

That employee said about the same conversation: 'I can only say that I told him I didn't know the seed and if he was satisfied it was suitable for the Irish market I would order it for him. I had not recommended it in any way.' He said that the plaintiff did not seek his advice and that he did not give it.

As to the clause exempting the defendant from liability, the catalogue for 1963, which the plaintiff had received from it, contained the following clause in the General Conditions of Sale.

Conditions of Sale

Hurst Gunson Cooper Taber Ltd. guarantee that all seeds offered or sold by them to which the *Seeds Act 1920*, and the regulations made thereunder applies (sic) have been tested in accordance with the provisions of the same. In accordance with the established custom of the seed trade, Hurst Gunson Cooper Taber Ltd. give no other guarantee. It is, therefore, not a condition of sale, neither do they warrant, expressly or impliedly or under the terms of the *Sale of Goods Act 1893*, or any statute or enactment, that the seeds, bulbs or roots shall correspond with the description under which they are sold, and Hurst Gunson Cooper Taber Ltd. will not be responsible for the crop. Notwithstanding anything herein contained, all accounts are payable at their head office. The giving or sending of any order to Hurst Gunson Cooper Taber Ltd. constitutes an acceptance of these terms by the purchaser, who if he does not accept these terms, must return the goods forthwith.

The invoice dated 4 March 1964, sent to the plaintiff in respect of the seeds the subject-matter of this action, contained a clause in somewhat similar terms. The defendant relied on both these clauses.

Now, I consider that the conversation between the defendant's employee and the plaintiff's director was sufficient to indicate to the plaintiff that the defendant had no such knowledge of the nature or quality of the goods as would entitle the plaintiff to rely on the skill and judgment of the defendant as to their suitability or fitness for the purpose for which they were sold, and that accordingly the statutory condition in s. 14 (1) of the *Sale of Goods Act 1893*, is not to be implied in this case. The goods were, however, goods sold by description, and were sold by a seller who dealt in goods of the description in question, namely seeds, and accordingly, unless otherwise excluded, the condition contained in s. 14 (2) of the Act is to be implied, namely a condition that the goods should be of merchantable quality.

The defendant seeks to exclude this condition by reason of the admissions made by the plaintiff's director as to his conversations with the defendant's employee, and his acceptance that the defendant was not accepting responsibility for the performance of the seed, and relies also on the condition in its catalogue and on the invoice.

I consider that the conversation was not such as to exclude the statutory condition. True, the plaintiff's director admitted that the defendant had represented to him that it knew nothing about the seed, and this is, as I have said, sufficient to exclude any implied condition as to fitness for a particular purpose. The defendant was, however, seed merchants, and it bought the seed for the plaintiff and resold it to it. By so doing, it put itself in a position where in my opinion the condition implied by s. 14 (2) applied to the contract of sale.

As to the written condition excluding liability, I consider that this does not suffice to exempt the defendant from liability. In the first place, the condition contained in the catalogue clearly had no application to this sale, since the defendant made it clear in the negotiations with the plaintiff that the opening part of the clause had no application to these particular goods, in as much as it knew nothing about the goods and they had not been tested in accordance with the *Seeds Act 1920*. Secondly, a clause of this kind is read strictly, and the provision that the vendors 'will not be responsible for the crop' is not an exclusion of a condition that the goods will be of merchantable quality.

As to the conditions on the invoice, the contract between plaintiff and defendant was made in or about the month of November, and I consider that it was not open to the defendant to insert into it at the time of delivery a fresh condition with the proviso that if the purchaser did not accept this new condition he must return the goods. Accordingly, I consider that the condition on the invoice had no applicability. Furthermore, if it does apply, I consider, for the reasons above indicated, that it was not sufficient to exclude the statutory conditions as to merchantable quality . . .

Case 44. Draper v Rubenstein
Circuit Court (1925) 59 I.L.T.R. 119

The defendant was a butcher of many years experience. He purchased some cattle which were for human consumption from the plaintiff who was a seller of cattle. The cattle proved to be unfit for human consumption. When the plaintiff sued for the price of the cattle the defendant argued that there had been a breach of the implied condition as to fitness.

Held that while the goods were purchased for a particular purpose within s. 14 (1) of the *Sale of Goods Act 1893* (now s. 14 (4) of the combined Acts) the defendant relied not on the seller's skill and judgment but on his own knowledge and experience and that accordingly the defendant could not rely on the protection of the section and the plaintiff was entitled to succeed.

Judge Pigot:

As shortly stated in the opening, it would appear to raise the question whether a salesman in a cattle market, innocently selling a fat beast to one whom he knows to be a butcher, gives an implied warranty that the animal is sound and in a condition fit for killing for human food. It appears to me, however to turn on a question of fact. The plaintiff is a cattle salesman. Three beasts were brought to his yard for sale on 15 January 1925. The defendant is a butcher of 17 years' experience who had had many dealings with the plaintiff, and was known by him to be a butcher. On this occasion there can be no doubt that he knew that the defendant was attending the market to buy for the purposes of his business as a butcher . . . It was proved, and was admitted, that when the animal in question, one of the three sold, was killed, it was infected with tuberculosis and was certified by the proper authority to be unfit for human food. There was no evidence that either vendor or buyer could by examination have ascertained its condition when sold in the market . . .

It may be taken as certain that the 'goods' were bought for a 'particular purpose' within the meaning of section 14 (1) of the *Sale of Goods Act 1893* (now s. 14 (4) of the combined Acts). The seller knew that the sale was for the purpose of being used as human food. Then, it seems to me that the only question which I have to put to myself as a juror on the admitted facts is this: Did the defendant rely on the plaintiff's skill or judgment in the transaction? As I have said, the purchaser was an experienced buyer in the market. He had been 17 years at the trade. I have no hesitation, looking at all the circumstances of the case, at the knowledge and experience of the defendant, and in the absence of any evidence to the contrary, that he was relying on his own power of bargaining on the subject matter, and was not relying on the skill or judgment of the plaintiff. I have no doubt that he inspected the animals which he was going to purchase, and used his own skill in the purchase. I am also satisfied that no usage has been proved, or attempted to be proved, which, as suggested by FitzGibbon L.J. in *Wallis v Russell*, (Case 42), might induce liability where the buyer had relied on the skill or judgment of the seller. Applying the principles enunciated in the judgments of the learned judges in the Court of Appeal in the above mentioned case, I have come to the conclusion that this is not a case coming within the exception expressed in section 14 (1) of the *Sale of Goods Act 1893* (now s. 14 (4) of the combined Acts) and that the defendant is in the wrong, and that this action should be dismissed.

---

c. Exclusion of Implied Terms

The *Sale of Goods Act 1893* permitted the exclusion of all the implied terms. To effectively do so the party relying on the exclusion must prove that it was incorporated into the contract. The exclusion of these terms was held to be effective in the cases of *Wicklow Corn Co. Ltd v Edward Fitzgerald Ltd* (Case 45), and *Tokn Grass Products Ltd v Sexton & Co. Ltd* (Case 46) though not effective in *O'Connor v McCowen & Sons Ltd* (Case 47) because the seller had failed to fulfil the terms of the exclusion clause, and *E.P. Sholedice & Co. Ltd v Hurst Gunson Cooper Taber Ltd* (Case 43). Though the *Sale of Goods and Supply of Services Act 1980* modifies the rule relating to the capability of the seller to exclude the implied provisions of the statute, the cases prior to this statute continue to be relevant.

Case 45. Wicklow Corn Co. Ltd v Edward Fitzgerald Ltd
Circuit Court [1942] Ir.Jur.Rep. 48

The plaintiff contracted to purchase from the defendant a consignment of seed wheat with respect to which it was expressly stated in the invoice that no warranty was given by the seller expressly or by implication as to its quality or fitness. The plaintiff took delivery and re-sold quantities of the wheat to some of its customers who found it to be of inferior quality and who subsequently by legal proceedings compelled the plaintiff to reimburse them for their loss of a satisfactory crop. The plaintiff sued the defendant for breach of contract.

Held that in the absence of an express warranty the plaintiff could not rely on any implied warranty in that such implied warranty was excluded by the invoice sent to the plaintiff by the defendant.

Judge Davitt:

There is an absence from the plaintiff's correspondence of any complaint based upon the breach of an express warranty and the evidence given on behalf of the defendant as to the warranty alleged to have been expressed over the telephone appeared to me to be more credible than that to the contrary effect offered on behalf of the plaintiff. The plaintiff, accordingly, cannot, rely upon any express warranty, while any implied warranty as to fitness is excluded by the invoice sent by the defendant to the plaintiff. Accordingly, counsel for the plaintiff is forced to rely on the allegation that a different commodity had been supplied to that which the defendant purported to supply, as in the cases he cited. There is, however, no case to show that the principle underlying those decisions can be applied where the defect complained of is one of quality only, as distinct from the supplying of a different substance. The plaintiff is, therefore, not entitled to succeed on any of the grounds put forward, and the civil bill must be dismissed with costs.

Case 46. Tokn Grass Products Ltd v Sexton & Co. Ltd
High Court, unreported, 3 October 1983

The defendant supplied machinery to the plaintiff which proved to be defective. The contract was made by a number of letters on the back of which were printed conditions which excluded the provisions of the *Sale of Goods Act 1893*. The plaintiff sued for damages for loss incurred by it and claimed that the sale was one by description and that the machinery supplied did not correspond with the description and was not fit for the purpose for which it was supplied. The defendant claimed that the conditions implied by the *Sale of Goods 1893* had been expressly excluded by the terms of the contract.

Held that the clause in question was sufficiently wide and explicit to exclude the protections implied by the statute, and that the plaintiff's claim must be dismissed.

Doyle J.:

. . . The contract between the parties was contained in four typewritten sheets each of which was dated 27 February 1978. The face of each sheet consisted partly of printed matter naming the defendant company, and also the printed words 'Specification and Tender'. At the bottom of each sheet appeared the words 'Terms and Conditions of Sale overleaf' and below that in smaller print the names of the directors of the defendant. The reverse of each of the four sheets, upon which no typewritten legend appeared, exhibited printed terms and conditions of sale numbering 13 in all. These printed terms and conditions of sale differed in certain respects from the typewritten script of the contract and in certain respects were incompatible. The sales director of the defendant had signed his name at the end of the typescript on the last of the four sheets of the contract.

To deal briefly with the nature of the discrepancies which I have mentioned between the written terms and conditions and the typed provisions in the body of the contract, I may perhaps exemplify, in the first place, the printed term and condition number 4 which reads as follows: 'Payment: Cash on or before Delivery' However the typewritten portion of the contract on page 4 contains a heading:

Terms of Payment
20% Deposit with Order
70% On delivery of the equipment to site
5% When erected or 30 days from date of delivery
5% When started.

As stated, the reverse of the sheet, upon which these typewritten provisions occur and upon which same sheet the sales director's signature also appears, contains the conflicting printed arrangement for payment. Having regard to the view which I take as to which of these conflicting arrangements is to predominate in my construction of this contract, it may not be necessary for me to consider other examples of discrepancies between the printed words and the typewritten ones.

There was oral evidence in the course of the trial, not contested, which indicated that the parties were following the typewritten terms of their arrangement as being the binding ones, rather than the printed terms and conditions on the back of the sheets containing the provisions of the contract. This is not to say that the printed terms and conditions of sale are out of the case. In fact the parties purported to rely on certain of them which, as will appear, were not in conflict with the typed arrangements, and arguments were addressed to me as to the effect of and implications to be drawn from certain of these terms and conditions by both parties to this case. In particular, a good deal of argument was directed to the effect of clause 5 of the printed terms and conditions, which provided: 'No condition as to quality is implied and no guarantee or warranty expressed or implied is given under the *Sale of Goods Act 1893* or otherwise in respect of any goods, vehicles or equipment sold. All goods, vehicles and equipment are sold with the benefit only of the manufacturers' guarantee if any.'

Reliance was also placed inter alia upon the provisions of clause 12 of the printed terms and conditions which provides: 'The company will not be liable for any consequential loss arising from the operation of any equipment or plant supplied.'

I propose to adopt the following method of construction of the arrangement between the parties in so far as it is evidenced in writing. I look first to the typed four-page contract of 27 February 1978 as setting out what was agreed. However I do not disregard the printed terms and conditions of sale on the back of each typewritten sheet, in so far as such terms and conditions of sale are not in clear or obvious conflict with the typewritten arrangement; and where no such conflict appears I must give them their ordinary legal meaning and construe their effect in binding the parties to the contract. In particular I must have regard to the principles stated by Willes J. in *Mody v Gregson* (1868) when he stated:

> The doctrine that an express provision excludes implication does not affect cases in which the express provision appears upon the true construction of the contract to have been super-added for the benefit of the buyer.

. . . To summarise, it may be said that the statutory provisions and the dicta of judges in the recognised authorities are really to afford assistance in the construction of the agreement and its true terms as arrived at between the parties. They do not in any way restrict the parties in the type of contract or bargain into which they may wish to enter. They merely afford help in deciding precisely what that contact or bargain may be . . . This was, I conclude, a sale of the grain drying equipment by description since the plaintiff relied to some extent on the description given by the defendant: see the observations of Judge Davitt in *O'Connor v Donnelly* (Case 36). It would however, be vain to regard the plaintiff as an innocent in the operation of grain dryers. It had been in the business in a substantial way and was sufficiently familiar with grain drying machines to specify a particular make of control panel—the Allen-West—in place of that normally incorporated in it. I can find nothing in the typewritten pages in the 'Contract Quotation' which runs counter to the printed term and condition number 5 endorsed on each page. It would be unreal to suggest that the plaintiff was taken by surprise or that it became aware of it only at a late stage . . .

The plaintiff alleges a contract for the sale of the grain dryer made in circumstances sufficient to bring into operation the provisions of s. 14 of the *Sale of Goods Act 1893*, especially sub-sect. 1, and alleges an implied condition and a warranty by the defendant that the grain dryer should be reasonably fit for the plaintiff's purpose, known to the defendant. I am satisfied that it was not so fit when delivered once erected and that it continued to be unfit during the 1978 harvest season whereby it suffered loss.

The defendant denies that the circumstances of the sale gave rise to the condition or warranty alleged. It relies upon the express negative contained in clause 5 of the printed terms and conditions. It further relies upon clause 12, exempting it from consequential loss, which if effective . . . would exclude most of the damage claimed by the plaintiff. The plaintiff has claimed both a condition and a warranty that the dryer should be reasonably fit for its purpose. It would appear that the circumstances relied upon give rise only to a condition . . .

The *Sale of Goods Act 1893* was a codifying statute and its construction requires consideration of the previous state of the law as stated by Palles C.B. in *Wallis v Russell* (Case 42). In this connection judges before and after the *Sale of Goods Act* have construed exemption clauses strictly, *contra proferentem*. The maxim '*expressum facit cessare tacitum*' was departed from according to particular circumstances in *Mody v Gregson* by Willes J. as earlier cited . . . Applying the strictest scrutiny to the wording of clause 5, I consider it to be sufficiently wide and explicit to exclude the provisions of s. 14. I am also satisfied that the plaintiff knew of the terms of the clause, in fact, the defendant as earlier stated in its accompanying letter, requested the plaintiff 'to study the 'Contract Quotation' carefully'. Thus I am constrained with regret to dismiss this claim . . .

Case 47. O'Connor v McCowen & Sons Ltd
High Court (1943) 77 I.L.T.R. 64

The plaintiff contracted to purchase from the defendant a quantity of turnip seed. It was expressly stated in the sale docket, signed by the plaintiff's agent, that the defendant selected its seeds with the greatest of care and that no express or implied warranty as to description or productiveness of any seeds sold was given. Before the plaintiff's agent received the seed, he was told that the defendant had not got its seeds from its usual suppliers and consequently could not guarantee it. When sown the seeds produced a crop with a wild leaf and with a root similar to a cabbage root but which crop was useless to the plaintiff. The plaintiff sought damages from the defendant for breach of the condition as to description.

Held that this was a sale by description and that the seed supplied did not correspond with that description. The words used at the time of sale were not sufficient to warn the plaintiff that the seed might not be turnip seed. The conditions of sale were not applicable as the defendant had not selected it seeds with the greatest of care but had taken what it was able to get.

Overend J.:

The plaintiff was a farmer, and was ill at the time of the transaction. He sent his son to buy the seed. The son went into the shop and saw the supervisor who was in charge of the seed department. He told the supervisor of his requirements, and a discussion arose as to the amount of seed that would be sufficient. There was no doubt that the nature of the purchase was clear. The amount having been arrived at, the supervisor told the assistant to fill out 14 lbs Blue Top Turnip seed, and the supervisor made the entry on the blue paper. This transaction was sale by description. The purchaser had no opportunity of examining the seed and if he had it would be no use for him. When he had filled up the blue docket, and before the plaintiff's son had signed it, the supervisor told the plaintiff's son that they had not got their seeds from their usual suppliers and could not guarantee them. These words were not sufficient to warn the buyer that the seeds might not be turnip seeds at all, and contained nothing to indicate that they would not produce turnips. If purchasers were to be precluded, when they purchased articles by description, and got different goods, then the very clearest words must be used by the seller, such as: 'You may be purchasing seeds that are not turnip seeds at all.'

The supervisor then asked the plaintiff's son to sign the Conditions of Sale—the usual Conditions which the defendant had on their dockets for a considerable time. At the time of the sale it had not entered into the supervisor's head that what he was selling was not turnip seed at all. The buyer, however, got something that was not turnip seed, and, quite apart from the *Sale of Goods Act*, he had a cause of action. Counsel for the defendant had put forward the proposition that in the Conditions of Sale all the risk was covered. But it was not. The Conditions said that they selected their seeds with the greatest care. These Conditions were not applicable to the case where the defendant had not selected its goods with the greatest care, which in this case it had not, as it took what it could get.

Under the circumstances the decision had to be made that the defendant was liable. It was a serious case for both the plaintiff and the defendant. One of two innocent parties would suffer, but since the plaintiff did not get what he bought, the defendant, though not morally liable, was legally so . . .

d. Where the Buyer Deals as Consumer

Where the buyer deals as consumer, the implied terms under the statute cannot be excluded (s. 55 (4) of the combined Acts). Where goods are sold to the buyer dealing as consumer and in relation to the sale an agreement is entered into by the buyer with a finance house for the repayment to the finance house of money paid by the finance house to the seller in respect of the price of the goods, the finance house is deemed to be a party to the contract and liable for breach of the contract of sale (s. 14 of the 1980 Act): *O'Callaghan v Hamilton Leasing (Ireland) Ltd* (Case 48) and *Cunningham v Woodchester Investments Ltd* (Case 49).

Case 48. O'Callaghan v Hamilton Leasing (Ireland) Ltd
High Court [1984] I.L.R.M. 146

The plaintiff owner of a take-away food shop purchased a machine which produced fruit drinks containing crushed ice which were dispensed by the plaintiff before serving them to the customer. The purchase was financed by the defendant on foot of a leasing agreement. The machine proved to be defective and after two payments the plaintiff sued for a refund of these monies and damages for loss of profits. While the defendant did not dispute the machine's defectiveness, it argued that since the plaintiff was not dealing as a consumer he was not entitled to the protection of the implied conditions contained in the *Sale of Goods and Supply of Services Act 1980*.

Held that the contract was made in the course of the plaintiff's business and accordingly he did not deal as a consumer within the meaning of the statute.[*]

McWilliam J.:

The defendant can only be liable to the plaintiff under s. 14 of the *Sale of Goods and Supply of Services Act 1980*, if the plaintiff was a buyer dealing as a consumer within the meaning of subsection (1) of s. 3 of the Act. [This section is quoted in Case 49.]

It seems to me that this contract was made in the course of the plaintiff's business. It was certainly made for the purposes of his business although I appreciate the point made on behalf of the plaintiff that this business does not in any way include a re-sale or further dealing with the goods dealt with by the contract before me.

[*][The plaintiff recovered the monies, and damages, against the supplier of the machine.]

In order to interpret the words of s. 3 otherwise I would have to amend paragraph (a) of subsection (1) by reading it as though it provided 'in the course of a business which includes a further dealing with the goods' or some words of that sort.

I cannot depart from the clear words of a statute and try to construe it in accordance with my view of an unexpressed intention of the legislature although I suspect the legislature was more concerned with the business of engaging in further dealings with the goods.

With regard to paragraph (c) of the subsection, I am of opinion that the expression 'ordinarily supplied for private use or consumption' should be contrasted with use for the purposes of a business rather than contrasted with use for the purpose of re-sale of or further dealings with the goods. These goods were supplied for the purpose of a business and it has not been suggested that they would ever be supplied for use other than for the purpose of a business.

Accordingly, although these goods were supplied for the personal use of the plaintiff and he is the consumer in the ordinarily accepted meaning of the word, I must hold that, in this transaction, he did not 'deal as consumer' within the meaning of the Act.

Case 49. Cunningham v Woodchester Investments Ltd
High Court, unreported, 16 November 1984

The plaintiff bursar of an argicultural college, which produced a large annual turnover on its farming activities, leased a telephone system from the defendant. The system, which proved to be faulty, had been sold and installed by a third party. The plaintiff, having regard to s. 14 of the *Sale of Goods and Supply of Services Act 1980*, sought to make the defendant, a finance house, responsible for the breach of contract by the third party, the seller of the goods.

Held that to gain the benefit of the section the plaintiff must prove that he acted as a consumer within the meaning of the statute. Since the goods supplied were of a type not ordinarily supplied for private use and were to be used mainly in the course of the farming business, the plaintiff was not dealing as a consumer when the contract was made and the claim under the statute failed.

McWilliam J.:

The plaintiff stated that the college is a non-profit making venture but, in addition to training students in agriculture, the college sells very considerable quantities of farm produce, including cattle, pigs, vegetables, mushrooms and eggs, with a turnover approaching £1,000,000. The plaintiff stated that all money earned was put back into the farm . . .

The plaintiff relies on the provisions of s. 14 of the *Sale of Goods and Supply of Services Act 1980* which provides as follows:

Where goods are sold to a buyer dealing as consumer and in relation to the sale an agreement is entered into by the buyer with another person acting in the course of a business (in this section referred to as a finance house) for the repayment to the finance house of money paid by the finance house to the seller in respect of the price of the goods, the finance house shall be deemed to be a party to the sale and the finance house and the seller shall, jointly and severally, be answerable to the buyer for breach of the contract of sale and for any misrepresentations made by the seller with regard to the goods.

The plaintiff was the buyer within the section and, to benefit from its provisions, must have been buying as consumer within the meaning of the Act. 'Consumer' is construed at s. 3 of the Act. This section provides:

(1) In the Act of 1893 and this Act, a party to a contract is said to deal as consumer in relation to another party if—

    (a) he neither makes the contract in the course of a business nor holds himself out as doing so, and

    (b) the other party does make the contract in the course of a business, and

    (c) the goods or services supplied under or in pursuance of the contract are of a type ordinarily supplied for private use or consumption.

The defendant relied on the . . . contention that the plaintiff was not a 'consumer' within the meaning of the Act. I was referred to my own decision in *O'Callaghan v Hamilton Leasing (Ireland) Ltd* (Case 48) . . .

Whatever may be done with the profits accruing from the extensive agricultural activities carried on at Warrenstown, I do not see how it can be said that engaging in these activities with a turnover of the amount indicated does not constitute carrying on a business. The evidence indicated that the equipment to be supplied was mainly or largely to be used in the course of the farming activities, although I am sure it was also to be used for other purposes of the college as well. Furthermore, the equipment was quite clearly not of a type ordinarily supplied for private use or consumption.

No argument has been advanced in this case which persuades me that I should alter the view I formed in *O'Callaghan's Case* (Case 48).

Finally, it was suggested on behalf of the plaintiff that he was entitled to succeed at common law on the grounds that he did not get what was agreed to be supplied, that the equipment was not merchantable or fit for the purpose for which it was supplied and that what was delivered was not complete. This may be correct as against the supplier of the goods but, with regard to the defendant, I was not referred to any authorities and I am not satisfied that there is any liability on a finance house in circumstances such as these.

CHAPTER 9.

DELIVERY OF THE GOODS

Section 27 of the *Sale of Goods Act* provides that it is the duty of the seller to deliver the goods and delivery is defined, in s.62, as the voluntary transfer of possession. A seller is bound to deliver at the places stipulated in the contract: *Board of Ordnance v Lewis* (Case 50). The mere selection of goods may not constitute delivery: *Bonner v Whelan* (Case 51).

Delivery of the wrong quantity entitles the buyer to reject all of the goods. *Tarling v O'Riordan* (Case 52), *Wilkinson v McCann, Verdon & Co.* (Case 53) and *Norwell & Co. Ltd v Black* (Case 54).

Where there is a stipulation as to the time of delivery it must be observed. In the absence of agreement, delivery must be made within a reasonable time: *MacAuley v Horgan* (Case 55).

Section 32 of the *Sale of Goods Act 1893* provides that delivery to a carrier is *prima facie* deemed to be delivery to the buyer, but this rule may be displaced by the facts in a particular case: *Michel Frères Societé Anonyme v Kilkenny Woollen Mills (1929) Ltd* (Case 56).

Case 50. Board of Ordnance v Lewis
Queen's Bench (1855) 7 Ir.Jur. (o.s.) 17

The defendant agreed to deliver certain quantities of coal under terms as to quality, condition and price to the plaintiffs. The plaintiffs required the defendant to deliver certain quantities of coal at several places. The defendant delivered different quantities which the plaintiffs refused to accept and sued the defendant for damages for non-delivery of the coal because they were compelled to purchase other coals at prices in excess of the contract price.

Held that the defendant ought, according to the terms of the contract, have tendered the coals at the particular places demanded by the plaintiffs.

Lefroy C.J.:

There was a contract to deliver at certain specified places quantities of coal, with a proviso that 'all fuel offered for delivery (not *to be ready* for delivery, and thereby showing that the parties contracted for an actual offer,) should be *such* coals, in the quantities specified in the notice, as should be finally approved of by the board of officers.' The breach then is, that although the defendant received such notice he did not deliver the coals at a single place therein mentioned. The plaintiffs did not say that the defendant failed to deliver coals 'approved of', because they say he did not deliver any at all. They were not bound to allege a breach with respect to the insufficiency of the coals, inasmuch as they say that they were not offered at all. At one place, indeed, it would appear that though 1200 tons had been ordered, about 120 were tendered, and these are not stated to have been approved of by the officers.

At the other places there is no allegation of delivery or anything approaching to it, but only of the *readiness* of the defendant to deliver.

Crampton and Perrin JJ. concurred.

Case 51. Bonner v Whelan
County Court (1905) 34. I.L.T.R. 24

The defendant offered some cattle for sale at a fair, and the plaintiff bought them. The animals were driven into a corner where the defendant's employees and the plaintiff marked each animal. Later when the cattle were being weighed the defendant refused to allow the plaintiff to take the cattle and the plaintiff sued for damages.

Held that selecting, marking and weighing of goods did not constitute delivery within the *Sale of Goods Act 1893*.

Judge Barry:

I hold that the marking and weighing did not constitute delivery under the *Sale of Goods Act 1893*, accordingly I must dismiss the action on the merits.

Case 52. Tarling v O'Riordan
Court of Appeal (1878) 2 L.R. Ir. 82

The defendant ordered a quantity of goods from the plaintiff, which were delivered in two consignments. The first consignment was in order and was accepted. When the second consignment arrived, some of the goods were not in accordance with the order and the defendant rejected all the goods in the second consignment. The plaintiff sued for damages, for non-acceptance of these goods.

Held that the defendant was not bound to select and accept those goods which corresponded with the order but was entitled to reject all of the goods in the second consignment notwithstanding that he had accepted the first consignment.

Ball L.C.:

On 26 November, one bale was delivered in perfect conformity with the
order. The goods in it were taken into stock, and mixed with other goods
in the retail dealer's shop.

On 8 December a second bale arrived, containing trousers, vests, and
knickerbockers, agreeing with the order given; and coats, not of the
prescribed size, and therefore not in conformity with the order. The retail
dealer returned the entire bale. The decision of three judges of the
Queen's Bench is that he was not justified in this course; that he should
have kept what did agree with his order. Judge O'Brien dissented, and we
are of opinion that he was right.

It has not been controverted that if the second bale were the whole
extent of the original order, that order being joint, the retail dealer could
have returned the whole of the goods, when he found such a portion of
them as occurred in the present instance (about half in value) not
according to order.

In such a case, since *Levy v Green*, the law may be taken to be as
expressed by the judges in the Court of Error. If there is any risk of being
charged with an acceptance of all the goods sent, or any difficulty in
severing them, or any risk incurred as to extra articles being connected
with the others, in any of these three cases the delivery is vitiated, not
being a performance by the seller of his contract. The buyer is not bound
to incur risk of charge, or inconvenience, or danger of damage to the
articles, and may return the whole.

It is because the second bale was not the whole extent of the contract,
but that there was also in pursuance of it a first bale, and that this first
bale was accepted, that the case is sought to be distinguished. I think it
must be admitted that the acceptance of the first bale waived any objection
to the goods not being all delivered together, if such an objection were a
valid one, which I doubt. But I do not see how it could be held to entitle
the seller to transmit the second bale with substantial deviations from the
order, and, if he did, then to relieve him from the otherwise legal
consequences. In *Champion v Shortt* the purchaser ordered plums, brown
sugar, and white sugar. The plumbs and the brown sugar, not the white,
were forwarded. He used the plums, and desired, nevertheless, to rescind
the contract, returning the brown and refusing to receive the white sugar,
on the ground that all were not delivered together. This, it was held, he
could not do, and rightly, as it appears to me; for the ground of rescission
existed as to all or none, and acceptance of any one article was a waiver of
the right to act upon the particular ground. But here how could acceptance
of the first bale, which conformed to the order, lead to any inference that
the purchaser assented to the second bale deviating from it? If it did not,
was not the seller bound to send the second bale also substantially agreeing
with the order? Then the principles, which, whenever there arises either
risk of being held to accept all, or inconvenience in severing and separating

enable the return of the whole bale, apply, . . . are adequate to justify the course pursued by the present defendant.

Morris C.J., Christian and Deasy L.JJ. concurred.

Case 53. Wilkinson v McCann, Verdon & Co.
Court of Appeal [1901] New Ir.Jur.Rep. 14

The plaintiff agreed to supply the defendants with a quantity of goods which were to be delivered as soon as possible. The goods were sent in two consignments, the first of which was received in due time and was accepted and paid for though it contained more goods than were ordered. The second consignment arrived late and the defendants refused to take delivery of it. In a letter written by the defendants to the plaintiff it was stated that more goods than were ordered were received. The plaintiff sued for the price of the goods.

Held that the fact of a wrong quantity having been delivered entitled the defendants to reject all the goods.

Lord O'Brien L.C.J.:

. . . What evidence there was in this case that the defendants elected to keep the goods? They first said that they came too late and then that too many were sent. There was no evidence of a new contract created by accepting the goods, and there was no question on this point left to the jury. I am, therefore, of opinion that if this case rested on the cases before the *Sale of Goods Act* the plaintiff must fail, and the *Sale of Goods Act* was equally clear and strong against the plaintiff, particularly s. 30 of the Act. In this case there was no evidence that the buyer accepted any goods; the evidence was entirely the other way . . .

Madden and Barton JJ. concurred.

Case 54. Norwell & Co. Ltd v Black
Circuit Court (1931) 65 I.L.T.R. 105

The defendant ordered certain goods from the plaintiff. A delivery of part of the order was made. Two days later an invoice arrived stating 'remainder to follow'. The invoice did not sufficiently correspond with the order to satisfy the defendant who, accordingly, refused delivery of the goods. No agreement had been made for delivery in instalments. The plaintiff subsequently sent goods which had in fact formed part of the original order, and the defendant accepted and paid for them as a separate order. The plaintiff sued for the amount lost on the re-sale of the refused goods.

Held that the defendant was entitled to refuse the first delivery on the ground that the contract had not specified delivery by instalments. The defendant was not bound by the whole contract because of his acceptance of the later delivery.

Judge Roche:

On a scrutiny of the Act and the cases on the point and having heard the arguments, I hold that the plaintiffs are not entitled to succeed. Orders for certain goods were given to a traveller of the plaintiff firm by the defendant and by him in the ordinary course sent on to the plaintiff. The orders were clear on their faces. If accepted, delivery in the ordinary way would be in one lot. No provision was made for delivery by instalments. Correspondence took place concerning the orders and eventually the plaintiff wrote to the defendant making a new suggestion to them concerning the orders. That constituted a new offer, contained in a letter of 19 September. The defendant did not accept, but in answer to that offer he made what amounted in my opinion to a fresh or counter offer. This did not provide for delivery of the goods, if the offer were accepted, in other than one delivery or lot. There was no actual acceptance in writing by the plaintiff of that new offer but following upon its receipt the plaintiff forwarded some goods forming only portion of the orders. On discovering that only part of the goods had been forwarded, the defendant refused to take delivery. Section 31 of the *Sale of Goods Act 1893*, was passed to meet cases of that kind. It lay with the defendant to accept or reject the goods so forwarded. In fact he repudiated them. The goods were brought to his place of business and it was found that no invoice had been sent. It was perfectly reasonable to refuse the goods under the circumstances. The burden of proof was on the plaintiff to show when the invoice was sent out, and I have no reason to refuse to accept an employee's evidence for the defendant that there was no invoice sent with the consignment. Later the invoice arrived. In the meantime the defendant was afforded a chance to inspect the goods actually sent, and this chance was availed of. It was found that they did not correspond with the order, in that (1) the whole had not been sent or tendered together in one lot and (2) as regards several items the consignment did not correspond with the order. The plaintiff's traveller who might have thrown light on the facts so far as disputed, is not here. It is not sufficient merely to try to explain away the discrepancies. On these grounds the defendant was entitled to repudiate the goods immediately, which he did, and that put an end to the transaction. Later, subsequent to the repudiation, the plaintiff decided it would send on certain of the rest of the goods originally ordered—viz. 'Pabco'. After some days the 'Pabco' parcel arrived and on comparison with the invoice the parcel was found to be correct and the defendant took possession and paid for it. I am asked to hold that that set up the whole of the original order, and though at one stage I was in doubt I am satisfied now that that is not so. The defendant was not bound to communicate directly with the plaintiff, but the shipping company through whom the goods were forwarded and tendered to the defendant did communicate the repudiation to the plaintiff, whereupon, the plaintiff wrote to the defendant saying that it was surprised to hear from the shipping company that the first consignment had been refused as 'not ordered'. Counsel for the plaintiff insists that the defendant is bound by those words, but that I think, is no answer. It was fairly correct to say 'not ordered'—though the defendant, as he says, probably meant by that, 'not as ordered', but little turns on that. The order being then at an end, 100 pieces of 'Pabco' which were in fact ordered in the original orders of the defendant forwarded and delivered to the defendant and were in accordance with the invoice. This transaction was distinct. There was no reference to the prior order or dispute. This, in my opinion, constituted a new offer of these goods—viz. 'Pabco'—by the plaintiff which the defendant was entitled to accept or refuse as a distinct transaction as he might choose. He accepted it, took delivery and paid for the goods. That did not in my opinion set up the previous transaction. The defendant is right in law, though, I do not commend his failure to communicate or answer the sympathetic letters sent to him. He chose and was entitled to adopt a policy of masterly silence, and did nothing immoral in ethics or wrong in law. The law is clear. It is regrettable that this dispute should have occurred, but I have merely to decide the law on the point at issue. I therefore dismiss the action with costs.

Case 55. MacAuley v Horgan
High Court [1925] 2 I.R. 1

The parties, in a series of telegrams, entered into a contract for the sale of goods. No date was fixed for delivery of the goods. When the defendant failed to deliver the goods the plaintiff sued for damages. The defendant contended that s. 28 of the *Sale of Goods Act 1893* provided that delivery and payment were concurrent conditions and that as the plaintiff neither sent a cheque nor tendered cash for the goods that a failure to deliver the goods could be alleged.

Held that since no time for delivery was stipulated by the parties, the delivery should have been made within a reasonable time. Failure by the defendant to so so amounted to a breach of contract. Accordingly, the damages were fixed at the difference between the contract price and the market price at the date of the defendant's refusal to deliver, less the cost of carriage.

Sullivan P.:

But there was no time fixed for delivery. As no time was fixed for delivery, it was the duty of the seller to deliver the goods free on rail within a reasonable time. This brings me to the second argument of counsel for the defendant namely, that delivery and payment are concurrent conditions, and that, as the plaintiff neither sent a cheque nor tendered cash for the wool, he cannot allege a failure to deliver, or that there was a breach of contract. I cannot accept this view. It was the duty of plaintiff to be ready and willing to pay for the goods; and I am satisfied that the plaintiff was in fact ready and willing to pay, and I am also equally satisfied that the defendant was not ready and willing to put on rail and deliver the wool which had been ordered. In fact, the wool ordered was never despatched. I accordingly hold that defendant broke his contract . . .

I hold that a reasonable time for delivery had elapsed by 5 December, and that the wool should have been delivered on or before that date. I further hold that the refusal or neglect of defendant to answer the plaintiff's letters of 5 December and the 18 December amounted to a refusal by the defendant to perform his contract, one month prior to his receipt of the letter of 18 January 1924, from the plaintiff's solicitors.

The measure of damages is prescribed by s. 51 of the *Sale of Goods Act 1893*. That section provides that where the seller wrongfully neglects or refuses to deliver the goods to the buyer, the buyer may maintain an action against the seller for damages for non-delivery (sub-s. (1)). The measure of damages is the estimated loss directly and naturally resulting, in the ordinary course of events, from the seller's breach of contract (sub-s. (2)). And then sub-s. (3) provides: 'Where there is an available market for the goods in question the measure of damages is prima facie to be ascertained by the difference between the contract price and the market or current price of the goods at the time or times when they ought to have been delivered, or, if no time was fixed, then at the time of the refusal to deliver.' The section, it will be seen, states two alternative dates for ascertaining the measure of damages, namely, 'when the goods ought to have been delivered.' or, if no time was fixed, then 'the time of the refusal to deliver'.

I have held that the conduct of the defendant in not answering the letters of the plaintiff amounted to a refusal to deliver, that before the end of December there has been a refusal by the defendant to deliver the wool to the plaintiff, and that the plaintiff was not entitled to wait until the end of January before accepting such refusal. Accordingly, the next question is, was there an available market for the goods in question, and, if so, what was the difference between the market price and the contract price at that time? There was no evidence as to the existence of an available market for wool at Cahirciveen where delivery was contracted for, but, having regard to the previous dealings between the parties and the inter-communication between Cahirciveen and Dublin, I think that the market price at

Cahirciveen may, for the purposes of the measure of damages, be taken to be the market price at Dublin, less the cost of carriage, and, accordingly, I hold that the plaintiffs can rely on the market price at Dublin . . .

Accordingly, I hold that the price of wool in Dublin at the end of. December was £100 over that contracted for, and from this I deduct £50 for the cost of carriage to Dublin, and I therefore assess damages at £50.

Case 56. Michel Frères Societé Anonyme v Kilkenny Woollen Mills (1929) Ltd
High Court [1961] I.R. 157

The plaintiffs in France contracted to sell goods to the defendant in Ireland. The contract was cash against documents and included an express term as to the date of delivery but no term as to the place of delivery. Before the date of delivery, the plaintiffs delivered the goods to carriers in France for transmission to the defendant. The bill of lading was made out to 'order' and was endorsed by the carriers. The goods arrived in Dublin after the stipulated date for delivery and five days later the documents were presented for payment. The defendant refused to accept delivery of the goods and the plaintiffs sued for damages for breach of contract.

Held that delivery of goods to the carriers in France was not delivery to the defendant in accordance with the contract. The contract was that the defendant was not intended to take delivery of the goods until payment was made. Since the goods were not delivered to the defendant in accordance with the terms of the contract the claim was dismissed.

Davitt P.:

In their statement of claim the plaintiffs plead that they delivered the goods to a carrier for transmission to the defendant on 13 July, and that this was delivery in accordance with the contract. The defendant pleads that the contract was that the goods would, within the period of two months, be delivered at Kilkenny, or alternatively at an Irish port, or in the further alternative that they would be shipped within that period. It denies that delivery to a carrier as pleaded would be delivery in accordance with the contract.

In their reply, the plaintiffs deny that it was a term of the contract that the goods would be delivered at Kilkenny, or at an Irish port, or that they would be shipped within two months of the order.

It seems to me that when the defendant's telegram is read together with the agent of the plaintiffs' letter of 23 May, it constitutes an offer to buy the yarn if delivered at an Irish port within two months. This is not accepted *simpliciter* by the defendant, who, by its confirmation note of 28 May, made a counter offer to deliver at Kilkenny by 15 August 1951. This counter offer was never accepted by the defendant and so the matter of the place of delivery was left open, to be decided, in my opinion, by the law applicable.

Section 32 of the *Sale of Goods Act 1893*, provided in sub-s. 1:
(1) Where, in pursuance of a contract of sale, the seller is authorised or required to send the goods to the buyer, delivery of the goods to a carrier, whether named by the buyer or not, for the purpose of transmission to the buyer is *prima facie* deemed to be a delivery of the goods to the buyer.

I now revert to the facts. On acceptance of the defendant's order, the plaintiffs arranged . . . to have the yarn spun. The matter was put in hand and the order completed by 6 July, when the yarn was despatched to the public conditioning house at Tourcoing. The plaintiffs were notified of this, and they arranged with . . . an international transport agents throughout the world, to collect the yarn at the conditioning house and despatch it to the defendant at Kilkenny.

The carriers collected the goods at the conditioning house on 11 July and brought them to their own warehouse at Roubaix where they remained until 23 July. They were then taken by motor lorry to Antwerp where they were shipped by *S.S. City of Cork* (of the Saorstát and Continental Steamship Co.Ltd) for conveyance to Dublin. The ship arrived at Antwerp . . . on 26 July and left for Dublin the same day. The goods could have been taken on board only on that day, as they arrived at Dublin on 28 July. In accordance with the plaintiffs' instructions, the bill of lading was made out to 'order' and endorsed in blank by the carriers, who sent it to the plaintiffs. They in turn sent it, together with the certificate of insurance and the invoice to the Westminster Bank, who in turn sent the documents to their agents in Kilkenny, the Ulster Bank, for the purpose of exchange against the price of the goods. They were received in Kilkenny on 4 August. On 30 July the defendant had received an advice note from the shipping company that the goods had arrived in Dublin. On 2 August they wrote to the agent of the plaintiffs refusing to accept the goods, as they had not been delivered within two months in accordance with the contract.

The net point for decision is whether the delivery of the goods to the carriers who took possession of them on 11 July was delivery in accordance with the contract. By s. 62 of the *Sale of Goods Act* 'delivery' is defined as meaning the voluntary transfer of possession from one person to another. In this case there was of course an actual transfer of possession of the goods to the carriers. The question arises whether there was a constructive transfer of possession to the defendant. If at the time they received them, the carriers owed any duty to the defendant to receive or hold the goods on its behalf and dispose of them according to its directions, then clearly the actual delivery to the carriers would be constructive delivery to the defendant. I cannot see, however, how the carriers were under any duty to the defendant. I feel certain that they would not have complied with any instructions of the defendant to dispose of the goods. If, for instance, the defendant had told them that it had sold the goods to Messrs 'X' of Brussels, and to deliver them accordingly forthwith, I am quite certain the carriers would have done nothing of the kind unless and until they had got the plaintiffs' instructions in the matter. They acted throughout under, and in accordance with, the plaintiffs' instructions. In particular, they took the bill of lading made out to 'order', endorsed it in blank, and sent it to the plaintiffs. This was in accordance with the contract which provided for the exchange of the documents against cash. The whole intent of the contract was that the defendant was not to get possession or control of the goods until it had paid for them. It could not get actual possession of the goods until it got the documents. I cannot see how, either, it could have exercised any control over the goods before it got the documents. In these circumstances, it seems clear to me that the carriers received the goods as agents for the plaintiffs, and not as agents for the defendant, and that delivery to them made no change in the possesion of the goods. They held them at the disposal of the plaintiffs, and the goods while actually in their possession were still constructively in the possession of the plaintiffs. As long as the plaintiffs by themselves or their agents retained possession and control of the documents, and particularly the bill of lading, the defendant had no constructive possession of the goods. They never had actual possession. In my opinion, accordingly, there was never any delivery of the goods to them.

This view of the matter is consistent with the provisions of s. 32, sub-ss. 1 and 2, of the *Sale of Goods Act* . . .

For the foregoing reasons I am of opinion that the delivery of the goods to the carriers was not delivery to the defendant in accordance with the contract or at all. There was never in fact any delivery of the goods in accordance with the contract. There was never any tender of the goods within the two months period, and the defendant was quite entitled to refuse to accept the goods when they arrived in Dublin on 30 July. There was no breach of contract on its part and it is entitled to judgment.

CHAPTER 10.

ACCEPTANCE OF THE GOODS

Section 35 of the combined Acts provides that the buyer is deemed to have accepted the goods when he intimates to the seller that he has accepted them or when the goods have been delivered to him and he does any act in relation to them which is inconsistent with the ownership of the seller. Whether or not there is acceptance is a question of fact to be ascertained from all the circumstances: *Hopton v McCarthy* (Case 57) and *Jennings v C.E. Macaulay & Co. Ltd* (Case 58).

Section 34 of the combined Acts provides that where goods are delivered to a buyer, which he had not previously examined, he is not deemed to have accepted them unless and until he has had a reasonable opportunity of examining them: *Marry v Merville Dairy Ltd* (Case 59). Once a reasonable opportunity has been given to examine the goods a rejection, to be effective, must be performed immediately: *White Sewing Machine Co. v Fitzgerald* (Case 60) and *Gill v Thomas Heiton & Co. Ltd* (Case 61).

Case 57. Hopton v McCarthy
Queens Bench Division (1882) 10 L.R.Ir. 266

The defendant verbally ordered goods from the plaintiff. The invoice was forwarded with the goods but was immediately returned to the plaintiff with a letter stating that it did not correspond with the agreement and notifying the defendant's refusal to collect the goods from the local railway station. The plaintiff sued for the price.

Held that there was no acceptance of the goods by the defendant and that in the absence of a written contract an action for the price could not be maintained.

Fitzgerald J.:

This action was brought for goods sold and delivered, and I suppose also, though this was not stated, for goods bargained and sold, and money paid, and at the close of the evidence on the part of the plaintiff, counsel for the defendant asked for a direction for the defendant, on the ground that there was no signed contract, and nothing to take the case out of the *Statute of Frauds*; but the learned judge declined to direct a verdict, being of opinion that there was evidence to sustain the claim for goods sold and delivered. What the question left to the jury does not appear, only that the case was left to the jury, and that they found for the plaintiff for the amount claimed. The question now before us is under the 13th section of the Irish *Statute of Fraud (1695)* and corresponds with the 17th section of the *Statute of Frauds (1677)* in England, by which it is provided, that 'no contract for the sale of any goods, wares, or merchandises, for the price of £10 sterling, or upwards, shall be allowed to be good, except the buyer shall accept part of the goods so sold, and actually receive the same, or give something in earnest to bind the bargain, or in part payment; or that same note or memorandum in writing of the said bargain be made, and signed by the parties to be charged by such contract, or their agents thereunto lawfully authorized.' [This section corresponds with section 4(1) of the *Sale of Goods Act 1893*].

The case is one of some importance to the commercial community, though the amount involved is small . . . The question before us is whether there was any sufficient evidence of the receipt and acceptance to be left to the jury. The evidence as it stood at the trial was, first, that of the plaintiff, who proved that he called on the defendant, at his place in Tipperary, in October 1879, when he told him about goods he wanted, and ordered some, partly in stock, and others to be specially manufactured for him. He also said that there were other goods which he did not deal in, and the defendant asked him to get them for him. So far we have it established that there was a verbal contract for the sale of goods in stock, and for the manufacture of other goods by the plaintiff for the defendant, and some to be purchased by the plaintiff, and to be sent forward to the defendant. The plaintiff further proved that he got some of the goods specially made for the defendant in Birmingham, and dispatched all on 17 December 1879, by the route agreed upon; and that he sent on the invoice, amounting to £35 18s. 8d. net, as per agreement. The plaintiff also referred to a correspondence, including the invoice, and commencing with a letter from the defendant, of 18 December, complaining that the prices in the invoice were too high, and ending with a letter of 18 April 1880, in which the defendant objects to take the goods because trade was bad. It was at this stage of the case that counsel asked for a direction. Now we have to consider whether, on the correspondence, there was a receipt and acceptance by the defendant. The goods were delivered to the carrier on 17 December 1879, and sent forward, and there was receipt of the goods by the defendant. In some of the cases receipt and acceptance seem to be considered the same. The goods having been delivered to the carriers on 17 December, and the defendant having received the invoice on 18 December, then wrote the letter of that date, as follows:

Bank-Place, Tipperary,
December 18th, 1879.

Sir,—I have received your invoice to-day, which caused me to reply at once, as it does not appear as per agreement. I return your invoice by first post. The quoted prices do not agreeably appear. Do not send on your goods before I hear from you, or I shall not receive them.—I remain yours respectfully,

Barth. McCarthy

There is no evidence of acceptance in that letter, which the plaintiff got on 19 December. There was a postscript to that letter: 'My objection is the prices are too high.'

The plaintiff, having got that letter of 18 December repudiating the whole transaction, wrote a letter on the 20th to the defendant, who

answered that on the 22nd, and says: 'I have marked opposite the goods
you will be kind enough to send me. I find business rather slack just now,
and I shall not take more goods from you at present.'

This may refer to something on the margin of the invoice, and that
therefore the defendant would be bound by; and in point of fact the goods
which the defendant seems to admit that he ordered would amount to
about £10 or £12, and that is what he refers to in his letter. Then there was
another letter from the plaintiff, of 24 December:

> In reply to your letter of 22 December, the goods sent are exactly as
> ordered by you, and a copy of the order. In your first letter you said it
> was a question of some of the goods being dear, but as you have not
> said anything in regard to that in your letter just to hand, I presume you
> are perfectly satisfied upon that point. The goods were sent off last
> week, and will be delivered to you in due course, as ordered by you,
> and as per invoice. I hope you will find an improvement in trade after
> Christmas, especially as this mischievous agitation appears to be killing
> itself out.

Then on 2 January 1880, the defendant writes: 'Having received intimation
from the railway that goods are arrived, I consider the carriage exorbitant,
being nearly £2. Is that fair? If so, please advise.'

And this was the letter most relied upon by the plaintiff as evidence of
acceptance.

I regret to say that we are of opinion that there was no evidence of
acceptance proper to be submitted to the jury. A good deal has been said
as to the delivery to the carrier named by the defendant; but that, I think,
has been met by the case of *Norman v Phillips*. In that case the defendant
gave the plaintiff a verbal order for timber, directing it to be sent to the
Paddington Station of the Great Western Railway, to be forwarded to him,
as had been the practice between the parties on previous dealings. The
timber was accordingly sent, and arrived on 19 April; and the defendant
was informed by the railway clerk of its arrival, upon which he said he
would not take it. An invoice was sent a few days after, which the
defendant received and kept, without making any communication to the
plaintiff himself until 28 May, when he informed the plaintiff that he
declined taking the timber; and it was held that, although there might be a
scintilla of evidence for the jury of an acceptance of the timber within the
Statute of Frauds, yet there was not sufficient to warrant them in finding
that there was such an acceptance. Certainly that was a much stronger case
than that before us. No repudiation of the contract was notified to the
plaintiff, and no notice of not taking the timber for a long time. In the
course of the argument in that case, the delivery to the railway company
was relied upon; and Alderson B. says: 'He must accept the goods, and
actually receive the same, to constitute an acceptance within the meaning
of the statute. Here the goods are sent in the usual way, but when they
arrive at the carriers' warehouse the defendant refuses to take them. That
can scarcely be said to be an acceptance.' And again, when it was further

pressed that the receipt by the carriers was an acceptance, Alderson B. says: 'No; he was not his agent to accept them. An acceptance is not complete until the party has precluded himself by what he does from objecting to the quality of goods.' Upon a full discussion, the court decided that there was not sufficient evidence of acceptance to justify the jury in finding a verdict for the plaintiff. In the case of *Morton v Tibbett*, Lord Campbell says, amongst other things: 'The acceptance is merely instead of a memorandum.' And again he says: 'There may be an acceptance and receipt within the meaning of the Act, without the buyer having examined the goods, or done anything to preclude him from contending that they do not correspond with the contract,' but he adds: 'the effect is merely to waive written evidence of the contract, and to allow it to be established by parol.'

. . . The only other authority that I will refer to is the case of *Coombs v Bristol & Exeter Railway Co.* in which Bramwell B. says:

Where there is a verbal contract for goods within the 17th section of the *Statute of Frauds*, and no earnest or note in writing of the bargain, there must be some affirmative act of acceptance to make the contract good. I think it would be more sensible to hold that any delivery and receipt is sufficient, unless there is a subsequent refusal to accept.

Upon examination of the evidence, it appears to us that, in place of any affirmative acceptance of the goods, there was from the beginning to the close a repudiation of the contract. We think, therefore, the verdict cannot be supported . . .

Barry J. concurred.

Case 58. Jennings v C.E. Macaulay & Co. Ltd
High Court [1937] I.R. 540

The plaintiff delivered a quantity of wool to the defendant which was rejected on the ground that the consignment contained more wool than was ordered. Letters passed between the parties and the plaintiff claimed that portion of this correspondence constituted a sufficient note or memorandum in writing of the terms of the contract. The letter of the defendant relied on by the plaintiff contained a reference to reducing the contract price by a sum which, it was alleged, was owed from a previous transaction. When the plaintiff wrote to the defendant that it was proposed to sell the wool at a reduced price and sue the defendant for the loss on the contract price, the defendant tele-grammed, 'Don't sell wool till we call tomorrow.' It was alleged by the plaintiff that this was a recognition by the defendant that it (the defendant) owned the wool. The plaintiff sued the defendant for damages for the failure to take delivery of the goods.

Held that while the court was prepared to hold that a contract existed for the lesser quantity of wool, the fact was that the contract as established did not contain any stipulation relating to the previous transaction. Accordingly, the defendant's letter did not constitute a sufficient note or memorandum in writing to satisfy the *Statute of Frauds*. Even if the telegram was a recognition by the defendant that it owned the wool it did not afford any evidence of receipt so as to negative the statutory requirement of having the contract evidenced in writing.

Sullivan P.:

. . . The final stage of the correspondence, which was conducted by a solicitor for the plaintiff and a solicitor for the defendant, continued from the month of February 1930 to the month of October 1934. Of the letters written during that period only two are relied on by the plaintiff as containing a note or memorandum of the contract. These two letters are as follows:

On 18 February 1930, the plaintiff's solicitor wrote to the defendant's solicitor: 'Messrs. C.E. Macaulay & Co., Wool Merchants, of 15 Haymarket, Dublin, have given me your name in connection with a contract for the purchase of wool between Mr. Martin Jennings of Ballinrobe and Messrs Macaulay. Messrs Macaulay purchased a quantity of wool at 1s.2¾d. per pound of which they have refused to take delivery. I write to notify you further that unless within a week from this date your clients take delivery of the wool my client will proceed to sell the wool at the best price that can be obtained, and will sue Messrs. Macauley for any loss or damage he may suffer by reason of their failure to carry out the contract.' The reply of the defendant's solicitor dated 28 February, was as follows: 'With reference to your letter of the 18th inst., we have now considered this matter with our clients. As we are instructed, in September last our clients inspected a quantity of wool representing about 20 bags in your client's store in Ballinrobe and agreed to purchase same. The quantity of wool was sufficient for our clients' requirements and they never had any intention of purchasing more than this amount, and, under the circumstances, our clients cannot see their way to take delivery of 40/50 bags which your client states he sold them. We are further instructed that the sale was subject to the payment to our clients of the sum of £14 3s. 1d. being the value of shortweights of a consignment of Scotch wool which sum has not yet been paid.' It will be noted that the contract alleged by the plaintiff's solicitor in his letter is a contract to purchase 'a quantity of wool at 1s.2¾d. per pound' and that the defendant's solicitor's reply does not contain any reference to the price, but alleges 'a contract to purchase a quantity of wool representing about 20 bags' subject to the payment to their clients (the defendant) of £14 3s. 1d. the amount of shortweights on previous consignments. I would be prepared to take the view that, as this latter letter does not contradict the statement in the plaintiff's solicitor's letter as to price, it should be interpreted as agreeing with it that the price was 1s.2¾d. per lb., and further to hold that it admits a contract to purchase an unascertained quantity of wool, which the defendant believed to represent about 20 bags, at that price. But there remains the difficulty that the sale is stated to have been subject to the payment by the plaintiff of the sum of £14 3s. 1d. . . . The contract pleaded [does not] contain any such stipulation and I am, therefore, unable to hold that the note or memorandum contained in those two letters is a note or memorandum of the contract. I am satisfied on the evidence that the contract did not, and could not, have contained any such stipulation, but that is, in my view, quite immaterial in considering the question whether there is a note or memorandum of the contract signed by the defendant or its agent. Having come to that conclusion, it is not necessary to consider the argument that the defendant's solicitor was not an agent authorised by the defendant to sign a note or memorandum of the contract.

The only remaining question is whether in this case the defendant accepted part of the wool sold and actually received the same. The matters relied on by the plaintiff to establish such acceptance and receipt are as follows: On 27 March 1930, the plaintiff's solicitor wrote to the defendant's solicitor notifying him that his client had been trying to dispose of the wool and had been offered 9d. per lb. for it, and that he intended to accept that offer unless he could get a better price, and sue the defendant for the loss on the resale. On the following day the defendant telegraphed to the plaintiff 'Don't sell wool till we call to-morrow,' and confirmed that telegram by a letter of the same day. It is said that that telegram recognises a pre-existing contract of sale of the wool, as unless the defendant was owner of the wool it would have no right to direct that the wool should not be sold. I do not think that the telegram should necessarily be read as imperative in its terms, it is at least equally capable of being interpreted as a request. But even if it be read as imperative and as evidence that the defendant *owned* the wool, I cannot see that it affords any evidence of receipt of the wool either actual or constructive.

Accordingly I have come to the conclusion that there is no note or memorandum of the contract sufficient to satisfy s. 4 of the *Sale of Goods Act*, and that the defendant did not accept and actually receive any part of the wool sold.

O'Byrne J. concurred.

Case 59. Marry v Merville Dairy Ltd
Circuit Court (1954) 88 I.L.T.R. 129

The parties entered into a contract for the supply of milk. The milk was to be pure whole milk, sweet, clean and marketable with all its cream and to be delivered at a place adjacent to the plaintiff's farm. It was deemed to be accepted by the defendant, subject to examination, upon delivery there. The defendant tested a quantity of milk supplied by the plaintiff at its premises and found it to be unwholesome and refused to pay for it. The plaintiff sued for the value of the milk and argued that the milk should have been examined at the place of delivery rather than at the defendant's premises.

Held that delivery was to take place subject to examination by the defendant and as the contract did not expressly specify where or when that examination was to be made it was reasonable that the defendant should examine it at its premises. Since the plaintiff supplied milk which failed this examination the action for the price must be dismissed.

Judge Shannon:

. . . The plaintiff submits that the correct interpretation of this clause is that if the defendant wishes to make an examination of any consignment so delivered it must be done at the place of delivery before it is taken from there by it.

The defendant urges that the correct view is that it is not to be deemed to have accepted a delivery unless and until it has had a reasonable opportunity of examining the consignment for the purpose of ascertaining whether it is in conformity with the contract, and that this reasonable opportunity arises only when the consignment reaches its premises, always provided, of course, tha there is no undue delay in collecting and carrying from the place of delivery to the defendant's premises.

The contract in question is in the form prescribed in accordance with the [relevant statute] and because of this it may be described as a statutory contract. I think it was agreed at the hearing before me that it was the defendant who filled in and named in the appropriate clause (clause 1) the place for delivery, and it is consequently urged by counsel on behalf of the plaintiff that this clause must be construed most strongly against the defendant. I accept this proposition as correct, but it cannot conclude the matter if the intention of the parties can be gathered from the whole of the agreement to be adverse to the submission of the plaintiff.

In my opinion clause 1 does not expressly specify where or when the examination mentioned is to be made if an examination is desired. The words 'upon delivery there' do not govern the preceding words in brackets 'subject to examination'. It was always agreed between the parties that delivery was made when the can was placed upon the roadside for collection. It was well known to the plaintiff that the collection of the can would not be made until some time after this delivery, and consequently examination could not be made 'upon delivery'. But quite apart from any such view of the facts the clear construction of clause 1 does not permit of the words 'upon delivery there' controlling the time and place of examination.

The agreement between the parties must receive the construction which its language admits, and which will best carry out the intention of the parties to be gathered from the whole of the agreement.

I cannot find in the whole of the document any expressed or implied intention that any examination made must be by the roadside at the place of delivery. I do find in the words of clause 1 an implied intention that the defendant was to have a reasonable opportunity of examining each consignment. I find this from the fact that no time or place for examination is expressly mentioned in the document. In these circumstances I do not find myself at liberty to go outside the agreement, and guess what was in the minds of the parties when they made the contract. What, then, is the reasonable time and place for examination? I do not think that anyone could seriously suggest that the defendant's driver, or his helper, if he has one, would be suitable persons to make the examination on the roadside. Apart from their competence to make tests, the nature of their employment makes them unsuitable. A test could be made on the roadside by a person with expertise, but I accept the expert opinion that whilst this would be possible, it is not practical. If the milk was delivered in sealed cans this becomes more apparent . . .

Case 60. White Sewing Machine Co. v Fitzgerald
Queen's Bench Division (1895) 29 I.L.T.R. 37

The defendant purchased a bicycle on credit from the plaintiff which proved to be defective. On two occasions the bicycle was returned to be put in proper repair, but each time it was returned in bad condition, though stated to have been fully overhauled and refitted. The defendant sought to repudiate the contract and demanded the return of the sum already paid, which return the plaintiff refused to make. When the defendant refused to pay the remainder, the plaintiff sued.

Held that where faulty goods are not at once returned and the contract repudiated, the implied condition that they are fit for the purpose for which they were purchased is waived. But the implied warranty of fitness remains, on which an action for damages may be brought.

Gibson J.:

I hold that the right to repudiate the contract depended on the implied condition in the contract of sale. The implication was negatived by the defendant not at once repudating the contract, and returning the goods instead of sending them to be repaired, and if the condition could be implied the defendant had waived it. The machine was defective, and a claim for breach of the implied warranty under the *Sale of Goods Act 1893* lay. This claim was pleaded as a set-off, of which notice had been given, and on that, there should be allowed £2 for damages. A decree should go for the amount sued for, less the £2 damages for breach of warranty, and defendant should, of course, retain the bicycle.

Case 61. Gill v Thomas Heiton & Co. Ltd
High Court [1943] Ir.Jur.Rep. 67

The plaintiff wholesale fuel merchant agreed with the defendant retail fuel merchant for the sale of a barge-load of turf. The turf was sent by barge to the defendant's wharf and shortly after the unloading had commenced the defendant's employee observed that the turf was, in his opinion, unfit for sale. He notified his superiors of this fact but the unloading continued until the entire load was unloaded. On the following day the defendant informed the plaintiff that the turf was useless and that they wished him to remove it from the wharf. The plaintiff contended that the defendant accepted the turf and accordingly he sued for the full price of the turf.

Held that the sale was by description and the turf as delivered not corresponding in quality with the description; therefore the defendant had a right to reject the goods at the time of delivery or within a reasonable time afterwards. Such right had not been exercised with sufficient promptness or in a manner consistent with the continued ownership of the seller and accordingly the plaintiff was entitled to damages.

Geoghegan J.:

. . . I have come to the conclusion that this was a sale by description within the meaning of s. 13 of the *Sale of Goods Act 1893*. The defendant, by virtue of s. 34 of this Act, had a right of examining the goods and, if justified by their examination, of rejecting the goods. The examination was carried out while the turf was being unloaded from the barge, and at about 11 o'clock in the morning the defendant was notified by its employee who was watching the unloading that the turf was of very bad quality. At this time only a small quantity had been discharged but it is conceded the quantity was enough for purpose of examination. No step, however, was taken at any time to suspend the unloading with the result that the whole of the consignment was removed from the barge on to the defendant's wharf. I think that the defendant was at fault in allowing this to happen if it wished afterwards to reject the turf, and in my opinion, it lost its right of rejection by not exercising it with reasonable promptness at this stage. The continuation of the discharge of the cargo after the defendant's foreman had informed it of the quality of the turf was not consistent with the ownership remaining in the sellers. Accordingly, the defence to this action, so far as it is based upon the defendant having purported to reject the goods, must fail . . .

PART THREE

HIRE-PURCHASE

According to the *Hire-Purchase Act 1946* a hire-purchase agreement is defined as an agreement for the bailment of goods under which the bailee may buy the goods, or under which the property in the goods will or may pass to the bailee. The property in the goods, as distinct from possession, will pass to the hirer should the hirer decide to pay all the sums due under the agreement. It is a hiring agreement with an option to purchase.

Invariably there are three parties to a hire-purchase arrangement; the seller of the goods, a finance house and the hirer. The goods which the hirer is anxious to acquire are bought by a finance house, which becomes the owner of them, and the finance house enters into a hire-purchase agreement with the party wishing to buy the goods and who is termed the hirer until all obligations under the agreement are terminated. The hire-purchase contract is between the owner and the hirer: *Dunphy v Blackhall Motor Co. Ltd* (Case 62).

Case 62. Dunphy v Blackhall Motor Co. Ltd
Circuit Court (1953) 87 I.L.T.R. 128

The parties agreed on the sale of a motor van. The plaintiff was not disposed to paying cash for it. The defendant contacted a finance company and it was arranged that it would advance the purchase price while in return the plaintiff would pay a deposit and discharge the balance through instalments. The plaintiff entered into a hire-purchase agreement with the finance house and the defendant invoiced the van to it and were paid by the finance house. The van was delivered by the defendant to the plaintiff. The van was involved in an accident and the plaintiff sued the defendant for relief under the *Sale of Goods Act 1893*.

Held that there was no contractual relationship between the parties and the action must be dismissed.*

Judge McCarthy:

On the facts before me I cannot hold that there was contract of sale [between the plaintiff and defendant]. There was, however, a real transaction of hire [between the plaintiff and the finance house]. I must dismiss the action.

CHAPTER 11.

STATUTORY REQUIREMENTS

The *Hire-Purchase Act 1946* requires that a hire-purchase contract must be in writing and must contain material information on vital terms of the contract, such as the cash price, the hire-purchase price, details of the instalments, a list of the goods and a notice, which sets out protections for the hire, which must be as prominent as the rest of the agreement. Failure to comply with these statutory requirements prevents the owner from enforcing the agreement though the court has a discretion to waive these requirements should it be satisfied that non-compliance has not prejudiced the hirer and that it is just and equitable to do so.

The agreement must contain the statutory details when the contract is signed by the hirer: *British Wagon Credit Co. v Henebry* (Case 63). To fulfil a definition of a note or memorandum it must contain the essential details: *United Dominions Trust (Commercial) Ltd v Nestor* (Case 64).

Failure to comply with the statutory requirements renders the agreement unenforceable: *Mercantile Credit Co. of Ireland Ltd v Cahill* (Case 65), unless the court waives such compliance: *B.W.Credit Corporation v Higgins* (Case 66).

---

*The *Sale of Goods and Supply of Services Act 1980*, s. 32, provides that the party conducting antecedent negotiations to a hire-purchase agreement is jointly and severally liable to the hirer for any breach of the agreement where the hirer acts as consumer.

Case 63. British Wagon Credit Corporation v Henebry
High Court (1963) 97 I.L.T.R. 123

The defendant signed a hire-purchase proposal form for the purchase of a tractor. The agreement, in the form in which it was presented to the court, contained details which had been inserted in two distinct inks. There was evidence that the details required by the statute had not been inserted before the agreement was signed by the defendant. The tractor proved defective and the defendant successfully sued the plaintiffs for damages and refused to pay any further instalments. The plaintiffs sued for the outstanding instalments.

Held that to satisfy the statute it must be proved that the agreement contained the statutory details at the time it was signed by the hirer. Since the plaintiffs could not do so, there was not a note or memorandum in writing as required by the statute and the action should be dismissed.

Murnaghan J.:

. . . The *Hire-Purchase Act 1946*, s. 3 (1) provides that there is a proviso to sub-section (2) that if the court is satisfied in any action that a failure to comply with the requirements specified in paragraphs (b) or (c) of this sub-section has not prejudiced the hirer, and that it would be just and equitable to dispense with the requirement, the court may—not shall—subject to any conditions it thinks fit to impose, dispense with that requirement for the purposes of the action.

Now, dealing first with this proviso it is quite clear that the requirements of sub-section (2) remain unless compliance therewith is dispensed with by the court in a given case. There must be a note or memorandum which has been made and signed by the hirer and by or on behalf of all other parties to the agreement. Some difficulty arises as to the matters which this memorandum is to contain. It is clear that it must contain in addition to those items set out in paragraph (b) of s. 3(2), the names and descriptions of the parties sufficient to identify them. What is to be found here? I have no direct evidence that this hire-purchase agreement was made and signed by the defendant. A signature 'John Henebry' appears upon the hire-purchase agreement, the proposal form and the delivery receipt. But the signature of a witness to the hirer's signature appears on the hire-purchase agreement. The normal way of proving a party's signature upon a document is to call the person who was present when it was signed by him; and when I say 'the document' I mean the document in the form in which it was presented to him for signature. Alternatively, the party who is alleged to have signed the document may himself be called and asked in the witness box to acknowledge his signature. In this case, however, neither of these modes of proof was adopted. But there is still a third mode of proving signature—circumstantial evidence of signature will suffice if it is such as to satisfy the court. Having regard to the history of this case, and the evidence adduced, I am satisfied that this was the defendant's signature.

In my view, the onus is on the hire-purchase company to establish to the satisfaction of the court that a note or memorandum was made and signed according to the requirements of the sub-section and that it contains the items required by the sub-section unless compliance therewith is dispensed with. If the plaintiffs have discharged this onus in so far as the signature on the note or memorandum is concerned, the onus still rests on them to prove the existence of a sufficient note or memorandum at the time of the signature by the hirer. They have produced documents which are now complete and as such would be a sufficient note or memorandum and counsel for the plaintiffs submits that I should hold that these documents in that form are sufficient. I will not make any presumption of regularity with respect to the state of the documents when presented to the defendant for his signature. I doubt if the maxim '*omnia praesumuntur rite esse acta*' does apply in a case of this kind. It does not, in my opinion, apply if there are apparent irregularities in the completion of the documents such as there are for example here as to the filling in of one of the essential matters, the hire-purchase price, after the hirer had signed the proposal form and the hire-purchase agreement. It has been urged upon me that the requirements of s. 3 of the *Hire-Purchase Act 1946*, are analogous of those of s. 4 of the *Statute of Frauds* and that the requirements of this latter section are sufficiently complied with if a note or memorandum is shown to have been made before action brought. I do not think that any such analogy exists—there is a clear distinction. There is in the *Hire-Purchase Act* the requirement that a note or memorandum of the agreement is made and signed by the hirer; this is of real significance and it appears that the note or memorandum should be made at the time of the agreement. This is clear from the Act and from the requirements respecting the statutory notice which, it is provided, shall be at least as prominent as the other part of the agreement. Then there is another provision which requires that a copy of the note or memorandum shall be sent to the hirer by the owner within seven days of the making of the agreement. That provision would make no sense if the hire-purchase company could by delaying its signature, make the date of its signature the date of the agreement. I do not decide, however, this question, but I would have some doubt that the date of the agreement was the ultimate date upon which the signature of the hire-purchase company was affixed to the agreement. I am not satisfied on the evidence that there was a sufficient note or memorandum signed by the defendant. That being so the plaintiffs must fail in this action.

Case 64. United Dominions Trust (Commercial) Ltd v Nestor
High Court [1962] I.R. 140

By a written agreement, which contained all the relevant statutory requirements, the defendant agreed to take goods on hire-purchase from the plaintiff. By a subsequent verbal agreement the defendant purchased some of the goods and agreed to pay the outstanding balance of the hire-purchase price of all the goods by instalments. When the defendant defaulted on payment of the instalments, the plaintiff terminated the agreement and claimed the return of some of the goods, or their value, and payment of the unpaid instalments with interest.

Held that the earlier written agreement did not comply with s. 3 the *Hire-Purchase Act 1946* in relation to the subsequent verbal agreement. Accordingly there was no note or memorandum in writing which satisfied the statute. Had the written agreement constituted a sufficient compliance with the statutory requirements the circumstances were such that the court would not exercise its discretion to dispense with the requirements of the statute. The action was dismissed.

Murnaghan J.:

The proceedings arise out of a hire-purchase transaction which was the subject-matter of a hire-purchase agreement dated 17 February 1960. It appears from the statement of claim that in the month of August 1960, a further arrangement was entered into between the parties to the agreement; however, that arrangement was not reduced to writing in any shape or form.

Counsel for the plaintiff, as I would have expected from him, immediately drew my attention to the fact that the subsidiary agreement of August 1960 had not been reduced to writing. The fact is of importance because of the provision of s. 3 (2) of the *Hire-Purchase Act 1946*. In so far as material, the provisions of this sub-section are as follows:

An owner shall not be entitled to enforce a hire-purchase agreement . . . unless . . .

(*a*) a note or memorandum of the agreement is made and signed by the hirer and by or on behalf of all other parties to the agreement, and

(b) the note or memorandum contains a statement of the hire-purchase price and of the cash price of the goods to which the agreement relates and of the amount of each of the instalments by which the hire-purchase price is to be paid and of the date, or the mode of determining the date, upon which each instalment is payable, and contains a list of the goods to which the agreement relates sufficient to identify them . . .

The legislature has seen fit to lay down strict requirements in relation to hire-purchase transactions. I have, in other cases, held that there is an onus on a plaintiff suing on a hire-purchase agreement to satisfy the court that the statutory requirements have been complied with . . .

It is eminently clear in this case that there is not any note or memorandum of a hire-purchase agreement [made in August 1960]. In other words, there has not been compliance with the requirements set out in para. (b).

Counsel for the plaintiff, in these circumstances, points to the proviso to s. 3 which is in the following terms: 'Provided that if the court is satisfied in any action that a failure to comply with the requirements specified in the foregoing sub-section or any requirement specified in para. (b) . . . of this sub-section has not prejudiced the hirer, and that it would be just and equitable to dispense with the requirements, the court may, subject to any conditions that it thinks fit to impose, dispense with that requirement for the purposes of the action.'

He submits that the hirer has not been prejudiced and, further, that it would be just and equitable to dispense with the requirements set out in para. (b).

This submission involves the plaintiff in having to fall back on the agreement of 17 February 1960, for the note or memorandum required by para (a). Unless he can rely on this agreement counsel admits that the plaintiff must fail. The submission that this agreement is sufficient might be tenable if all that is required by para. (a) is an agreement in writing, signed by the parties thereto, containing the names of the parties and a reference to the goods in question. This brings into relief the question, which so far as I am aware has never yet been resolved in a reported case, of the true construction to be placed on the provisions of sub-s. 2, and in particular on paras. (a) and (b) thereof. The way this question is usually raised in argument is by posing the question: 'What is left in a case where the court is satisfied to dispense with the requirements of para. (b)?'

The consideration of this problem, if it be a problem, must start with one proposition which is clear, namely, that the requirements of para. (a) cannot be dispensed with. It follows therefore that there must be a note or memorandum of the agreement made and signed by the parties. If there is to be a note or memorandum it would seem that the normal contents of such note or memorandum would be the date of the agreement, the parties between whom it was made, the goods to which it related, the price to be paid therefor and the manner of payment. If this is so it can then be said: 'What is the reason for para. (b) which is joined to para (a) by the word, "and"?' The answer, in my view, is that the form of the sub-section was adopted not to indicate that what is included in para. (b) is excluded from para. (a), but to make assurance doubly sure and to ensure that the requirements set out in para. (b) shall be contained in the note or memorandum mentioned in para. (a), and also as a convenient method of proving 'that a failure to comply with . . . any requirement specified in para. (b)' might be dispensed with for the purposes of the action. It is in my view impossible to imagine a case in which the court, having to bear in mind that there must be a 'note or memorandum of the agreement . . . made and signed . . . ', would dispense with *all* the requirements specified in para. (b) . . .

My view of the interpretation of s. 3 being as I have stated, in my opinion there has not been a compliance with the requirements of para. (a) in this case. In other words, the agreement of 17 February 1960, ignoring the fact that it pre-dates the agreement of August 1960, is insufficient to comply with the requirements of para. (a) for the purpose of these proceedings. I go further and say that if it should happen that this view is erroneous I would not be prepared to dispense with the requirements of para. (b) as would be necessary for the plaintiffs to succeed.

The plaintiff, in the circumstances, fails in this application for judgment, but having regard to the fact that the defendant has seen fit to ignore the present proceedings I will accede to the request of counsel that the plaintiff should be allowed to discontinue them and I so order.

I hope that this case, in conjunction with what I said recently in Carlow when on circuit (see *British Wagon Credit Co. v Henebry* (Case 63)), will have the effect of bringing home to hire-purchase companies the advisability of a strict compliance with the statutory provisions in relation to hire-purchase agreements. I make this comment because I regret to say that it has been my experience that insufficient care is taken in many cases in the making and signing of these agreements.

Case 65. Mercantile Credit Co. of Ireland Ltd v Cahill
Circuit Court (1964) 98 I.L.T.R. 79

The defendant agreed to take a motor car on hire-purchase from the plaintiff. When the defendant signed the agreement the details required by the *Hire-Purchase Act 1946*, s. 3, had not been filled out though they were completed later by the plaintiff. The copy of the agreement given to the defendant differed materially from the original agreement. The car proved defective and the defendant refused to pay any of the instalments. The plaintiff brought an action for the full sum due under the agreement.

Held that the statutory requirement as to the necessity of a note or memorandum in writing of a hire-purchase agreement had not been fulfilled. In such circumstances it would not be either just or equitable to dispense with the statutory requirements. The action was dismissed. The effect of non-compliance with the statutory requirements was to render the agreement unenforceable and since the defendant was in lawful possession of the car no order would be made for its return to the plaintiff.

Judge Maguire:

. . . I am satisfied, on the evidence, that when the defendant was asked to sign the hire-purchase agreement none of the details was filled in.

It seems clear that in this particular transaction the offeror was not aware of the actual offer he was making to the offeree—and that while, strictly speaking, there is in evidence a note or memorandum of the agreement made and signed by the hirer, the hirer was not aware of the terms of the agreement at the time he signed. It is my view that in all the circumstances the agreement itself does not comply in law with the apparent intention of s. 3 sub-s. 2 of the 1946 Act.

There is a further piece of evidence to which I must refer. The defendant gave evidence that the car gave him considerable trouble after he bought it and he had in fact to spend over £140 on it a few months after he bought it. This could have given rise to other proceedings which might or might not have been successful. Apart from this latter piece of evidence I have come to the conclusion that this transaction did not comply with any single one of the requirements of s. 3 of the 1946 Act. Thus as to sub-s. 1: (a) There were no tickets showing the price and (b) There was no evidence that the goods were selected by reference to a catalogue, price-list, or advertisment.

Sub-s. 2: (a) The note or memorandum was not in my view completed or executed in a manner that complied with this requirement, and (b) The note or memorandum did not contain a correct statement of either the cash price or the hire-purchase price, and (c) The notice required by this paragraph did not comply with the requirements of s. 16 of the 1960 Act as to the prescribed sub-paragraph, and (d) a copy of the note or memorandum of the agreement sent to the hirer was not a true copy of the note or memorandum.

By the proviso to s. 3 I could dispense with one or possibly more of these requirements if I were satisfied that the hirer was not prejudiced and that it would be just and equitable to dispense with such requirement or requirements. If I were satisfied that he was prejudiced the agreement would not be enforceable. On the other hand, if I were satisfied that he was not prejudiced I would still have to be satisfied that it would be just and equitable to dispense with one or more of the statutory requirements. In all the circumstances I am not satisfied that it would be either just or equitable to dispense with the statutory requirements, which have not been complied with in this case. I therefore dismiss the plaintiff's claim.

Note: The judge refused the application for an order for the return of the car, but gave the plaintiff liberty to re-apply within one week in the event of their having authority for the making of the order sought. No such re-application was made.

Case 66. B.W. Credit Corporation v Higgins
High Court, unreported, 11 November 1968

The parties entered into a hire-purchase agreement. When the defendant fell into arrears the plaintiff sued and the defendant alleged, *inter alia* that the plaintiff had failed to comply with the requirements of s. 3 of the *Hire-Purchase Act 1946* in that (a) the mode of determining the date on which payments were to be paid was absent from the contract, (b) that the statutory notice was not at least as prominent as the rest of the contents of the contract and (c) that a copy of the contract had not been delivered to the defendant within fourteen days, and consequently the agreement could not be enforced. The plaintiff had obtained on another occasion judgment by default against the defendant in the Circuit Court. To do so it was necessary to swear that the statutory provisions had been complied with.

Held that the failure to comply with the statutory requirements had prejudiced the defendant and that it would be unjust and inequitable to overlook this default. The plaintiff's proceedings in the Circuit Court had compounded its disregard for the statutory requirements.

Henchy J.:

. . . .Paragraph (b) of s. 3(2) requires that the hire-purchase agreement (which is the note or memorandum relied on) should contain a statement of the date or mode of determining the date upon which each instalment is payable. It fails to do so. It provides for an initial rent of £350 payable on or before delivery 'and 3 November rents each of £320.6.8d the first of which shall be payable November after delivery and subsequent November rents on the same date in each subsequent November during the period of hire'. It gives neither the date nor a mode of determining the date upon which the rent is to be paid. It says no more than that it is to be paid in the month of November. Thus it falls short of what is required by the statute.

Paragraph (c) lays down that the note or memorandum should contain a notice, which is at least as prominent as the rest of the contents of the note or memorandum, in the terms prescribed in the Act (as amended by the *Hire Purchase (Amendment) Act 1960)*. The object of this provision is to ensure that the hirer's right to terminate the agreement and the restriction of the owner's right to recover the goods shall, in the interest of the hirer, be set out in the document in a manner which does not suggest that these matters are of any less importance that the rest of the contents of the document. In the present case, the hire-purchase agreement is printed mainly in black and partly in red, the matters in red thereby acquiring a prominence and emphasis. A number of different sizes of print are used in the document. Yet the statutory note is printed in black and in the smallest type used in the document. It requires good eyesight to read it, whereas other matters stand out clearly and boldly. This is a breach of the requirement that the notice should be as prominent as the rest of the contents of the document.

Paragraph (d) (as amended by the 1960 Act) requires that a copy of the note or memorandum be delivered or sent to the hirer within fourteen days. In the present case, a document purporting to be a copy of the hire-purchase agreement was sent to the defendant, but it differs from the original in six respects: (1) it purports to show the agreement as being dated 26 August whereas the original was dated 24 August; (2) it gives an incorrect chassis number of the machine; (3) it says that the rent shall be payable '3 months after delivery and subsequent November rents on the same date in each subsequent November during the period of hire', whereas the original says that the rent shall be payable 'November after delivery and subsequent November rents on the same date in each subsequent November during the period of hire'; (4) the copy purports to show the agreement as having been signed on behalf of the company by a person other than the person who in fact signed for the company; (5) the name of the person given in the copy as witnessing the signature on behalf of the company is different from that given on the original; (6) the defendant's christian name is correctly spelled in the copy but not in the original. Some of these deviations from the original are slight and may be mere typing errors, but the variation in the copy of the mode of determining the dates for payment of the rent is substantial and must have been intentional. The copyist must have realised that the original was defective in this fundamental respect and rectified the position to the company's advantage. The 'copy' is therefore a pseudo-copy, a fabrication. I hold there was a non-compliance with paragraph (d).

The position therefore being that the company has not complied with paragraphs (b), (c) or (d) of the sub-section, the present claim for rent due under the agreement cannot be allowed unless I am satisfied (a) that the non-compliance has not prejudiced the defendant and (b) that it would be just and equitable to dispense with the requirements that have not been observed. Counsel for the plaintiff contends that the alleged breaches have not been pleaded in the defence, but I consider that in the circumstances the defence was sufficient to put the company on notice that non-compliance with paragraph (b) would be relied on.

I consider that the absence from the hire-purchase agreement of a proper mode of fixing the dates for payment of the hire-purchase rent is the only non-compliance that raises the question of prejudice. The evidence does not suggest that any of the other forms of non-compliance affected the defendant to his detriment. The hire-purchase agreement provided for three November rents, starting in November 1964, without fixing any date in the month of November. In these circumstances, the plaintiff was not entitled to complain of a default in the payment of the first rent until the month of November 1964 had run out. I am satisfied that from the time the company sent to the defendant the so-called copy of the hire-purchase agreement they knew it contained no date for the payment of the rent. Nevertheless they arbitrarily fixed 24 November 1964 as the date for the payment of the first rent. The plaintiff issued to the defendant a so-called copy of the agreement which purported to show that the original provided for the payment of the first rent three months after the delivery of the machine. I must impute to the plaintiff knowledge that this was false.

A civil bill claiming an instalment of rent amounting to £320.6s.8d alleged to be due on 24 November 1964, with interest of £8, i.e. at 10 per cent per annum, was issued in the Galway Circuit Court. There was absolutely no justification for a claim for rent due on 24 November; it was not open to the plaintiff to allege non-payment until the month of November had run out; so interest could not begin to accrue until seven days later (as provided by the conditions of hiring). Judgment in default of appearance to that Civil Bill for £328.6s.8d was obtained in the office of the Circuit Court in Galway, and to get that judgment an affidavit must have been sworn on behalf of the plaintiff verifying the averment in the Civil Bill that 'all statutory requirements and provisions pursuant to the *Hire-Purchase Acts 1946 and 1960* were duly complied with'. That averment was false and the plaintiff knew or ought to have known that it was false. If the truth had been brought to light the plaintiff would have had to go before the Circuit Judge before judgment could be got and it would have had to serve a notice of motion on the defendant. If that had been done, it is not unlikely that the defendant would have gone to his solicitor and that the whole circumstances of this hire-purchase transaction would have been explored in the Circuit Court. Instead, the plaintiff by putting in an affidavit falsely stating that the requirements of the *Hire-Purchase Acts* had been complied with, improperly got judgment in the office and the defendant had to sell livestock so as to raise money to satisfy an execution order for £339 17s 8d. Moreover, if the proper course had been adopted, the present proceedings might not have been necessary.

In all the circumstances, I am not satisfied that the defendant has not been prejudiced by the plaintiff's default or that it would be just and equitable to overlook such default. This is not the case of a slip or an oversight on the part of the plaintiff. The hire-purchase agreement is printed in a manner which, in breach of the statute, relegates the statutory notice to the obscurity of the small print. The failure to provide in the agreement for dates for the payment of the hire-purchase rent may have been a slip, but the statutory copy sent to the defendant was fabricated so as to conceal this error. If the matter stopped there, one might consider relieving the plaintiff from such defaults. But when it proceeded to compound its disregard of its statutory obligations by obtaining judgment against the defendant in the Circuit Court office by falsely stating on oath that it had complied with its statutory obligations, it forfeits in my eyes any right to say that the defendant has not been prejudiced or that it would be just and equitable to allow it to succeed in a claim which might never have been necessary if its conduct had been otherwise. The claim will be dismissed, but without costs.

CHAPTER 12.

IMPLIED CONDITIONS AND WARRANTIES

The *Hire-Purchase Act 1946* implied a number of conditions and warranties which have been replaced by more comprehensive protections contained in the *Sale of Goods and Supply of Services Act 1980*. These relate to title, description, merchantable quality, fitness and sample.

Where the goods are defective the hirer may repudiate the agreement and seek the return of all moneys paid under the contract: *Butterly v United Dominions Trust (Commercial) Ltd* (Case 67), though the hirer may have to pay some amount for the use of the goods, *Bowmaker (Ireland) Ltd v Begley* (Case 68). Instead of repudiating the contract the hirer may sue for damages: *Murphy v Industrial Credit Co. Ltd* (Case 69).

Case 67. Butterly v United Dominions Trust (Commercial) Ltd
High Court [1963] I.R. 56

The plaintiff agreed to take a motor car on hire-purchase from the defendant. Almost immediately defects in the car became apparent. The agreement purported to exclude any implied condition as to fitness for the purpose for which the car was required. The plaintiff claimed that he was entitled to rescind the contract on the ground that it was not of merchantable quality and sought the return of his deposit and instalments and consequential damages.

Held that the implied condition as to merchantable quality and reasonable fitness for the purpose for which it was required had been broken, that the implied condition as to fitness had not been validly excluded and that the plaintiff was entitled to rescind the agreement and to recover his deposit and instalments, together with a sum for consequential damages.

Davitt P.:

Now, I think it is reasonably clear that s.9 of the *Hire-Purchase Act* was modelled upon certain provisions of the *Sale of Goods Act 1893*. Sub-s.1 (a) of s.9 corresponds word for word with s. 12 sub-s.2, of the *Sale of Goods Act*. Sub-s.1 (b) corresponds closely with s.12 sub-s.1. Sub-s.1 (c) corresponds closely with s.12 sub-s.3. Section 1 (d) corresponds with s.14 sub-s. 2. In each case there is to be an implied condition that the goods shall be of merchantable quality.

In the case of s.9 sub-s. 1 (d) of the *Hire-Purchase Act*, goods expressly stated to be secondhand are excluded; and no condition is to be implied as regards defects of which the owner could not reasonably have been aware, or as regards defects which an examination in fact carried out by the hirer should have revealed.

In the case of s. 14 sub-s. 2, of the *Sale of Goods Act* there is to be a condition that the goods shall be of merchantable quality limited to cases where the goods (a) are bought by description, and (b) are bought from a seller who deals in goods of that description; and there is a similar provision as to examination of the goods. Section 9 sub-s. 2, corresponds to s. 14 sub-s. 1, of the *Sale of Goods Act*. Section 9 sub-s. 2, provides that where the hirer expressly or by implication makes known the particular purpose for which the goods are required there shall be an implied condition that the goods shall be reasonably fit for that purpose. Section 14 sub-s. 1, contains an exactly similar provision, with the addition that the buyer must make known his requirements to the seller in such a way as to show that he relies on the seller's skill and judgment, and that the goods must be of a description which it is in the course of the seller's business to supply. There is taken an exception as to the sale of an article by its patent or trade name.

It will be seen, although there are significant differences, that s. 9 sub-s. 1, is modelled closely on these provisions of the *Sale of Goods Act*, and, in my opinion, was an attempt by the legislature to place the hirer, in the case of a hire-purchase transaction, in much the same position as a buyer in the case of a sale of goods, subject to certain essential differences on account of the difference in the nature of the transaction. Now, I do think that the corresponding sections can be reasonably said to be *in pari materia*. When we find the legislature using the same words in s. 9 of the *Hire-Purchase Act* as in s. 14 of the *Sale of Goods Act* it is to be presumed that they intend the same meanings to be applied to them as have been consistently applied for over half a century by the courts interpreting the *Sale of Goods Act*. Now, it is well settled—and I think it is conceded by counsel for the defendant—that s. 14 sub-ss. 1 and 2, of the *Sale of Goods Act* are not mutually exclusive; and that the words, 'particular purpose' as used in s. 14 sub-s. 1, do not mean a particular purpose as distinct from a general purpose, but mean a specified purpose, that is, the purpose which is either expressly or impliedly made known to the seller by the buyer. I think it is unnecessary to refer to reported cases on that point. One that comes to my mind at once is the famous 'sale of crabs' case in which this section was analysed and dealt with quite exhaustively by Chief Baron Palles. [See Wallis v Russell Case 42, p. 92.]

I take the view that s. 9 sub-s. 1 (d), and s. 9 sub-s. 2, are not mutually exclusive in the sense for which counsel for the defendant has contended, and that the section gives the hirer the double-barrelled remedy. If he fails with the first barrel under s. 9 sub-s. 1 (d), he may hit with the second under s. 9 sub-s. 2.

The next matter to be determined is whether the application of either sub-section is excluded by the terms of the hire-purchase agreement. Term 2 of the Agreement provides: 'The hirer's acceptance of delivery of the goods shall be conclusive that he has examined the goods and found them complete and satisfactory. Except as provided in section 9 (1) of the *Hire-Purchase Act 1946*, the owner gives no warranty as to the state or quality of the goods; and save as aforesaid any warranty as to description, repair, quality or fitness for any purpose is hereby excluded.'

As was held in *Baldry v Marshall* (1925), those words are apt to exclude warranties only, and are not apt to exclude conditions; they have not the effect in this case of excluding the conditions implied by s. 9 sub-s. 1 (d), or s. 9 sub-s. 2. Moreover, the provision that acceptance by the hirer is to be conclusive that he has examined the goods is a modification and, to that extent, a part exclusion of the condition implied by s. 9 sub-s. 1 (d), of the Act; and is in my opinion contrary to the first provision in sub-s. 3. Sub-s. 3 reads:

(3) The warranties and conditions set out in subsection (1) of this section shall be implied notwithstanding any agreement to the contrary and the owner shall not be entitled to rely on any provision in the agreement excluding or modifying the condition set out in subsection (2) of this section unless he proves that before the agreement was made the provision was brought to the notice of the hirer and its effect made clear to him.

It seems to me that when term 2 is read in connection with that section, it is clearly an attempt to evade the provisions of the statute and therefore invalid and ineffective.

The next matter to be considered is whether there has been any breach of either of these conditions. I have no intention of reviewing the evidence as to the alleged defects in the car in question in this case. We have heard a vast lot of evidence, expert and otherwise. I take the view that the car was not of merchantable quality . . .

All these matters taken together contribute to make the car unmerchantable. If the plaintiff were confined to whatever remedy he has under s. 9 sub-s. 1 (d), all these defects could not be taken into account. I think that the defect in the bonnet would be excluded. It must have been obvious to the plaintiff when he first looked at the car. The defects in the paint-work and spring-lock to the glove compartment should have been noticed on the customary garage check before delivery. The defects in the steering, braking, the water leak, and the defects in the crown wheel and pinion are such that the defendant could not have been reasonably aware of them at the time the agreement was made. Nor are they such that the plaintiff could have noticed them on examination.

If the plaintiff was entitled only to damages for breach of the condition implied with s. 9 sub-s. 1 (d), they would be quite small indeed.

I now turn to sub-s. 2. The car was clearly not fit for the purpose for which it was required . . .

The only question remaining is the main one, whether the plaintiff was entitled to repudiate the contract. He was always, of course, entitled to terminate the hiring under the provisions of clause 8, but, quite apart from that, he would be entitled to repudiate as soon as he discovered that the car was useless for the purpose for which he required it and that the condition implied in s. 9 sub-s. 2, had been broken. The principles which apply to the matter of repudiation under the *Sale of Goods Act* have no application in the case of a contract under the *Hire-Purchase Act*. In the case of the sale of goods, once the goods have been accepted and the property has passed to the buyer, he can not repudiate; and he is confined to the remedy by way of action for damages. The *Hire-Purchase Act* is entirely different and having regard to the submission on the point made by counsel on behalf of the defendants, and by counsel on behalf of the plaintiff, it would appear to be common case that the hirer can repudiate within a reasonable time of becoming aware of a breach of a condition which would entitle him to repudiate. In this case he was entitled to repudiate on 30 May 1958 and within a reasonable time thereafter. There was no repudiation in fact until the issue of the summons on 29 July, two months later, although I think that some time before that the plaintiff had told the defendant that he was not going to take the car. It seems to me that the question can be reduced to this: was the defendant substantially in any worse position as regards minimising its loss on 29 July than it was on 30 May? If not, then it seems to me they have no cause to complain of the delay. I cannot see that their position was in any way prejudiced. The interval between 30 May and 29 July was occupied in correspondence between the various parties concerned, in getting new parts from the manufacturer to replace the defective parts in the crown wheel and pinion, and in doing the necessary refitting. In fact, as a result of the manufacturer supplying the parts and the dealer fitting them, all free of charge, the defendant was in a better position on 20 July than it would have been if the plaintiff had repudiated on 30 May—certainly in no worse position. On 12 July the plaintiff's solicitor wrote to the defendant, threatening proceedings; and on 15 July received a reply that the matter was receiving urgent attention and that they would write further. It showed that the matter was still open, so far as the defendant was concerned. No further letter appears, on the file of correspondence put in evidence, before the issue of the summons. In my view the plaintiff was clearly entitled to repudiate the contract on 30 May and had not lost that right when the summons was issued on 29 July.

Case 68. Bowmaker (Ireland) Ltd v Begley
Circuit Court (1975) 109 I.L.T.R. 28

The defendant took a secondhand motor car on hire-purchase from the plaintiff. He had paid the instalments for over a year before he discovered that the car was in a dangerous condition and unroadworthy. He rescinded the contract, informed the plaintiff that it should take possession of the car and refused to pay any further instalments. The defendant did not use the car thereafter. The plaintiff sued for instalments due to date and the defendant counterclaimed for the amount he had paid under the agreement.

Held that the car was defective when the agreement was made and that this amounted to a breach of fundamental obligation on the plaintiff's part. The court dismissed the plaintiff's claim and allowed the defendant's counterclaim. The court refused to allow a set-off to be awarded to the plaintiff in respect of the defendant's use of the car.

Judge O Briain:

A witness, who was called on behalf of the plaintiff, agreed that these complaints in relation to the car would constitute serious defects. He gave evidence that the defendant had paid his instalments punctually.

On behalf of the defendant counsel has submitted that these defects constituted a breach of fundamental term of the agreement. I would prefer to treat it as a breach of fundamental obligation in the manner in which it is referred to in Cheshire and Fifoot on the *Law of Contracts*, 7th edn, at p. 121. Counsel referred me to *Yeoman Credit Ltd. v Apps* (1962). In that case clause 8 of the hire-purchase agreement provided as follows: 'No warranty whatsoever is given by the owner as to the age, state or quality of the goods or as to the fitness for any purpose and any implied warranties and conditions are hereby expressly excluded . . . .' In the present case there appears a clause which is rather similar to clause 8 in the *Yeoman Case* which reads as follows: 'The hirer has examined the goods described in the schedule and agrees that no warranty beyond that implied by section 9 sub-section (1) of the Act has been given, and further agrees that he has not expressly or by implication made known the particular purpose for which the goods are required . . . .' This is a very wide and sweeping clause but counsel for the defendant says that there has been a fundamental failure on the part of the plaintiff and that his client cannot be bound by the clause.

I accept the evidence of the defendant and I believe that if the plaintiff had been aware of the condition of the car as it was when the defendant discovered the defects it would not have purchased the vehicle or attempted to sell it on hire-purchase to the defendant. The critical date, however, is the date of the agreement and I must consider whether this motor car, having travelled six hundred miles since April 1965, and having been garaged in a barn, was safe and roadworthy on the date when the defendant took possession of it under the hire-purchase agreement. Taking into account the nature of the defects and accepting the facts that rust is progressive I am of the opinion that the vehicle was no more fit on the date of the execution of the hire-purchase agreement than it was on the date when the defects were discovered.

In the *Yeoman Case* there are the judgments of Holroyd Pearce, Harman and Davies L.JJ. I will content myself, however, by referring to the judgment of Harman L.J. as follows:

The difficulty and the artificiality about hire-purchase cases arises, I think, from the fact that the member of the public involved imagines himself to be buying the article by instalments from the dealer, whereas he is in fact the hirer of the article from a finance company with whom he has been brought, willy nilly, into contact, of whom he knows nothing and which, on its part, has never seen the goods which are the subject-matter of the hire. The finance company trusts, I suppose, the dealer for the condition of the goods. The member of the public does the like. If the finance company chooses to hire goods of which it has never seen the condition, nor decided the value, in reliance on the good faith of the dealer, it cannot complain if, there being a defect, it is called upon to be answerable for it.

I take it to be quite clearly the law that the hirer of a chattel does warrant that it is reasonably fit for the purpose for which he hires it—in this case that the motor car 'shall be a viable motor car'.

I am satisfied that this is the law and I am prepared to treat the defects in the present case as constituting a breach of fundamental obligation as is set out in Cheshire and Fifoot on the *Law of Contract* 7th edn, p. 121 to which I have already alluded. The defendant's defence, therefore, succeeds and the plaintiff's claim fails.

The defendant had counterclaimed. In the *Yeoman Case* Lord Justice Holroyd Pearce deals with the question of damages. In the present case the defendant claims that there has been a total failure of consideration even though he had the car for thirteen months before he repudiated the contract. However, once he discovered the defects he repudiated the agreement totally and, in my opinion, he was entitled to do so. There was no acceptance of the contract on continued use of the car once the defects were discovered. Accordingly, unlike the *Yeoman Case*, the present case is not one in which an allowance should be made and a set-off allowed against the defendant's counterclaim in respect of the defendant's use of the car during the thirteen months.

Case 69. Murphy v Industrial Credit Co. Ltd
High Court, unreported, 6 October 1980

The plaintiff took a motor lorry on hire-purchase from the defendant. The lorry gave constant mechanical trouble and repairs carried out under a guarantee did not resolve the problems which re-occurred. The plaintiff claimed that the lorry was not reasonably fit for the purpose for which it was required and was not of merchantable quality. He sought damages, including loss of earnings, because the plaintiff's livelihood depended on the use of the lorry.

Held that since there had been a breach of the implied conditions as to fitness and merchantable quality the plaintiff was entitled to damages, including those for loss of earnings.

Doyle J.:

. . . Without going into all the details of the plaintiff's evidence on his direct examination, on cross-examination and in the documents which were produced in support of the claim, I can perhaps summarise the plaintiff's complaints as follows, and also the defendant's comments upon those complaints.

The plaintiff complained about the starter mechanism of the lorry but conceded in cross-examination that that was made effective without any great delay. He states that the turbo-charger was not working properly but that that eventually was replaced in May 1976 and that it worked satisfactorily thereafter. The fuel injectors gave trouble from an early stage and were, apparently, the part of the mechanism that was causing the emission of smoke and I think also the loss of power complained of. These were changed when the vehicle had clocked up 1,000 miles. The plaintiff's complaint about the fuel pump was first made in August 1975 and apparently it transpired that the wrong type of pump had been fitted by the suppliers. An important element in his complaints related to the defective lifting gear. It was essential for the operation of the lorry that it should be able to tip out its contents without difficulty or delay and it seems that the gear which should have operated this part of the mechanism was defective from the start. It is noteworthy that the plaintiff complained in very clear terms, both orally and in writing, about this particular defect in the lorry and it does not appear that there was any clear repudiation of his claim. This defect as well as some of the other matters complained of are, of course, of importance if the plaintiff is entitled to succeed in his claim that the goods were not of merchantable quality or reasonably fit for the purpose for which he purchased them.

As I have already stated I have come to the conclusion that the plaintiff's complaints which I have detailed earlier in this judgment, have been substantially made out and I do not consider that the defendant's evidence on fact, and on the professional views of the persons called in support of the defence case, have been sufficient to displace the initial claim made by the plaintiff.

The plaintiff founds his case upon the provisions of s. 9 of the *Hire-Purchase Act 1946* . . .

In my opinion the evidence establishes that the scheme whereby the plaintiff's employers were assisting their drivers to acquire lorries as their own property or ultimately to become their own property was well known to the defendants and so the provisions of s. 9 sub-s. 2 are applicable, namely that the goods should be reasonably fit for such purpose. I consider also that the provisions of s. 9 sub-s. 1 (d) applied also to this transaction, and that the hirer was entitled to receive goods of merchantable quality. When received by him I am of the view that the goods were not of merchantable quality or reasonably fit for the purpose for which it was known by both parties they were required. In the case of *Butterly v United Dominions Trust (Commercial) Ltd* (Case 67), Davitt P. had to consider the effect of s. 9 sub-ss. 1(d) and 2 of the *Hire Purchase Act 1946*. That learned judge expressed his view that it was reasonably clear that s. 9 of the *Hire-Purchase Act* was modelled upon certain provisions of the *Sale of Goods Act 1893*. He concluded that the *Hire-Purchase Act* was an attempt by the legislature to place the hirer, in the case of a hire-purchase transaction, in much the same position as a buyer in the case of the sale of goods under the *Sale of Goods Act*, subject to certain essential differences on account of the difference in the nature of the transaction. He came to the conclusion that in the circumstances of the case which he was then considering, the plaintiff was entitled to relief. The learned judge expressed his opinion that s. 9 sub-s. 1(d) and s. 9 sub-s. 2 of the *Hire-Purchase Act* are not mutually exclusive and that the section gives the hirer a double-barrelled remedy. As Davitt P. expressed it, 'if he fails with the first barrel under s. 9 sub-s. 1(d) he may hit with the second under s. 9 sub-s. 2.'

Davitt P. went on to examine the question whether the application of either of these sub-sections in the case which he was then considering was excluded by the terms of the hire-purchase agreement, which were not greatly different in terms from the proviso in the agreement now under consideration, namely, and I quote from paragraph 5 of the hire-purchase agreement 'the hirer's acceptance of delivery of the goods shall be conclusive that the hirer has examined the goods and found them to be complete and satisfactory'. It went on to provide that 'except as provided in sub-section 1 of section 9 of the *Hire-Purchase Act 1946* the owner 'gives no warranty as to the state or quality of the goods'. Davitt P. held that these words were not apt to exclude conditions and in particular that they had not the effect of excluding the conditions implied by s. 9 sub-s. 1(d) and s. 9 sub-s. 2. The facts that I have found in my opinion establish that the defendant was in breach of these conditions in the present transaction and I consider therefore that the plaintiff is entitled to damages . . .

CHAPTER 13.

RECOVERING THE GOODS

The *Hire-Purchase Act 1946*, s. 12, provides that once one-third of the hire-purchase price has been paid or tendered by the hirer, the owner cannot enforce any right to recover possession of the goods from the hirer otherwise than by a court action. Should the owner contravene s. 12 the consequences are serious for the owner.

It is not considered a breach of s. 12 should the hirer voluntarily surrender goods on which at least one-third of the hire-purchase price has been paid: *McDonald v Bowmaker (Ireland) Ltd* (Case 70).

The court has considerable discretion in dealing with an action by the owner to enforce recovery of the goods. Where goods are divisible the failure by the owner to prove the relative value of each portion may be a ground on which the court will allow the hirer to retain the entire goods subject to payment of the balance due under the agreement: *United Dominions Trust (Commercial) Ltd v Byrne* (Case 71).

Case 70. McDonald v Bowmaker (Ireland) Ltd
High Court [1949] I.R. 317

The plaintiff took a motor lorry on hire-purchase from the defendant. The plaintiff fell into arrears with the monthly payment when a sum in excess of one-third of the hire-purchase price had been paid. When the defendant terminated the agreement and threatened to institute proceedings for the recovery of the lorry the plaintiff returned it. Subsequently the plaintiff sought to recover the sums already paid under the agreement, claiming that the defendant had recovered the lorry in breach of s. 12 of the *Hire-Purchase Act 1946*.

Held that the action should be dismissed. The plaintiff was entitled to waive the provisions of the statute which were enacted for his protection. The defendant had not enforced a right to recover possession within the meaning of s. 12, and that in accepting the plaintiff's voluntary return of the lorry the defendant had not contravened the provisions of the section.

Davitt J.:

I am quite satisfied that the plaintiff voluntarily agreed to the defendant resuming possession of the lorry in question in this case. There was no seizure of the lorry. It was returned to the defendant's premises by an agent upon the express instructions of the plaintiff. Counsel for the plaintiff sought to convince me that, because the return of the lorry followed upon the receipt by the plaintiff of two letters, one from the defendant, terminating the hiring and requiring its return, and the other from the defendant's solicitor, also requiring its return, and threatening legal proceedings in default, that therefore the plaintiff's action was not voluntary. I am not convinced. A period of a week or so elapsed between the receipt of these letters and the return of the lorry, during which the plaintiff had an interview with the defendant's representative, and the possibility of the plaintiff obtaining some work for the lorry, and so being able to resume payment of the instalments, was discussed. It is clear that these discussions were not genuine on the part of the plaintiff, and were used by him merely as a means of temporising.

It seems obvious that several considerations led the plaintiff to his decision to return the lorry. He was considerably in arrears with his instalments, was quite unable to make any payment whatever, and the defendant had terminated the hiring. There were several prosecutions pending against him in respect of unlawful dealings in petrol coupons, and at least while these were pending he had no lawful means of obtaining petrol and could not operate the lorry. He had no other means of earning any money.

For some considerable time, four or five weeks, before he received these letters he had the fixed intention of seeking work in England and had made the necessary arrangements. He did, in fact, leave the country the very day the lorry was returned. I believe he was quite aware that the fact that he had paid a certain number of instalments modified, in some way, the defendant's right to resume possession, though his knowledge was in no way precise or certain. He was not, apparently, concerned to seek advice as to what his rights were, exactly. Quite clearly he did not act precipitately; and I do not believe that he was overawed or intimidated in any way by the threat of legal proceedings. I believe he came to the conclusion that the best thing he could do in the circumstances in which he found himself was to cut his losses and return the lorry. It seems to me that what happened in reality was that the plaintiff, by his actions, in effect said to the defendant, 'There is no need for you to take proceedings to enforce your rights to resume possession of the lorry. I am returning it.'

That conclusion disposes of the net question which arises for decision in this case, viz., whether it can reasonably be said that the defendant has enforced its right to take possession of the lorry, within the meaning of s. 12 of the *Hire-Purchase Act 1946*. In my opinion it cannot.

The submission made on behalf of the plaintiff is that, once one-third of the hire-purchase price is paid, there exists no lawful means whereby the owner can again become possessed of his property, other than by the judgment of the court in an action by the owner to recover possession. This is a proposition with which I am not disposed to agree . . .

The *Hire-Purchase Act 1946*, was passed to regulate the legal rights of the parties to hire-purchase transactions and sales of goods on credit. Section 12 seems specifically designed to give to a hirer certain rights which he would not otherwise possess. So to a certain extent is s. 13. I do not see that in the application of these sections to the facts of any particular case the rights of any person other than the parties to the transaction in question, whether as principals or sureties, can be involved. In these circumstances it is surely competent to a hirer to decide, as he thinks best, whether or not he will avail himself of the provisions of these sections. It would clearly not be to the interest of hirers, generally, if the effect of the Act were that they would never waive their rights thereunder. It would surely be an intolerable hardship upon a hirer if, in every case in which one-third of the hire-purchase price had been paid, he could not safely allow the owner to resume possession of goods until he had initiated and prosecuted to judgment an action at law for their recovery. If such were held to be the true effect of ss. 12 and 13, then it would seem that these provisions were enacted for the benefit of the legal profession, and not for the benefit of hirers. I am quite satisfied that such was not the intention of the legislature.

An application by a hirer to the court to exercise in his favour the power it possesses under s. 13 may not be successful. Must he, nevertheless, run the risk of adding to the obligation which he has already found himself unable to meet, the costs and expenses of an action? That, surely, would be a peculiar consequence of an enactment designed for his benefit.

For these reasons I am of opinion the plaintiff cannot succeed in the action.

Case 71. United Dominions Trust (Commercial) Ltd v Byrne
High Court [1957] I.R. 77

The defendant took some farm machinery on hire-purchase from the plaintiff. He fell into arrears with the instalments when in excess of one-third of the hire-purchase price had been paid. The plaintiff terminated the agreement and took legal proceedings to recover the goods and outstanding instalments. After these proceedings began the defendant paid further instalments. The defendant did not appear at the hearing of the case.

Held that where there is *prima facie* evidence which shows that the goods are divisible into parts, and that the court would be entitled to exercise its powers under s. 13 (4) (c) of the *Hire-Purchase Act 1946* which allowed for the transfer of the owner's title in part of the goods to the hirer and ordering the return of the remainder to the owner. It is the duty of the owner to furnish evidence showing whether or not the goods are divisible into parts, and if so, what are the relative values of the parts into which the goods may be divided. The failure of the owner to furnish such evidence may, where the balance due under the agreement is relatively small, be a ground on which the court may in its discretion allow the hirer to retain the entire goods, subject to payment of the balance due under the agreement. In this case since the plaintiff refused to furnish such information the court declined to order the return of the goods but granted a decree for the outstanding instalments.

Murnaghan J.:

Section 12 sub-s. 1 of the Act provides that when one-third of the hire-purchase of goods, let under a hire-purchase ageement, has been paid, the owner shall not enforce any right to recover possession of the goods from the hirer otherwise than by action.

This section seems to me to contain one of the fundamental restrictions imposed by the legislature on hire-purchase transactions, and stipulates in the circumstances mentioned in the section that an owner of goods let under a hire-purchase agreement cannot recover possession of such goods otherwise than by action.

The legislature cannot have thought his provision necessary, unless on the basis that the courts would not permit injustice.

Section 13 sub-s. 4 of the Act provides that, on the hearing of the action contemplated by s. 12 sub-s. 1, the court, without prejudice to any other power, may (*inter alia*)

(b) make an order for the specific delivery of all the goods to the owner and postpone the operation of the order on condition that the hirer or any guarantor pays the unpaid balance of the hire-purchase price at such times and in such amounts as the court, having regard to the means of the hirer and any guarantor, thinks just, and subject to the fulfilment of such other conditions by the hirer or a guarantor, as the court thinks just, or

(c) make an order for the transfer to the hirer of the owner's title to a part of the goods and for the specific delivery of the remainder of the goods to the owner, subject, if the court thinks fit, to the condition that the hirer or any guarantor pays to the owner within a specified time such further amount in respect of the hire-purchase price as the court, having regard to the amount already paid in respect thereof, the price of that part, the use which the hirer has had of the remainder of the goods and their depreciation in value, thinks just.

It is to be noted that this sub-section recognises that the court has other powers than those thereby conferred.

Section 13 sub-s. 5 of the Act provides that no order shall be made under s. 13 sub-s 4 (b) aforesaid, unless the hirer satisfies the court that the goods are in his possession or control at the time when the order is made. This provision, in practice, requires that the defendant (the hirer) should appear on the hearing of the action, because the onus is on the hirer to satisfy the court in the terms of s. 13 sub-s 5. It has been my experience, during the past eighteen months, when I have been dealing with applications of this kind, all of which have been in relation to motor vehicles, that no defendant has appeared in court. The result is, as far as my experience goes, that the provisions of s. 13 sub-s. 4 (b) are a dead letter.

Turning for the moment to the clause in the notice on the agreement [the statutory notice] it is evident that in the light of s. 13 sub-s. 5 this clause is illusory and misleading, because, for the reasons I have indicated, the court cannot do what the said notice in this clause says it can do, namely, allow the hirer to keep all the goods, on terms, where the hirer does not appear in court on the trial of the action.

No such restriction is placed on the operation of s. 13 sub-s. 4 (c), as is placed by s. 13 sub-s. 5 on the operation of s. 13 sub-s. 4 (b).

Having had regard to (i) clause 3 of the agreement [which sets out the statutory notices]; (ii) section 13 sub-s. 4 (c) of the Act; (iii) the fact that the hirer had paid approximately 5/6ths of the hire-purchase price; (iv) the fact that a comparatively substantial payment had been made by the defendant after the notice terminating the agreement; (v) the fact that *prima facie* it would be possible in this case to operate s. 13 sub-s. 4 (c) of the Act, as it would seem possible to deal with part of the goods in one way and with the remainder of the goods in another way, I indicated to counsel for the plaintiff that I thought that, in the circumstances, it would be just to the defendant, if possible, to allow him to keep a fair proportion of the goods, but that I had not sufficient evidence before me to enable me to decide, in the first place, whether it was possible to deal with a proportion of the goods, and if so, the relative values of the several parts into which the goods might reasonably be divided, and in the second place any matter comprised in s. 13 sub-s. 4. (c) which the plaintiff might consider material, if I saw fit to operate the said section; and I offered such counsel an opportunity to provide me with such evidence. Counsel, however, declined my said offer and submitted that I should, on the case as it stood, give judgment for the plaintiff for payment of the sum of the balance of the sum . . . outstanding after giving credit for the sum [paid since procedings began] and for the return and delivery of the goods to the plaintiff, and as I followed his argument, submitted that I was bound to give such judgment.

If the plaintiff's counsel is correct on these submissions, then the court dealing with applications of this kind is nothing more than a form of rubber stamp. I cannot accept these submissions. To do so would, in my opinion, be in the teeth of the intention of the Act as expressed in the provisions to which I have referred, and would ignore the provisions hereinbefore specifically set out of the notice on the agreement.

I am not prepared to order the defendant to return all the goods to the plaintiff as to do so would not, in my opinon, be just. I am unable to exercise the jurisdiction conferred on me by s. 13 sub-s 4. (c) due to lack of evidence. I am satisfied that the plaintiff is in a position to produce sufficient evidence to enable me to exercise such jurisdiction and has declined to do so. In the circumstances I make no order in relation to the goods . . .

PART FOUR

INSURANCE

A contract of insurance is a contract whereby one party, called the insurer, agrees in return for a payment called the premium, to pay a sum of money to another party, called the insured, on the happening of a certain event, or to idemnify the insured against the loss caused by the risk which is insured against.

CHAPTER 14.

THE DUTY OF DISCLOSURE

The general principle of contract law is that silence is golden. Generally a party can suffer no liability where he or she makes no representation. But the rule acknowledges a major exception in insurance law. Because a contract of insurance is *uberrimae fidei*—of the utmost good faith—the law casts a duty of disclosure on the party seeking insurance. The duty extends only to material facts and what is material in each case is not a matter for the insurer or an expert but for the courts.

Where there is a proposal form it is generally provided that this form is to be the basis of the contract. Generally it has been the non-disclosure in the proposal form which has lead to litigation though this duty to disclose may continue up to the assumption of risk by the insurer.

Failure to disclose a refusal to reinsure by another insurer was material: *Taylor v Yorkshire Insurance Co. Ltd* (Case 72). Previous damage to the insured's motor car was material: *Furey v Eagle, Star & British Dominions Insurance Co.* (Case 73). The incorrect statement of age in a life assurance policy was material: *Irish National Assurance Co. Ltd v O'Callaghan* (Case 74). The failure to disclose that the insured had tuberculosis was material: *Griffin v Royal Liver Friendly Society* (Case 75) as was the omission that the insured had suffered an epileptic manifestation shortly before the effecting of the policy: *Curran v Norwich Union Life Insurance Society* (Case 76). The failure to state that the insured had been suffering from influenza was not material: *Harney v Century Insurance Co. Ltd* (Case 77).

The failure to disclose that the insured had suffered loss in a previous fire was material: *Chariot Inns Ltd v Assicurazioni Generali SPA* (Case 78).

Failure to disclose a petty criminal conviction gained some twenty years prior to the effecting of the policy was not material: *Aro Road & Land Vehicles Ltd v Insurance Corporation of Ireland Ltd* (Case 81).

It is a general rule of contract law that a written contract is construed against the party that drafted it and insisted on its inclusion into the contract. This is known as the *contra proferentem* rule and it is applied in insurance cases: *In re Sweeney and Kennedy's Arbitration* (Case 79).

Where the insured expressly warrants the accuracy of the answers and agrees that they are made the basis of the contract, there must be strict and exact compliance with the obligation or statement which is warranted, independently of any question of materiality: *Keenan v Shield Insurance Co. Ltd* (Case 80).

The consequence of non-disclosure is that the insurer may avoid all liabilities under the policy. But in instances where the insured is not presented with a proposal form the insurer cannot, in the absence of fraud on the part of the insured, repudiate the policy on the ground of non-disclosure: *Aro Road & Land Vehicles Ltd v Insurance Corporation of Ireland Ltd* (Case 81).

Case 72. Taylor v Yorkshire Insurance Co. Ltd
King's Bench [1913] 2 I.R. 1

The plaintiff insured a horse with an insurance company but on the expiry of the policy that company refused to reinsure the horse. The plaintiff filled out the defendant's proposal form which contained several questions to be answered by the plaintiff and at the foot a declaration by the proposer that he warranted the truth of the statements made by him. One of the questions was, 'Have you had a proposal for livestock insurance declined?'. No answer was given. The policy was issued and on the death of the horse the defendant repudiated the policy on the ground of non-disclosure. The plaintiff sued for the sum for which the horse was insured.

Held that the withholding of the information relating to the previous refusal by another company to insure amounted to non-disclosure and accordingly the defendant was entitled to repudiate the policy.

Palles C.B.

. . . As to the second question, I agree with the learned judge that material information within the knowledge of the plaintiff, not disclosed in the proposal, was 'withheld', within the meaning of that word in the proposal.

One of the objects of a proposal is to lay before the insuring company such facts within the knowledge of the proposer as, in the opinion of the company, are material in valuing the risk they are asked to undertake. The mode adopted by the company in attempting to obtain knowledge of these facts is, first, by asking certain specific questions and requiring a warranty that the answers given to these are true. But that alone is not sufficient. It is essential to the true valuation of the risk that, not only shall there not be any false representation, but that there shall be no concealment of any material matter. So essential is this that the very nature of the contract involves a duty in the proposer to state all material facts within his knowledge; and Sir George Jessel, in *London Assurance Co. v Mansel* (1879), uses the words 'non-disclosure' and 'concealment' as synonymous in reference to matters which it is one's duty to disclose. 'Concealment', properly so called, says that very learned judge, 'means non-disclosure of a fact which it is a man's duty to disclose.'

Now, in my clear opinion, the effect of the words in the proposal, 'I have not withheld any important information', amounts to an express condition at least as extensive as that which is implied by law in a contract of insurance, that the information given is *all* the information, material to the insurance, within the knowledge of the proposer; and that, therefore, any such information not communicated is, within the meaning of the document, 'withheld', just as, within the meaning of the insurance law, it is concealed.

How does the contract provide that this information is to be communicated? To answer this we must look to the nature of the document. Its object was to communicate information for the purpose of valuing the risk. The risk, undoubtedly, was to be valued at the head office of the company—whether in Dublin or London does not appear—by the officials there; not in Mullingar by the agent. Therefore, the information to be communicated should be put in such a form that it should reach the head office. Again, the information was to be covered by a condition by the proposer in a document which was to bear his signature; and, therefore, the only mode of communication sufficient to satisfy the intention of the parties was disclosure in the proposal itself. I am therefore of opinion that the true meaning of 'I have not withheld' in the proposal is 'I have not withheld from this proposal,' and that everything material which was within the plaintiff's knowledge, and which was not disclosed in the answers, was withheld . . .

Gibson J. delivered a concurring judgment and Boyd J. concurred with both. (See also, Case 9, regarding an agent's knowledge to be imputed to a principal, and Case 82, the role of an agent in insurance).

Case 73. Furey v Eagle, Star & British Dominions Insurance Co.
Court of Appeal (1922) 56 I.L.T.R. 109

The plaintiff sought car insurance from the defendants. He filled out a proposal form which contained a question relating to previous accidents. He stated that there had been a previous accident whereby damages had been paid to a third party but he failed to mention a sum awarded to him for damage done to his car. He also failed to mention an accident he had when he was part-owner in another car. After the plaintiff was involved in an accident the defendants repudiated the policy and the plaintiff sued to enforce it.

  Held that the wilful misstatement invalidated the policy.

Molony L.C.J.:

The proposal is incorporated in the policy and is the basis of the contract . . . There had been other accidents, one of which occurred while the plaintiff was a half owner in partnership with his brother. I think that the insured should have stated in his proposal any accident which occurred while he was driving although he was not the owner of the car. There appears to me to be ample grounds in support of the finding of the learned judge. There was clearly a misstatement in respect of the accident in 1920 when the plaintiff concealed the payment in respect of injury to the car.

Ronan L.J. and Wylie J. concurred.

Case 74. Irish National Assurance Co. Ltd v O'Callaghan
High Court (1934) 68 I.L.T.R. 248

The defendant effected a policy of life assurance on his father's life with the plaintiff. An incorrect age of the life assured was given in the proposal form. When the plaintiff sought to avoid the policy the defendant claimed a sum which would have been payable had the correct age been given.

  Held the plaintiff was entitled to avoid the policy and that claim by the defendant was dismissed.

Hanna J.:

In cases such as this where the proposal form contains a declaration, signed by the proposer for insurance, that the answers to the questions contained in the proposal form are true, the truth of those answers is the basis of the contract with the company, and if the answers are untrue the policy is avoided. I am satisfied, on the evidence, that the plaintiff knew this side of insurance business thoroughly, as he had himself been an agent for an insurance company. I am satisfied also that the plaintiff supplied the ages which appeared on the proposal forms. Now it has been taken as common case here that those ages are untruly stated. The Circuit Court, nevertheless, appeared to have thought that it could disregard the untruth of the answers relative to the ages stated on the proposal form, and that it could adjust the proposals and the policies to the correct ages in order to calculate what was due, on the assumption that the correct ages had been stated on the proposal forms. I am of opinion, however, that the Circuit Court had no power to do this and that it should have dismissed the action on the ground I have already stated, namely, that the policies were avoided by the untrue statements . . .

Sullivan P. gave a concurring judgment.

Case 75. Griffin v Royal Liver Friendly Society
High Court [1942] Ir.Jur.Rep. 29

The plaintiff took out a policy of assurance on her husband's life with the defendants. She signed a proposal form before the policy was issued to her, and on the form the question, 'Is the proposed in good health?' had been answered in the affirmative. To a question as to the nature of the last illness, if any, of the proposed the answer had been 'None'. In fact the proposed had been receiving treatment for tuberculosis of the kidney for eight years prior to the signing of the proposal form. When the proposed died within two years of the effecting of the policy the defendants repudiated the policy on the ground that false statements had been made in answer to the questions given.

Held that the defendants were entitled to repudiate the policy despite the fact that the plaintiff had no fraudulent intention.

Murnaghan J.:

. . . The plaintiff's husband was quite a young man. He was born in 1909 and he was only about thirty years of age at the date of the proposal. He had been working for some months before the insurance was effected. One of the company's officials had seen him from time to time when he had called to collect premiums on another policy taken out by the deceased. The deceased man passed a medical examination as required by the insurance company. It was not the plaintiff who had initiated this policy. The deceased had had a similar policy . . . and the agents of the company suggested to the plaintiff that she should take a further insurance . . . What was the position before this policy was taken out? The official had seen the deceased man frequently and he made the declaration required by the company recommending the deceased as a good life. But it now transpires that . . . an eminent Dublin surgeon had had this man under his care at various times for the preceding eight years, and that he had had various operations, among them the excision of a kidney in 1931. In fact the deceased was suffering from a deep-seated disease of a tubercular nature from which he subsequently died. It is only fair to the plaintiff to point out that several people had seen her husband at regular intervals and had taken him to be quite a normal healthy man. There is no suggestion that the plaintiff took out the policy with full knowledge that he was stricken down by disease.

The question of law is whether the answers on the proposal form embodied in the contract contain misstatements of fact which would vitiate the contract. In the proposal form it is asked, 'Is the proposed in good health?' That is not a very searching question and does not go as far as many companies require in the case of life insurance. The second question is as to the nature of the last illness, and the answer given to that was 'none'. This answer is manifestly incorrect. The plaintiff does not justify her answers at all. She says she did not give the answers. The form handed to her was, she says, blank and she signed it in order to show that she was the wife of the proposed. The officials of the society say that the answers, down to the answer to the second question, were put in before the plaintiff signed the form, and that the purport of the questions was put to the plaintiff. They do not say that the exact words of the questions were put to her, but that is immaterial . . .

The second point against the plaintiff is that she signed a paper and she says that she did so without reading it. But she signed a declaration. She said that she just put her name to the paper. That may have occurred and people may sign forms without reading them, but when a number of witnesses tell me that the form was filled in before her signature and only the person signing it says the contrary, and that without having read the proposal form, I cannot accept that answer. I think that the substantial parts of the form were filled in before it was signed. It would have been better if the agents had not asked the plaintiff to sign the form before all of it was filled in. The agent was ill-advised to fill in the answers to certain of the questions after the form was signed. If the point were material I would have held that the plaintiff did not answer the other questions filled up after she had signed the form. The officers of the society say that they put the question about her husband working and that the plaintiff told them where he was working. She herself admits she mentioned where he was working. I am satisfied that there was on the form, when the plaintiff signed it, the answer to the question which, as I have said, was an incorrect answer. It is said on behalf of the plaintiff that the agents were the agents of the company to put in the answers to the questions. That point might possibly be made if the form were left empty, but if the answers were actually put in as a summary of the information the plaintiff gave to the agents of the company, it does not seem to me to be material. There is, of course, the criticism that the agents were too ready to fill in the desired answers to the questions in order to procure the issue of the policy.

. . . I find, as I have said, that the plaintiff had no fraudulent intention at all. But these clauses [of a British statute which formed part of the contract] contain the second proviso I have mentioned above regarding a misstatement with regard to the health of a person to be assured. I have examined this clause very closely and counsel for the defendants has given his comment on it, and I think that he is right, that if an innocent mistake is made where the form is filled in by the officials of the company, that point can be raised within two years of the date of the issue of the policy. That having been done in this case I must hold that, even though there was no fraud, there was an innocent misstatement of a material fact and that misstatement is sufficient to avoid the policy as the objection has been made within two years of the issue.

Case 76. Curran v Norwich Union Life Insurance Society
High Court, unreported, 30 October 1987

The plaintiff's late husband entered into a policy of insurance with the defendants. The insured made a written declaration which he duly signed that 'to the best of my knowlege and belief I am presently in good health and I am not in receipt of medical treatment'. The insured had suffered a head injury some years previously from which he appeared to have made a full recovery. A short time before effecting the policy in question the insured suffered a minor epileptic manifestation, unknown to himself, but observed by the plaintiff. He was prescribed daily medication for at least a year as a precautionary measure. The insured did not take this medication and when he died four months later the defendants repudiated on the ground that the declaration of good health on which the contract was based was untrue to the insured's knowledge at the time it was made.

Held that the defendants were entitled to repudiate the policy on the ground that the facts as to the insured's medical condition were material and should have been disclosed.

Barr J.:

In February 1985 the late husband of the plaintiff, entered into a contract with the defendants which was primarily an investment scheme but which also provided life cover in the sum of £12,330.00 payable should the insured die during the currency of the contract and while the market value of units purchased on his behalf from monthly instalments of £70 payable by him to the defendant was less than the sum insured.

The contract was based upon a written declaration dated 16 February 1985 and duly signed by the deceased which, *inter alia*, is in the following terms: ' . . . to the best of my knowledge and belief I am presently in good health and I am not in receipt of medical treatment.' No medical examinations or investigations were envisaged by the defentant as being necessary in the ordinary course in connection with such contract . . .

I am satisfied that although the contract in question is primarily a scheme for saving and investment, it contains in it a significant element of life insurance and that the declaration made by the applicant, which I have quoted, relates to the life cover which forms part of the parcel on offer. Accordingly, as with all forms of insurance contract the standard required of the declarant as to the disclosure of all information relevant to the insurance required is *uberrimae fides*.

The medical/surgical background to the declaration made by the insured is as follows:

In March 1984 he suffered a severe head injury in a traffic accident which necessitated intermittent lengthy hospitalisation for about six months. He was discharged from hospital in September 1984 and I am satisfied from the plaintiff's evidence that her husband had good reason to regard himself as having made a full recovery at that time subject to regaining strength and mobility. He was not warned of the risk of epilepsy in the future, nor was he advised to remain under any form of medical supervision or treatment. His rehabilitation proceeded uneventfully and by the following February he appeared to have been restored to his full pre-accident state of good health. Accordingly, having regard to the wording of the declaration, he would have had no obligation to disclose the head injury sustained by him in 1984 but for an event which took place shortly before the declaration was signed by him and submitted to the defendant. During the night of 13/14 February 1985, two days before the declaration was made, the insured while in bed asleep had a severe attack of shivering which was witnessed by his wife. He was unaware of having had the attack and seemed to be in good health and none the worse of it on the following morning. However, the plaintiff was disturbed by what she had seen and, contrary to her husband's wishes, she contacted the family doctor, who also gave evidence. He related the attack to the deceased's head injury and concluded that it was likely to have been a minor epileptic manifestation which might never occur again but which in his opinion required daily medication for at least one year as a precautionary measure. He visited the deceased on 14 February and believes that he explained to him his diagnosis and the necessity for taking the prescribed medication. In the event, unknown to his wife and doctor until after his death, the deceased did not take the tablets which had been prescribed for him.

On 16 February 1985 the insured signed the declaration and submitted it to the defendants, thus indicating to them that to the best of his knowledge and belief he was then in good health and was not receiving any medication. His application was duly accepted and the required policy document was issued. On 28 June 1985 the insured was found dead in his garage/workshop where he had been working alone for some hours. The plaintiff, who is the executrix of the estate of the deceased, claimed from the defendant the death benefit of £12,330.00 payable on foot of the policy. The insurer repudiated liability on the ground that the deceased's declaration of good health on which the contract was based was untrue to his knowledge at the time when it was made.

The standard of care required of a proposer for insurance as to the disclosure of facts material to the insurance sought by him has been laid down by the Supreme Court in *Chariot Inns Ltd v Assicurazioni Generali SPA* (Case 78), see in particular the opening paragraphs of the judgment of the court delivered by Kenny J. which are as follows: 'A contract of insurance . . . [this quotation is given in full on page 167] . . . is not to be determined by such witnesses.'

In the light of the foregoing it is clear that the insured had a duty to disclose to the insurers the fact that a few days previously he may have suffered a minor epileptic seizure for which his doctor deemed it wise to prescribe continuing medication and that he might be at risk of a further similar attact in the future. These were material facts which I am satisfied a prudent insurer would be likely to investigate further and to take into account in its assessment of the risk proposed. I accept the evidence of the defendant's principal underwriter in that regard. It was immaterial to the plaintiff's duty of disclosure in the circumstances of the case that the deceased himself may have *bona fides* believed, notwithstanding his doctor's diagnosis, that the episode on the night of 13/14 February was not epileptic in nature and had no connection with his prior head injury. The inescapable fact remains that he had good reason, based on professional medical advice, to believe that he may have had such an attack and that itself was a material fact which should have been disclosed to the insurers regardless of what his personal opinion as to his state of health may have been. Likewise, he had a duty to disclose that continuing medication had been prescribed for him by his doctor. Accordingly, in the premises I am obliged to hold that the defendants were entitled to repudiate the contract on the ground that the declaration of health made by the deceased was misleading in material particulars pertinent to the insurer's assessment of the risk proposed . . .

Case 77. Harney v Century Insurance Co. Ltd
High Court, unreported, 22 February 1983

When seeking a health insurance policy the plaintiff filled out a proposal form on 23 May, which contained the sentence: 'The office must be notified of any changes in the health and circumstances of the life of the insured prior to the assumption of risk.' When the policy was issued, the 'date risk assumed' was 31 August. On 9 August the plaintiff attended his doctor with a head cold, was given antibiotics, and continued to attend work. His condition worsened and when the insured claimed payment under the policy the defendant avoided it. The plaintiff sued for the benefits under the policy.

Held that the non-disclosure by the plaintiff of the visit to his doctor on 9 August was not material to the risk and the defendant was not entitled to avoid the policy .

McWilliam J.:

. . . On 9 August 1979, the plaintiff attended his doctor complaining of a head cold and some pain in his chest. The doctor found that he had an infection of the throat which he considered to be a common minor illness and he put the plaintiff on antibiotics for five days. The plaintiff returned to his doctor on 16 August complaining that he still had a cough and the doctor diagnosed an infection of the air passages in the lungs, a form of bronchitis, which he stated is a very common complication of a head cold and he put the plaintiff on different antibiotics for a further five days. He stated in cross-examination that bronchitis could be serious if chronic but that he had no reason to consider that this was chronic and still considered that the plaintiff had only a minor illness which was merely of nuisance value to the plaintiff at work. At no time during August was the plaintiff off work and the doctor did not make any such recommendation. Both the visits to the doctor took place before the effective date and about a fortnight before the date risk assumed. On 5 September the senior doctor in the practice, who had been on holiday during August, thought the plaintiff's symptoms were only minor although annoying to him at work.

In the middle of September 1979 the plaintiff's condition began to get worse and he was taken off antibiotics which the doctor thought might be the cause of the trouble. The doctor advised the plaintiff to go ahead with a holiday to America which had been arranged for the end of October. The plaintiff did go for his holiday but on his return, he became very much worse and did not recover until September 1980. It was accepted by the plaintiff's doctor that what happened in August was the beginning of the illness which incapacitated the plaintiff.

Evidence was given on behalf of the defendant by an independent insurance representative and by a representative of the defendant who both stated that they considered it material to the risk that the plaintiff had a cold which had not cleared up and had visited his doctor twice notwithstanding that no significance had been attached to the original information disclosed to the defendant's doctor that the plaintiff had a cold. I was somewhat unhappy about that part of the second witness's evidence which seemed to suggest that, because the plaintiff's cold was a viral infection, he would have thought of cancer because he had heard that cancer is a viral illness, although no medical evidence was called to establish any connection and no suggestion of any connection was put to the plaintiff's doctors. No medical evidence at all was called on behalf of the defendant.

Both these witnesses stated that an insurance company would postpone or suspend a risk if it was made aware that the proposer was attending a doctor for a cold and that antibotics had been prescribed without success. One of them also said that, if a company was made aware that a person was suffering from a cold the company would postpone the risk until it had cleared up. He agreed that he could refuse, load or accept the risk but said he would postpone to see if the infection cleared up.

On behalf of the plaintiff it is argued that the continuation of the plaintiff's cold was not material to the risk, particularly as there was a deferred period of thirteen weeks before any liability for illness could arise. It was urged that the test of materiality is whether knowledge of the continuation of a cold and the visits to the doctor would at that time have caused a prudent insurer to refuse the insurance and that the onus of proving materiality is on an insurer. I was referred to the cases of *Chariot Inns Ltd v Assicurazioni Generali SPA* (Case 78) and *Mutual Life Insurance Co. of New York v Ontario Metal Products Ltd* (1925).

It has not been disputed that the onus is on the defendant to establish materiality but it is urged that the evidence of the two insurance representatives does establish that the information which was withheld was material and would have been so considered by a prudent insurer. Although the amended defence suggests that this aspect was considered, no argument was advanced on the basis that there was a contractual duty to disclose the plaintiff's condition in August arising by reason of the statement at the foot of the proposal form and the recital in the policy that the proposal was delivered as the basis of the policy.

The submission and evidence on both sides related solely to the question of the materiality of the non-disclosure of the visits by the plaintiff to his doctor in August and I propose to confine myself to a consideration of this.

The following passage from the judgment of Kenny J. in the *Chariot Inns case* sets out how I must approach my consideration of this question. He said 'What is to be regarded as material to the risk [this quotation is given on page 167]?'.

In the case of the *Mutual Life Insurance Co. of New York*, which concerned a policy of life insurance, Lord Salvesen giving the judgment of the Privy Council said: 'The appellant's counsel . . . suggested that the test was whether, if the fact concealed had been disclosed, the insurers would have acted differently either by declining the risk at the proposed premium or at least by delaying consideration of its acceptance until they had consulted Dr Fierheller. If the former proposition were established in the sense that a reasonable insurer would have so acted, materiality would, their Lordships think, be established but not in the latter case if the difference of action would have been delay and delay alone.'

To this I would add that the options open to an insurer are to accept the contract, refuse the contract or make a new offer at an increased premium. There cannot be any course of accepting the premium and waiting until it was seen how the proposer's health progressed so that, if the infection cleared up the proposer would be held covered in future with this premium based for future reference as of the effective date but that if some complication developed, the proposer's premium would be returned to him and the policy cancelled.

Having regard to the decisions to which I have been referred I am of opinion that the evidence has not established the probability that the non-disclosure of the visits by the plaintiff to his doctor in August were material to the risk. On this assessment the plaintiff is entitled to succeed in his action.

Case 78. Chariot Inns Ltd v Assicurazioni Generali SPA
Supreme Court [1981] I.L.R.M. 173; [1981] I.R. 199

The plaintiff proposed to insure its licensed premises with the defendant. In answering questions contained in the proposal form, an employee of a firm of insurance brokers advised the plaintiff that it would not be necessary to answer a certain question contained under the heading of 'material damage'. The question required the plaintiff to detail any claims for loss experienced over the previous five years. The plaintiff had in fact suffered material damage to furnishings belonging to it which had been stored in premises owned by an associate company. The defendant issued the policy to the plaintiff. Subsequently a fire caused extensive damage to the licenced premises. The defendant repudiated liability because of the non-disclosure of the previous fire.

Held that the non-disclosure by the plaintiff that it had suffered loss in the previous fire was material to the risk which the defendant had been requested to undertake.

Kenny J.:

A contract of insurance requires the highest standard of accuracy, good faith, candour and disclosure by the insured when making a proposal for insurance to an insurance company. It had become usual for an insurance company to whom a proposal for insurance is made, to ask the proposed insured to answer a number of questions. Any misstatement in the answers given, when they relate to a material matter affecting the insurance, entitles the insurance company to avoid the policy and to repudiate liability if the event insured against happens. But the correct answering of any questions asked is not the entire obligation of the person seeking insurance; he is bound, in addition, to disclose to the insurance company every matter which is material to the risk against which he is seeking indemnity.

What then is to be regarded as material to the risk against which the insurance is sought? It is not what the person seeking insurance regards as material nor is it what the insurance company regards as material. It is a matter or circumstance which would reasonably influence the judgment of a prudent insurer in deciding whether he would take the risk and, if so, in determining the premium which he would demand. The standard by which materiality is to be determined is objective, not subjective. The matter has, in the last resort, to be determined by the court: the parties to the litigation may call experts in insurance matters as witnesses to give evidence of what they would have regarded as material but the question of materiality is not to be determined by such witnesses.

The generally accepted test of materiality in all forms of insurance against risks when property of any kind is involved is stated in s. 18 (2) of the *Marine Insurance Act 1906*: 'Every circumstance is material which would influence the judgment of a prudent insurer in fixing the premium or determining whether he will take the risk.' Although this test is stated in an Act dealing with marine insurance, it has been accepted as a correct guide to the law in insurance against damage to property or goods of all types.

The rule to determine the materiality of a fact not disclosed to the insurers was expressed by Lord Justice MacKinnon with his customary pungency in *Zurich General Accident & Liability Insurance Co. Ltd v Morrison* (1942):

> Under the general law of insurance an insurer can avoid a policy if he proves that there has been misrepresentation or concealment of a material fact by the insured. What is material is that which would influence the mind of a prudent insurer in deciding whether to accept the risk or fix the premium. If this be proved, it is not necessary further to prove that the mind of the actual insurer was so affected. In other words the insurer could not rebut the claim to avoid the policy because of a material misrepresentation by a plea that the particular insurer

concerned was so stupid, ignorant or reckless that he could not exercise the judgment of a prudent insurer and was in fact unaffected by anything the insured had represented or concealed.

The statement of Samuels J. of the rules relating to the law about materiality of facts not disclosed in insurance law in *Mayne Nickless Ltd v Pegler* (1974) has the authority of having been approved and followed by the Judicial Committee of the Privy Council in *Marene Knitting Mills Property Ltd v Greater Pacific General Insurances Ltd* (1976):

> Accordingly I do not think that it is generally open to examine what the insurer would in fact have done had he had the information not disclosed. The question is whether that information would have been relevant to the exercise of the insurer's option to accept or reject the insurance proposed. It seems to me that the test of materiality is this: a fact is material if it would have reasonably affected the mind of a prudent insurer in determining whether he will accept the insurance, and if so, at what premium and on what conditions.

. . . When the plaintiffs bought the licensed premises, it was insured with the General Accident Insurance Co. Ltd ('the General Accident') and this policy was renewed subsequently. The principal of the plaintiff's insurance brokers advised Mr W. (a director of the plaintiff) that a different and wider insurance cover was advisable in respect of the premises, but when the General Accident were asked to quote for this, they increased the premium which they would require by 50 per cent. Mr W. was most reluctant to pay such a large increase and decided to get his broker to ask for tenders for the insurance. The defendant, who is an Italian insurance company, is represented and carries on business in the Republic of Ireland through its agents, International Underwriters Ltd and it sent in the lowest tender. Mr H. (an employee of the insurance brokers) had remained on friendly terms with Mr W. and frequently called to his premises. The plaintiff wanted cover against fire risk, employers' liability, liability to the public and loss of profits. Separate proposal forms for each type of insurance were sent out by the defendant and Mr H. got these. On 22 February 1978 Mr H. called to the premises with these proposal forms. They were issued by International Underwriters Ltd. One related to material damage. Mr H. asked the questions necessary to fill in the answers to the questions and gave any other information required. It was not disputed by anyone during the trial that the handwriting in which the answers appeared was Mr H.'s. There was a discussion about the fire at Leeson Street and Mr H. said that it was totally unnecessary to disclose this on the proposal forms because (as Mr W. said) 'we were dealing with a separate company and only had to show what was relevant to the Chariot Inn'. In the form dealing with material damage this appeared:

> *Material Damage*
> Give claims Experience for loss over the last 5 years (i.e. Date, Nature of loss. Amount paid or outstanding. Brief details of how loss occurred). If none in any class say so.

The answer written in by Mr H. was 'None'.

Three experts on insurance business gave evidence. Their unanimous view was that the [previous] fire and the damage to the plaintiff's goods were matters that were material to the risk which the defendant was asked to insure. Their opinions were not conclusive on this matter. The question whether any of these matters were material is essentially an inference from facts established by evidence. The circumstance that Mr W. was director of the plaintiff and of an associate company would not of itself make a fire on the premises owned by the associate company a fact material to the risk undertaken by the defendant when it insured the plaintiff against fire in the latters' premises.

I think, however, that it was material to the insurance effected by the plaintiff with the defendant that goods belonging to the plaintiff were damaged by fire in premises owned by [an associate company]. The answer to the query about claims made by the plaintiff for loss over the last five years was literally correct, but though the plaintiff had no claim against the insurance company which had issued a policy in respect of the [fire damaged] premises, they were paid by an insurance company the sum negotiated in respect of the furnishings stored.

The circumstances in which the goods of the plaintiff were stored in the [fire damaged] premises and the fact that the plaintiff ultimately got payment in respect of them were, in my view, matters which would reasonably have affected the judgment of a prudent insurer in deciding whether to take the risk or in fixing the premium, particularly as Mr W. was a director of and managed and controlled the plaintiff and the associate company . . .

Henchy and Griffin JJ. concurred.

(Note: The plaintiff was awarded damages against the insurance brokers for the negligence of its employee. See Case 8.)

Case 79. In re Sweeney and Kennedy's Arbitration
High Court [1950] I.R. 85

A proposal form for a motor policy in respect of motor lorries, the property of the proposer, contained the question: 'Are any of your drivers under 21 years of age or with less than 12 months' driving experience?'. The answer given by the proposer was 'no' which was correct. The form also contained the following statement which the proposer was required to sign: 'I agree that this declaration shall be held to be promissory and so form the basis of the contract.' After the policy was effected the insured occasionally employed his son who was under 21 years of age to drive one of the lorries. Later his son was regularly employed. While under the age of 21 years but having 12

months experience the son was in charge of a lorry when a fatal
accident occurred. The insurers refused to accept liability on the
ground that the terms of the policy had been broken. On a reference to
arbitration, under the terms of the policy, the arbitrator held that the
insurers were liable to indemnify the insured and on request sought the
opinion of the High Court.

Held that the expression 'this declaration shall be held to be
promissory' was referable to the facts existing at the time the proposal
form was completed and did not refer to any time thereafter. Where
an insurer uses ambiguous language in a proposal form such language
will be strictly construed against him by the court.

Kingsmill Moore J.:

. . . Counsel for the insurer relied particularly on the sentence: 'I hereby
agree that this declaration shall be held to be promissory, and so form the
basis of the contract . . . ' In his contention the word 'promise' and its
cognate words must always refer to a future time. In this, I think, he is in
error. The most usual meaning of the verb 'to promise' is 'to undertake to
do or abstain from doing something in the future'. But there is a well-
recognised second usage in which 'to promise' means 'to assert confidently,
to declare'. Such an assertion usually refers to a future state of affairs, but
it may also refer to the present, as in the phrase, 'I promise you that it is
so'. It is true that the Oxford dictionary classes this latter usage as
colloquial or archaic; but an archaism or two in an insurance policy will
not give a lawyer familiar with their verbiage too violent a shock. Certain
marine policies seem compounded of little else but archaisms.

Counsel for the insured, in an argument as logical as it was devastating,
contended that the word 'promissory' was used in the second sense which I
have mentioned. It signified a positive declaration, applicable alike to
future, present, and past states of affairs, according to the wording of the
particular question, and of such a nature as to constitute, not merely a
representation, but a warranty, breach of which would, in insurance law,
avoid liability. For this meaning, said counsel, the sentence provided its
own dictionary. It did not end with the word 'promissory', but continued,
'*and so* shall form the basis of the contract'. A sentence introduced by the
words 'and so' must be either explanatory of, or a logical corollary of, the
preceding word or words. Thus, the meaning of the word 'promissory'
must be some meaning which made the declaration a basis of the
contract . . .

The interpretation so given by counsel for the insured to the word
'promissory' in the proposal form, though unusual, involves no violation of
grammar or language. In this interpretation the word can be applied
accurately and intelligibly to questions whether they refer to past, present
or future. If the question refers to the future the answer becomes a

warranty as to the existence of a state of affairs in the future. Where the question is so couched as to refer to the present or the past, then the answer is a warranty that a certain state of affairs exists in the present or existed in the past. Counsel for the insurer's interpretation, on the other hand, not merley tortures language, but involves a person who has answered an apparently straightforward question as to the present or past in a concealed warranty as to the future. Such a carefully camouflaged method of extracting a future warranty would hardly commend itself to the court, and I would be loth to attribute such an intention to the underwriters.

An attempt to apply counsel for the insurer's interpretation to other questions (and, I think, he was forced to admit that if it applies to one it applied to all) reveals manifest absurdities. Take, for instance, Question 2:—'Have you or your driver during the past 5 years been convicted of any offence in connection with a motor vehicle?' To this the answer correctly given was 'No.' If, as is argued, the subsequent provision that the declaration is to be promissory amounts to an undertaking that what was true for the past will remain true for the future, we arrive at the extraordinary position that the insured was undertaking that neither he nor any driver of his would in future be convicted of a motoring offence; and that if he or his driver subsequently was involved in a collision and was convicted of driving without due consideration, the underwriters could repudiate liability for any claims arising out of such a collision. It does not seem likely that anyone would knowingly propose for such a nugatory insurance.

It would be easy to show similar absurdities which would be produced by the application of counsel for the insurer's interpretation to other questions and answers. Indeed, it is difficult to see how any insurer could answer this vital Question No. 9 without involving himself in difficulties. The insured's answer of 'No' was correct in fact; but, according to the contention of the underwriters, this answer involved a promise never to employ a driver aged under 21 years or without 12 months' experience. Was the insured to safeguard himself by explaining that in certain circumstances he might be obliged, for a longer or shorter time, to employ a driver aged under 21? How far was he to elaborate the circumstances, which had not yet arisen and which might be difficult to forsee. I cannot conceive that an applicant for insurance who is asked a specific question is bound to do more that give a truthful answer to such questions or that there is any obligation to provide answers to questions which are not asked. In saying this I am not forgetting the overriding obligation to make full disclosure of all facts clearly material to the risk, but as a qualification I would adopt the words of Lord Shaw in *Condogianis v Guardian Assurance Co.* (1921):

> In a contract of insurance it is a weighty fact that the questions are framed by the insurer, and that if an answer is obtained to such a question which is upon a fair construction a true answer, it is not open to the insuring company to maintain that the question was put in a sense

different from or more comprehensive than the proponent's answer covered. Where an ambiguity exists, the contract must stand if an answer has been made to the question in a fair and reasonable construction of that question. Otherwise the ambiguity would be a trap against which the insured would be protected by courts of law.

For the reasons given I am of opinion that counsel for the insured's interpretation of the sentence, 'this declaration shall be held to be promissory,' is a correct interpretation and that the interpretation urged by the counsel for the insurer is unsustainable. But, even if I am wrong in my conclusion that the interpretation is reasonably free from doubt, the case must be decided against the underwriters if the words are ambiguous. The wording of the proposal form and the policy was chosen by the underwriters who knew, or must be deemed to have known, what matters were material to the risk and what information they desired to obtain. They were at liberty to adopt any phraseology which they desired. They could have provided clearly and expressly that no driver should be employed who was under 21 years of age or had less than 12 months experience, and they could have done this by means of a special condition or by an addition to the final proviso under the heading, 'Description of Drivers', in the policy. Indeed, they could have secured their object (if it was their object) with perfect clarity in half a dozen ways. If, then, they choose to adopt ambiguous words it seems to me good sense, as well as established law, that those words should be interpreted in the sense which is adverse to the persons who chose and introduced them.

Assuming, then, that the interpretation is not so clear as I think it is, and that counsel for the insurer's interpretation of the words may be as feasible as counsel for the insured, I must still decide against the underwriters who chose words raising such ambiguity. I would like to associate myself with the opinion of Lord Greene M.R. in *Woolfall & Rimmer Ltd v Moyle* (1942) where he says:

> . . . if underwriters wish to limit by some qualification a risk which, *prima facie*, they are undertaking in plain terms, they should make it perfectly clear what that qualification is. They should, with the aid of competent advice, make up their minds as to the qualifications they wish to impose and should express their intention in language appropriate for achieving the result desired. There is no justification for underwriters, who are carrying on a widespread business and making use of printed forms, either failing to make up their minds what they mean, or, if they have made up their minds what they mean, failing to express it in suitable language. Any competent draughts-man could carry out the intention which [counsel] imputes to this document, and, if that was really intended, it ought to have been done.

This is but the latest expression of a sentiment which judge after judge has uttered for nearly a century. In *Anderson v Fitzgerald* (1853) Lord St. Leonards says:

A policy ought to be so framed, that he who runs can read. It ought to be framed with such deliberate care, that no form of expression by which, on the one hand, the party assured can be caught, or by which, on the other hand, the company can be cheated, shall be found upon the face of it.

Lord Wright adopted this passage in *Provincial Insurance Co. v Morgan* (1933), and in that case also Lord Russell of Killowen says:

For myself I think it is a matter of great regret that the printed forms which insurance companies prepare and offer for acceptance and signature by the insuring public should not state in clear and unambiguous terms the events upon the happening of which the insuring company will escape liability under the policy. The present case is a conspicuous example of an attempt to escape by placing upon words a meaning which, if intended by the insurance company, should have been put before the proposers in words admitting of no possible doubt;

and in *Glicksman v Lancashire & General Assurance Co.* (1927) Lord Atkinson says: 'I think it is a lamentable thing that insurance companies will abstain from shaping the questions they put to intending insurers . . . in clear and unambiguous language.'

It is useless for me to attempt to add to the words of such great judges, and I content myself with recording them once more and pointing out that the result of using ambiguous expressions is generally a decision against those who deal in such ambiguities.

Case 80. Keenan v Shield Insurance Co. Ltd
High Court [1987] I.R. 113

The plaintiff applied to the defendant for fire insurance. In reply to a question on the proposal form as to whether the plaintiff had ever sustained loss or damage by any of the risks he wished to insure against, the plaintiff answered 'no'. The plaintiff signed a declaration at the foot of the proposal form that the particulars therein contained were 'true and complete in every respect and that no material fact had been suppressed or withheld' and agreed that the declaration and the answers given on the proposal form should be the basis of the contract between the parties. The defendant disputed its liability to pay the plaintiff when he made a claim on the ground that the plaintiff had failed to disclose that he had, within the previous year, been paid a small sum in respect of fire damage to the premises.

Held that as a matter of construction the declaration made by the plaintiff entailed two statements: first, that the particulars and answers given were true and complete in every respect and second, that no material statement had been suppressed or withheld. Since the plaintiff had expressly warranted the accuracy of his answers and agreed that they would be made the basis of the contract, these must, independently of any question of materiality, be strict and exact compliance with an obligation or statement which he warranted.

Blayney J.:

Counsel's principal submission on behalf of the plaintiff was that, in view of the finding that the inaccuracy and incompleteness of the answer to Question 8 did not amount to a misrepresentation or concealment of material fact by the plaintiff, the arbitrator was wrong in law in making an award in favour of the defendant. His argument might be summarised as follows. The declaration made by the plaintiff at the foot of the proposal form commenced as follows; 'I hereby declare that the above particulars are true and complete in every respect and that no material fact has been suppressed or withheld . . . 'This amounted to a declaration that the plaintiff, in answering the questions, had not withheld or suppressed any material fact. It was only answers which withheld or suppressed a material fact which would be a breach of the declaration. The answer to Question 8 did not suppress or withhold any material fact. That the plaintiff had within the previous year been paid £53 in respect of a claim for fire damage to a pump was not material to the insurance being sought, and so the plaintiff had correctly answered 'no' to Question 8 which had asked whether he had 'ever sustained loss or damage by any of the risks or liabilities' he wished to insure against.

The basis on which this argument reposes is the construction that counsel gives to the sentence I quoted from the declaration, but it seems to me that this construction cannot be supported. In my opinion the sentence in question contains two separate statements: Firstly, that the 'particulars and answers are true and complete in every respect' and, secondly, 'that no material fact has been suppressed or withheld'. The first statement relates to the obligation of the plaintiff to give correct answers, since these are made the basis of the contract, and the second relates to his obligation at common law, arising from the nature of a contract of insurance, to make full disclosure of all material facts. Counsel's contention was that the two parts of the sentence should be read together with the result that the second part would be imported into and qualify the first. But in my opinion the language does not lend itself to such a construction. If counsel's contention were to be accepted it would involve treating the second part of the sentence as if it read 'and that *in the answers to the questions* no material fact has been suppressed or withheld'. I can see no justification for adding in this qualification and, accordingly, I must reject this submission.

Counsel referred me to a passage in the judgment of Kenny J. in *Chariot Inns Ltd v Assicurazioni Generali SPA* (Case 78) in support of his contention that it is only inaccurate replies which relate to material matter affecting the insurance which entitle an insurance company to repudiate a policy. At first sight one of the statements in the passage does appear to have this effect but on further consideration it seems clear that Kenny J. was not dealing with what is in issue here, namely, answers which by agreement were being made the basis of a contract of insurance. In the absence of such an agreement it is only a misstatement of a material fact which would entitle an insurance company to repudiate. The passage in question is: 'A contract of insurance . . . (this quotation is given above on page 167).

While Kenny J. refers to misstatements in answers to questions, it seems clear that he is doing so in the broad context of the common law obligation to make full and complete disclosure and he is not referring to the situation which exists in the present case, namely, one where the insured has warranted that the answers to the questions are complete and accurate. As will appear later from this jugment, in such a situation the materiality of the subject matter of the questions is irrelevant.

Counsel further submitted that the inaccuracy in the reply to Question 8 was trivial, and that because of this the defendant would have to show that it was prejudiced before it would be entitled to repudiate. In support of the contention he referred me to MacGillivray and Parkington on *Insurance law* (7th edn) paragraph 586, where the learned authors say;

> If a misstatement is trivial, the court may well form the opinion that it could not have affected the mind of a reasonable underwriter at all, or induced him to enter into the contract, as where premises were described as roofed with slate whereas a small part of them was roofed with felt, but the misdescription was immaterial.

This paragraph occurs in the chapter dealing with fraud and misrepresentation and is in the section of that chapter which is entitled 'Characteristic of Actionable Misrepresentations'. It is concerned with the nature of a misstatement which on its own would entitle an insurance company to repudiate. It is not concerned with inaccuracies in replies to questions which, as here, have been warranted by the insured to be true and complete in every respect. The relevance of inaccuracies in that context is dealt with by the learned authors in paragraph 725:

> It has always been the law since Lord Mansfield's day that there must be a strict and exact compliance with the obligation or statement which is warranted, so that, as he himself said in *Pawson v Watson* (1778): 'Nothing tantamount will do or answer the purpose.' It is, therefore, not open to the assured to say that the obligation has been substantially complied with, or that the answer he made to a question was more or less accurate. This rule is presumably related to the general doctrine that a warranty is independent of any question of materiality, since an assured who gave an answer which was false only in a trifling detail, and contended that it was accurate, might in a sense be contending that the difference was not material or important to the insurer's calculations.

It is this principle which applies in the present case and not the principle set out in paragraph 586 on which counsel sought to rely. So even if I were to conclude that the inaccuracy in the reply to Question 8 was trivial, that would be no obstacle to the defendant repudiating the policy in view of the accuracy of the answers in the proposal form having been warranted by the plaintiff.

Counsel also referred me to paragraph 724 of the same work, but this equally is of no assistance to his case, and in fact the opening sentence of the paragraph is wholly against his submission that it is only inaccurate replies in regard to matters which are material that enables an insurance company to repudiate for breach of warranty. That paragraph is as follows:

It is convenient to bear in mind two exceptions to the general rule that materiality is of no account in warranty law. First, when the intention of the parties to give a particular term the status of a warranty is in doubt, the fact that it is material to the risk is, as we have seen, a good indication that a warranty was intended. Secondly, the effect of a breach of warranty may be cut down by a proviso which states that the policy can only be avoided for untrue statements or concealment of material facts. In that case, the materiality of the false answer is made a relevant issue. There is also a possible third exception, in as much as the court may be more ready to construe a warranty in the assured's favour, in order to find that he had complied with it, if the matter warranted was trivial and not fundamental to the risk.

The facts of the present case do not bring it within any of these exceptions with the result that the general rule applies, namely, that the materiality of the answers to the questions in the proposal form is of no account . . .

Case 81. Aro Road & Land Vehicles Ltd v Insurance Corporation of Ireland Ltd
Supreme Court [1986] I.R. 403

The plaintiff agreed to supply goods to a firm in Northern Ireland and arranged with CIE to transport these goods. The goods were to be carried at owner's risk. A CIE employee suggested insurance and offered to arrange it. He had blank insurance certificates from the defendants and, without disclosing the identity of the defendants, he explained over the telephone the extent of the cover that would be provided, namely against the risks of fire and theft. The plaintiff's managing director reluctantly agreed to take out the proffered insurance. Before the goods were transported the relevant certificates were completed by CIE as agents for the defendants though these were not issued to the plaintiff, nor was the identity of the defendants made known to the plaintiff. CIE as agents for the defendants did not require a proposal form from the plaintiff or make any inquiries except as to the names and addresses of consignor and consignee and the nature and value of the goods. Part of the consignment was hijacked in Northern Ireland and destroyed by fire. The defendant repudiated the policy on the ground that the plaintiff's managing director had not disclosed that over twenty years previously he had been convicted for receiving stolen property and sentenced to imprisonment. The plaintiff sued the defendants for an indemnity under the policy for the loss.

Held that the petty criminal convictions of over twenty years previously were not material. Since no questions were asked of the plaintiff the defendants were not, in the absence of fraud, entitled to repudiate the policy on the ground of non-disclosure.

McCarthy J.:

The managing director and principal shareholder of the plaintiff had in 1962 been convicted on ten counts of receiving stolen motor parts and sentenced to twenty-one months' imprisonment. Not merely was the fact of these convictions not disclosed to the insurers; not merely did it not occur to the managing director, a reluctant insured, to disclose them; they never occurred to him at all; they were a part of his past which he understandably preferred to forget. Although a great number of different matters were canvassed in the course of the trial, at the conclusion, the sole issue was the right claimed by the insurers to repudiate liability on the ground of non-disclosure of these convictions, which, it is said, was a non-disclosure that a reasonable and prudent underwriter would regard as material and, therefore, on ground of moral hazard, a valid reason for refusing the risk. I think not.

Consideration of this appeal is not helped by the fact that the master policy, the open policy, was not produced in evidence. There was no evidence to suggest that between 15/16 July and 20 July (the day of the hijack) there was any communication passing to the insurers concerning this particular risk. Carroll J. [in the High Court] considered that the convictions could not be material, particularly, to the type of insurance where the risk only attached while the goods were in the custody of CIE. Nonetheless, accepting that [an underwriting expert] was expressing the view of a reasonable and prudent underwriter, she felt that the defendants had discharged the onus on them to prove a material non-disclosure; she felt obliged, so to speak, to suppress her own view of materiality in favour of that of the expert, once she assessed him to be a reasonable and prudent underwriter. Notwithstanding that she still held to her view that the convictions were not material, Carroll J. deferred to the view of the expert; in my judgment, she was incorrect in so doing, being herself the sole and final arbiter.

In my view, if the judgment of an insurer is such as to require disclosure of what he thinks is relevant but which a reasonable insured, if he thought of it at all, would not think relevant, then, in the absence of a question directed towards the disclosure of such fact, the insurer, albeit prudent, cannot properly be held to be acting reasonably. A contract of insurance is a contract of the utmost good faith on both sides; the insured is bound to disclose every matter which might reasonably be thought to be material to the risk against which he is seeking indemnity; that test of reasonableness is an objective one not to be determined by the opinion of the underwriter, broker or insurance agent, but by, and only by, the tribunal determining the issue . . .

The learned trial judge depended part of her judgment upon the decision of this court in *Chariot Inns Ltd v Assicurazioni Generali SPA* (Case 78). In his judgment, with which Henchy and Griffin JJ. agreed, Kenny J. stated: 'A contract of insurance . . . (this quotation is given above on page 167) . . . is not to be determined by such witnesses.' These observations were made in a case in which there was a proposal form, there were questions asked by the insurer and, as this court held, there was a non-disclosure of a matter material to the risk. In the High Court (in *Chariot Inns*) Keane J. said:

> The most widely accepted test of materiality in all forms of insurance on property and goods appears to be that set out in s. 18 sub-s. 2, of the *Marine Insurance Act 1906*, which is in the following terms: 'Every circumstance is material which would influence the judgment of a prudent insurer in fixing the premium, or determining whether he will take the risk.'
>
> That test has been frequently stated to be applicable to non-marine insurance as well: see *Joel v Law Union & Crown Insurance Co* (1908) and *March Cabaret Club & Casino Ltd v London Assurance* (1975). Another test has sometimes been proposed, i.e. the test of whether a reasonable man in the position of the assured and with knowledge of the facts in dispute ought to have realised that they were material to the risk. But this test has been confined normally in its application to cases of life insurance and, possibly, burglary insurance: see *MacGillivray & Parkington* on Insurance Law (6th edn—paras. 749, 750). It was not suggested by any of the parties as the appropriate test in the present case and, accordingly, I propose to apply the test set out in s. 18, sub-s. 2 of the Act of 1906.

Kenny J. did not expressly advert to this proposition but it reflects the argument advanced by the plaintiff here touching on what the insured might consider relevant or material. Keane J. referred to the judgment of Fletcher Moulton L.J. in *Joel's case*. There it was said:

> Over and above the two documents signed by the applicant, and in my opinion unaffected by them, there remained the common law obligation of disclosure of all knowledge possessed by the applicant material to the risk about to be undertaken by the company, such materiality being a matter to be judged of by the jury and not by the court.'

The same Lord Justice had some critical comments to make on the practices on the part of insurance offices of requiring that the accuracy of the answers to the proposal form should be the basis of the contract. I point to this so as to emphasise that *Joel* was a case concerned with a proposal form and insurance effected on foot of it as was *Chariot Inns*. This is not such a case, but the test remains one of the utmost good faith. Yet, how does one depart from such a standard if reasonably and genuinely one does not consider some fact material; how much the less does one depart from such a standard when the failure to disclose is entirely due to a failure of recollection? Where there is no spur to the memory, where there is no proposal form with its presumably relevant questions, how can a failure of recollection lessen the quality of good faith? Good faith is not raised in its standard by being described as the utmost good faith; good faith requires candour and disclosure not, I think, accuracy in itself but a genuine effort to achieve the same using all reasonably available sources, a factor well illustrated by Fletcher Moulton L.J. in *Joel*. If the duty is one that requires disclosure by the insured of all material facts which are known to him, then it may well require an impossible level of performance. Is it reasonable of an underwriter to say: 'I expect disclosure of what I think is relevant or what I may think is relevant but which a reasonable proposer may not think of at all or, if he does, may not think is relevant'? The classic authority is the judgment of Lord Mansfield in *Carter v Boehm* (1766) where in terms free from exaggeration he stated:

> The reason of the rule which obliges parties to disclose, is to prevent fraud and to encourage good faith. It is adapted to such facts as varied the nature of the contract; which one privately knows, and the other is ignorant of, and has no reason to suspect. The question therefore must always be whether there was, under all the circumstances at the time the policy was underwritten, a fair representation; or a concealment; fraudulent, if designed; or, though not designed, varying materially the object of the policy, and changing the risk understood to be run.

If the determination of what is material were to lie with the insurer alone I do not know how the average citizen is to know what goes on in the insurer's mind, unless the insurer asks him by way of the questions in a proposal form or otherwise. I do not accept that he must seek out the proposed insurer and question him as to his reasonableness, his prudence, and what he considers material. The proposal form will ordinarily contain a wide-ranging series of questions followed by an omnibus question as to any other matters that are material. In the instant case, if the managing director had ever had the opportunity of completing a proposal form, which, due to the convenient arrangement made between the insurers and CIE, he did not, there is no reason to think that he would have recounted petty convictions of about twenty years before the time. For the reasons I have sought to illustrate, in my view, the learned trial judge failed correctly to apply the very stringent test; in my judgment, the insurers failed to discharge the onus of proof that lay on them.

There is a second ground upon which, also, in my view the plaintiff is entitled to succeed. Without detracting from what I have said in respect of the general law of insurance, in my judgment, that law is materially affected by over-the-counter insurance such as found in cases of the present kind, in other forms of transit and in personal travel, including holiday, insurance. If no questions are asked of the insured, then, in the absence of fraud, the insurer is not entitled to repudiate on grounds of non-disclosure. Fraud might arise in such an instance as where an intending traveller has been told of imminent risk of death and then takes out his life insurance in a slot machine at an airport. Otherwise, the insured need but answer correctly the questions asked; these must be limited in kind and number; if the insurer were to have the opportunity of denying or loading the insurance one purpose of the transaction would be defeated.

Expedition is the hallmark of this form of insurance. Counsel for the defendant suggested that the whole basis of insurance could be seriously damaged if there was any weakening in the rigidity and, I might add, the severity, of the principle he sought to support. The force of such an argument as a proposition of law is matched by the improbability of the event . . .

Walsh and Hederman JJ. concurred and Henchy J. delivered a concurring judgment, with which Griffin J. concurred.

CHAPTER 15

THE AGENT'S ROLE

It is quite common for insurance to be effected by an employee of the insurer, who often fills in, or assists in filling in, the proposal form. In doing this the agent is only regarded as the insurer's agent where he fills out the proposal form accurately. Should the agent suppress material information or carelessly fill in the form the agent is regarded as the insurer's agent. The insured will be bound by the answers as if he or she had filled the proposal form personally: *Taylor v Yorkshire Insurance Co.Ltd* (Case 82) and *Connors v London & Provincial Assurance Co.* (Case 83).

Case 82. Taylor v Yorkshire Insurance Co. Ltd
King's Bench [1913] 2 I.R. 1

The plaintiff insured a horse with an insurance company and on the expiry of the policy that company declined to reinsure the horse. The plaintiff insured with the defendant and on the proposal form no answer was given to the question, 'Have you had a proposal for livestock insurance declined?'. On both occasions the proposal forms were filled out by the same agent who acted for both companies and was aware of the refusal of the other company to reinsure. On the death of the horse the defendant repudiated the policy on the ground of non-disclosure. The plaintiff sued for the insured sum and alleged that the agent's knowledge must be imputed to the defendant.

Held that when the defendant's agent filled out the proposal form and withheld material information he was then acting as the plaintiff's agent and not as the defendant's agent. Accordingly, the action should be dismissed.

Palles C.B.:

. . . The proposal for the insurance bears the date 29 October 1909, and is signed by the plaintiff; but the answers are in the agent's handwriting. The plaintiff and the agent differ as to the circumstances of the preparation of this document. The plaintiff says that the agent filled up the answers; that he (the plaintiff) did not read them; that he told the agent all he knew; that he was not dealing with the company direct, but with the agent; that if he had been allowed to fill the form he would have filled it differently, and given all the information in his power.. The agent, on the other hand, swore that the plaintiff told him to fill up the form; that he read out the questions; and that the plaintiff answered them.

For the purposes of this case, I deem the difference between these two accounts immaterial; but, in the determination of this motion, I assume, as I am bound to do , that the plaintiff's account is the correct one. It is, to my mind, undoubted, and, indeed, was ultimately admitted by plaintiff's counsel, that, in filling up the answers, the agent must be taken to have acted as the plaintiff's agent, and that the plaintiff is bound by the declaration he signed, as if he had read it, and knew the answers it contained: *Biggar v Rock Life Assurance Co.* (1902).

As, however, during the early part of the argument, it was suggested that this decision, which was that of a single judge—the late Mr Justice Wright—was inconsistent with the previous decision of the Court of Appeal in *Bawden v London, Edinburgh & Glasgow Assurance Co.* (1892) and must, therefore be taken not to be law, I do not like to altogether abstain from referring to this question.

In *Bawden's Case* the plaintiff was an illiterate man, and, to the knowledge of the defendant's agent, was almost unable to read or write, although he could write his name. He had but one eye. The company's agent saw this when the plaintiff applied to him to be insured. The form of the proposal was a complicated one, and contained a note: 'If not strictly applicable, particulars of any deviation must be given at back '; which may well be taken to have been a direction, not to the proposer, but to the agent. Lord Esher M.R. rested his judgment on the imputation to the company of the knowledge acquired by their agent during the negotiations for the policy, that the proposed had but one eye. Lindley and Kay L.JJ., however, in addition to relying on this imputation of notice, held that a duty lay upon the agent, in reference to the filling up of the proposal. Lindley L.J. stating it was his duty 'to put it in shape,' and Kay L.J., that it was his duty to see that it was filled up correctly, and to have written at its back that the proposer had but one eye—a fact which rendered the form not strictly applicable. Thus, one Lord Justice expressly and certainly, and the other probably, bases the duty which it is alleged makes the company's agent an agent of the proposer to fill up the answers, on the special circumstances of that particular case. This is the view taken of it by Wills and Phillimore JJ. in *Levy v Scottish Employers' Insurance Co.*

Agreeing, as I do, with them, I hold not only that, as a general rule, no such duty devolves upon an insurance company's agent, but that the expressions relied on do not indicate an opinion that it does. On the contrary, I hold with Mr Justice Wright that, although 'he may have an agent to put the answers in form,' the agent of an insurance company cannot be treated as their agent to invent the answers to the questions in the proposal form; and that, if he is allowed by the proposer to invent the answers, and to send them as the answers of the proposer, the agent is, to that extent, the agent, not of the insurance company, but of the proposer. In arriving at this conclusion, I have not overlooked the fact that both in *Biggar's Case* and *Levy's Case* there was a provision in the proposal that verbal statements to the agent should not be imputed to the company; but, in relation to this question of authority, as distinct from that of imputations of notice, this is immaterial . . .

Gibson J. delivered a concurring judgment and Boyd J. concurred with both. (See also Case 9, regarding an agent's knowledge to be imputed to a principal, and Case 72, regarding disclosure in insurance.)

Case 83. Connors v London & Provincial Assurance Co.
High Court (1913) 47 I.L.T.R. 148

The plaintiff insured his two and a half year old child with the defendants. The proposal form was signed in blank by the plaintiff and the defendants' agent completed the form and stated the age of the child to be twelve years. The sum insured was in excess of that which statute permitted. The policy provided that the agent's authority was confined to submitting proposals and that the company was not bound by any statement or representation of the agent. When the child was killed in an accident the plaintiff claimed on the policy. The defendants then became aware of the true age of the child and refused to pay. The plaintiff sued.

Held that where a policy purports to provide for the payment of a sum in excess of the maximum payable under a statute on the death of a child it is void *in toto* and not even the sum which might legally have been assured is payable. Where the defendants' agent with full knowledge of the facts carelessly fills up the proposal form stating the insured's age inaccurately after obtaining the proposer's signature the agent must be taken as acting on behalf of the proposer and the defendants are not affected with this knowledge. But the agent may be personally liable to the proposer for the amount for which the policy might legally have been issued.

Gibson J.:

The facts are startling. The child insured was only two and a half years of age, and was insured at the suggestion of the agent who saw him, and persuaded his father, the plaintiff in this action, to sign a proposal form in blank, which the agent undertook to fill in. This he did by stating the age as twelve, and the child as a scholar. He alleges this was a mistake, and for the purpose of this case I shall so assume. The policy was issued in February, 1912, stating the age as twelve. The mistake was not noticed by the insurer, the plaintiff. The policy was an 'Endownment and Accident Policy', maturing after twelve years or upon an accidental death, and securing a payment of £16 10s. for a weekly payment of 6d. It contained, *inter alia*, the following conditions: (1) The agent's authority is confined to submitting proposals; the company is not bound by any statement or representation of the agent, and the agent has no power to vary, cancel, or waive any of the terms or conditions of the company's prospectus or policies. (2) The proposal is the basis of the contract, and the policy contains all and the only conditions by which the company is bound. Any untrue statement in the proposal makes the policy null and void. (3) In the event of an accident directly resulting in death the full sum payable at maturity becomes at once payable. (4) This policy is absolutely final and indisputable except in clear cases of fraud, misrepresentation or non-disclosure of any material fact.

Section 6 of the *Friendly Societies Act 1896*, forbids insurance for payment on the death of any child under five years of any sum exceeding £6, or on the death of any child under ten years of age exceeding £10. Section 84 makes payment on the death of a child under ten years of age otherwise that as provided in the Act an offence. This appears to refer to s. 63, which contains special provisions as to the person to receive payment in each case.

It was stated that in case of endownment policies on children coming within s. 62 the defendants had a special form of policy omitting the clause as to accident accelerating payment, and merely providing for a partial refund of the premiums actually paid at the time of death.

The child having died shortly after the issue of the policy from an accident—a fall—the plaintiff sued on the policy and obtained a decree. Counsel for the defendants contends (1) The the clause as to acceleration upon death by accident brings the policy within the provisions of s. 62 of the Act and that the policy is illegal, (2) That the agent had no authority from the defendants to act as he did.

Counsel for the plaintiff, argued (1) That the policy was not illegal. (2) That the defendant company was affected by the knowledge possessed by their agent, and was precluded from relying on his mistake. (3) That the plaintiff could, at least, recover £6.

In my opinion this policy does come within s. 62. In the event of death by accident—an event which actually occurred in this instance—it insured a payment of £16 10s. The maximum limits is £6, which is prescribed by the section in order to avoid giving parents any substantial pecuniary interest in the death of young children. Whether the death is due to negligence, accident, or otherwise is a matter which cannot be investigated. The prohibition is comprehensive and based on public policy. Had the assurance in this case stated the child's age correctly on its fact it would have been manifestly illegal, and the plaintiff cannot be in a better position by reason of the child's age being incorrectly stated. The plaintiff cannot, therefor recover £16 10s., nor £6, for which sum a policy could have been legally issued. The policy purports to insure the entire sum of £16 10s., and it cannot be treated as one insuring £6. The condition, therefore, making the policy indisputable cannot be sustained, the contract being by statute illegal.

Hence the question as to whether the fault of the agent can be imputed to the company does not arise in this case. The last decision on this point is *Taylor v Yorkshire Insurance Co.* (Case 82), where *Bawden's Case* (1902) and *Biggar's Case* (1902) are discussed.

This condition in this policy expressly restricting the agent's authority would make it difficult to take the case out of the decision in *Biggar's Case*, even were the statutory difficulty out of the way.

I reverse the decree with regret, but as regards the agent personally the plaintiff may have cause of action against him, as, had the age been properly stated, a policy for £6 would have been legal. The agent undertook to fill up the proposal form correctly, and therein acted as plaintiff's agent. The plaintiff may not be without a remedy to this extent; but as the agent is not now before me I express no concluded opinion as to the degree of his liability.

CHAPTER 16.

INSURABLE INTEREST

The essence of a contract of insurance is the protection of some interest of the insured. This is known as an insurable interest. To prevent contracts of insurance from being used as instruments of gaming the law provides that insurance contracts are void unless the insured has some insurable interest in the item insured: *Church & General Insurance Co. v Connolly* (Case 84).

Case 84. Church & General Insurance Co. v Connolly
High Court, unreported, 7 May 1981

The plaintiffs insured the defendant, who was a tenant at will of premises used as a youth club, against loss resulting from fire damage. When a fire damaged the premises the plaintiffs repudiated liability on the ground that the defendant had no insurable interest in the premises. The dispute was referred to arbitration, which found that the plaintiff, as tenant at will of the premise, was entitled to be indemnified so as to include the loss and damage caused to the owners of the fee simple of the premises. When the arbitrator stated a case for the opinion of the High Court, the plaintiffs not alone claimed that the arbitrator was wrong but argued that to allow the finding to stand would amount to the enforcement of an illegal contract in that the relevant statute law made it unlawful to enter into a policy of fire insurance without inserting the names of all persons interested in the policy.

Held that the *Life Assurance Act 1774*, as applied to this country by the *Life Assurance Act 1866*, did not extend to fire insurance policies on premises and that the contract was therefore not illegal. The court also found that the arbitrator's finding as to the plaintiff's insurable interest should stand.

Costello J.:

. . . The plaintiffs' submissions on this part of the case can be summarised as follows. The arbitrator found that the insurable interest of the defendant in the premises was that of a tenant at will. But he also found that they were entitled to be indemnified not only in respect of the damage sustained to this insurable interest but also in respect of loss and damage caused to the interests of the owners in fee of the premises. This determination was incorrect, the plaintiffs claim. As part of their argument my attention was drawn by the plaintiffs to a proposition of law contained in Halsbury's

Laws of England 4th (Halisham) edn. vol. 25 at paragraph 641 dealing
with insurances taken out for the benefit of several interests which reads as
follows:

> Warehousemen and other bailees effect policies which will enure* for
> the benefit of their bailors and similar insurances are effected by
> mortgagors or mortgagees, tenants for life or remaindermen, lessors or
> lessees and a company, its contractors and subcontractors, for the
> benefit of other persons interested in the same property. Insurances of
> this latter kind may be made in the performance of some contract or in
> the discharge of some duty, although this is not necessary . . . All that is
> required to make the insurance effective is that *at the time of insuring it
> is his* (i.e. the person effecting the insurance) *intention (was) to cover
> their interests as well as his own* . . . If the requisite intention is
> established, the insurance is a valid insurance enuring for the benefit of
> all persons interested.

The plaintiffs say that that part of the statement which I have italicised is
incorrect. They refer to *Hepburn v A. Tomlinson (Hauliers) Ltd* (1966)
and claim that this establishes that a unilateral intent on the part of one
person to a contract of insurance to confer a benefit on an unnamed third
party will not suffice to confer such a benefit, that extrinsic evidence on
this point should not be permitted, and that the intention to confer a
benefit on the owner of an insurable interest other than that of the insured
must be gleaned from the policy itself. Applying this principle (and not the
proposition of law in Halsbury which I have quoted) the plaintiffs say that
I should look at the terms of the policy, that it is apparent from these that
there was no intention to benefit anyone but the Bandon Youth Club, and
that as there was no intention to benefit the fee simple owner it follows, it
is claimed, that there is an error of law on the face of this award. I was
referred to Australian authority, *British Traders Insurance Co. Ltd v
Monson* (1964) as an example of a case in which the tenants under a lease
for one year could only recover in respect of the actual loss sustained by
them.

To succeed on this submission the plaintiffs must not only establish that
the arbitrator made an error of law but that this error appears on the face
of the award . . .

In examining the determination made by the arbitrator I can find no
error of law on its face. He found that the defendant had an insurable
interest in the property as tenants at will, that they are entitled to be
indemnified under the policy by the company, and that such indemnity
should cover not only the loss and damage they suffered to their limited
interest but also the damage caused to the owners in fee of the premises.

The law permits a person with a limited interest in a property to insure
not only his interest but the interests which others may have in the same
property, and what the arbitrator has found in this case is that the

* enure: come into effect (*law*)

defendant has done what the law permits him to do. There seems to be nothing erroneous therefore on the face of this award . . .

I now come to the second 'misconduct' argument under s. 38 of the *Arbitration Act 1954* and to the suggestion that the arbitrator's award should be set aside because it has the effect of enforcing an illegal contract . . . The plaintiffs' argument . . . is based on the *Life Assurance Act 1774* and they submit (a) the provisions of this Act apply to fire insurance; (b) they were applied in this country by the *Life Assurance Act 1866*; (c) the 1774 Act makes it unlawful to enter into a policy of fire insurance without inserting the names of all persons interested in the policy. In the present case the name of the fee simple owner was not inserted on this policy. The arbitrator's award, it is submitted, has the effect of enforcing an illegal contract, and should therefore be set aside.

To consider this argument I must first examine the 1774 Act. It is entitled as 'Act for regulating insurances upon Lives, and for prohibiting all such Insurances, except in cases where the persons insuring shall have an Interest in the Life or Death of the Persons insured'. It would seem from this that it was intended that the Act should only apply to life assurance and that it has nothing to do with fire insurance. However, the Act has a preamble which recites that 'whereas it hath been found by experience that the making of insurances on lives *or other events* where the assured shall have no interest hath introduced a mischievous kind of gaming' and s. 2 of the Act provides that 'It shall not be lawful to make any policy or policies on the life or lives of any person or persons, *or other event or events* without inserting in such policy or policies the person or persons' name or names interested therein, or for whose benefit, or on whose account such policy is so made or underwrote.'

The plaintiffs say that the words in the phrase italicised '*or other event or events*', mean that it is not lawful to effect a policy of insurance either on the life of any person, or other event unless the names of persons interested therein are inserted on it, and that the 'other events' referred to include policies of fire insurance. But the problems of construction which this case presents are not exhausted by the 1774 Act. The 1774 Act was applied to this country by the *Life Assurance Act 1866*. This was entitled 'An Act to amend the Law relating to Life Assurances in Ireland' and having recited the title of the 1774 Act to which I have already referred it provided in two short sections as follows:

1. From and after the commencement of this Act the provisions of the said recited Act shall extend to Ireland.

2. This Act shall commence and take effect from and after the first day of November in the year one thousand eight hundred and sixty six, and shall apply to all Policies of Insurances upon lives entered into upon and after that date.

It will become immediately apparent that in the construction of these two Acts two problems of some magnitude arise. The first is: does the 1774 Act apply to fire insurance policies? The second is: even if the 1774 Act is to be so construed did s. 2 of the 1866 Act apply to this country only those provisions of the earlier Act which related to life assurance policies?

. . . In my view if the attention of the court is drawn to an arbitration award whose enforcement would be contrary to public policy the court might well consider that it should in the exercise of its discretion remit the award even though the point had not been raised before the arbitrator. And so it seems to me that I should consider the arguments I have just summarised and reach a conclusion firstly on the application of the 1774 Act to fire insurance policies on buildings and secondly as to the application of the 1774 Act to this country.

MacGillivray, on *Insurance Law*, 6th edn, paragraph 144, asserts that the 1774 Act applies to insurances on buildings and finds support for this view from *In Re King decd.* (1963). But the passage referred to (a passage from the judgment from Lord Denning M.R.) seems to me to be clearly obiter, and, strange as it may seem, it has not been finally or authoritatively decided in England that the 1774 Act applies as MacGillivray suggests. Ivamy, on *Fire and Motor Insurance* (1973 edn) holds a view contrary to that of the editors of the latest edition of MacGillivray and states that the right of an insured who has a limited interest only in houses and buildings to cover the interests of other persons as well as his own is not affected by the 1774 Act (see pages 177 to 181). The latest editor of Halsbury's *Laws of England* (see 4th (Hailsham) edn. vol. 25, paragraph 633, footnote 9) agrees with him. Ivamy points out (1) that the statute in practice has never been treated as applicable to fire insurance and although questions on the lawfulnes of fire policies have frequently been raised no court has suggested that the 1774 Act applied, the judicial silence on the point is, it is suggested, significant; (2) that the mischief which the statute was intended to remedy did not at the time of its passing exist in connection with fire insurance; (3) the amount recoverable by the insured under a policy of life insurance is calculated on a different basis to that recoverable on a policy of fire insurance, and if the same construction is applied to the latter type of policy as to the former this would mean that a policy of fire insurance would not be regarded as a contract of indemnity—a conclusion contrary to all the authorities on the subject.

I find the arguments advanced by Ivamy persuasive and it seems to me that the 1774 Act should not be construed as applying to fire insurance policies on buildings. But even if they did the plaintiffs must show that they were applied in this country by the Act of 1866. MacGillivray suggests that this was the effect of the 1866 Act (see paragraph 30 of the sixth edition), but I do not interpret the Act in this same sense. The Act is entitled 'An Act to amend the Law relating to Life Insurances in Ireland' and makes no references to amending the law relating to other forms of insurances. Although s. 1 applied the provision of the 1774 Act to this country, s. 2 provided that after the commencement date the 1774 Act 'shall apply to all Policies of Insurance upon lives entered into upon and after that date'. It made no provision that the Act was to apply to any other type of policies of insurance after that date. And so I conclude that the 1774 Act only applies in this country to policies of life insurance. It follows therefore that there was nothing unlawful in the manner in which the policy was entered into by the parties, that it would not be contrary to public policy to enforce it and that the plaintiffs' illegality argument fails.

CHAPTER 17.

THE RISK INSURED AGAINST

It is vital for the insured to know precisely the extent of the risks which are covered. Where property is insured against loss, an insured will not have a claim unless he or she can prove, first, that there has been a loss, and secondly, that the loss was caused by the risk insured against. The onus of proving that the loss comes within the risk covered is on the insured and should he or she discharge this onus the insurer must indemnify the insured: *Kelleher v Christopherson* (Case 85). Should that onus not be discharged the insurer is not responsible under the policy: *Ashworth v General Accident & General Assurance Corporation Ltd* (Case 86).

Case 85. Kelleher v Christopherson
Circuit Court (1956) 91 I.L.T.R. 191

The plaintiff was awarded damages and costs in respect of a motor accident caused by a party insured by the defendant. When the insured refused to honour the award the plaintiff sued the defendant as insurer. The defendant pleaded that the policy did not cover the incident which caused the plaintiff's damage in that the insured was engaged in an activity connected with a business which was not covered by the policy of insurance.

Held that the fact that the insured was at the time of the incident using his car in accordance with the terms of the policy, the fact that the insured was conveying material which was used in a business venture carried on by him did not alter the nature of the user of the car and that accordingly the plaintiff was entitled to succeed.

Judge Shannon:

. . . Shortly stated, the facts are that the insured, who is employed as a labourer at Haulbowline, insured the motor car with the Equitable Motor

Policies, and the use of the car covered by the policy was for social, domestic and pleasure purposes, and the use by the insured personally in his business. His business is described as a builder's labourer. The insured used the car to bring him to work every day. In his spare time he carries on pig farming in a small way. It is contested whether this is a business or a hobby. I have come to the conclusion that the pig farming carried on by the insured is in the nature of a business and not a hobby or an amusement. For the purpose of feeding the pigs, the insured got swill about three times per week at the canteen at his place of employment. The swill he carried home in containers in his motor car, the back seat having been removed to make way for them. When the accident occurred he was returning home from work and was carrying some swill in the containers in the car.

In respect of this accident the insurance company has repudiated liability under the policy on the grounds that in carrying the swill the insured was not using the car for the business covered by the policy. The question argued before me was, what was the effect on the policy of the fact that the insured was carrying swill in his car at the time of the accident? It was accepted that when the insured used the car for the purpose of getting to and from his place of work merely, he was covered by the insurance policy. At the hearing in support of their repudiation of the policy the insurance company relied upon a number of authorities, but the chief case upon which reliance was placed and which, it was argued covered the present case entirely was the case of *Jones v Welsh Insurance Corportion* (1937). In that case the wording of the clause regarding user in the policy was similar to that of the policy now under consideration. The insured was a motor mechanic and the business for which his car was insured was that of a motor mechanic. He was also engaged in sheep farming. On the date on which the accident occurred he asked his brother to take his car and bring two sheep and two lambs to their father's house where he had made arrangements regarding the grazing for the animals. While the sheep were being conveyed the accident occurred. The court held that the sheep farming was a business carried on by the insured and that as the car was at the time of the accident being used for the purpose of that business the insurance company was not liable under the policy in respect of the accident.

It appears to me, however, that this cited case differs materially from the present case. The insured in the cited case was not driving the car at the time of the accident. The car was being used for the purpose of a business clearly not covered by the policy. As I have already pointed out in the present case, it was admitted that when the insured drove his car to and from his work he was covered by insurance. Thus, if the insured had not swill in his car on the date when the accident occurred, his driving would have been covered. I have come to the conclusion that his carrying of swill made no difference to the insurance cover in this case. I cannot accept the proposition that by carrying swill he thereby converted a journey which was covered by insurance into one which was not so covered. It appears to me that when a person is using his car for a purpose which is apparently covered by his policy of insurance, there is a very heavy onus on the insurance company to discharge before it can establish that such a user has ceased to be insured by reason of some action of the insured. As in this case, it is a fact that the insured was returning home from work and thus is covered by insurance. To deprive him of this benefit it must be proved that he had done something which alters the nature of the journey or user of the car.

In my opinion the insurance company has fallen far short of discharging that onus. I am compelled to hold that on the evidence in this case firstly, that on the date when the accident occured, the car was being used by the insured to bring him to and from his work and, secondly, that that user was covered by insurance, and that the mere carrying of swill did not alter the nature of the use of the car.

Case 86. Ashworth v General Accident Fire & General Assurance Corporation Ltd
Supreme Court [1955] I.R. 268

A ship was insured against perils of the sea under a policy of marine insurance. The ship left Cork to pick up a cargo at Wexford. On the way a defect occurred in an exhaust pipe and she put into Youghal. While there she was also fited with a new starboard propellor. Continuing the journey to Wexford she gave another ship in trouble assistance as a result of which she went on the rocks, remaining there for a number of days. Following repairs she got off the rocks and continued her voyage. When some miles out of Youghal the port engine went out of commission and she continued to run on her starboard engine. This in turn stalled and she was towed to Wexford. She was found to have taken six inches of water. The hole was repaired with concrete by the crew. With a view to having her dry-docked for examination and overhaul she was sent to Dublin. On this journey the ship was found to be taking water and she put in to Arklow. On leaving Arklow she was again found to be taking water, the engine overheated and when it was stopped the ship drifted with the tide. Repairs could not be made for some hours until the engine cooled. Because it was appreciated that she could not be kept afloat until daylight it was decided to beach her. Before the repairs could be undertaken the weather deteriorated and despite attempts to refloat her she was eventually abandoned as a total loss. The plaintiff sought to recover for the loss of the ship under the policy.

Held that the ship was not seaworthy, that it put to sea in an unseaworthy condition with the privity of the insured and that the loss was due to the ship's unseaworthiness and not to any peril of the sea.

O'Byrne J.:

. . . The question whether the ship was sent to sea in an unseaworthy condition is a pure question of fact and I am of opinion that not only was the judge's finding [in the High Court] on this question justified by the evidence, but that the finding was, on the facts of the case, inescapable. The facts are not seriously in dispute and have been set out in such detail by the trial judge that I do not consider it necessary to recapitulate them. The journey from Cork is one trail of misfortune due, not to any unusual perils of the sea, but to the condition of the vessel. In dealing with the latter portion of this journey, the trial judge says:

> This ship left Wexford in a leaky condition. She had a hole clean through her bottom plating well below the water line. This had been crudely patched with concrete by McD. who, however willing he might be and whatever may have been his experience in mixing mortar, had no previous experience whatever of this class of work, work which for some unexplained reason was not undertaken by the two masons from Staffords'. McD.'s patch had to be supported by sacking kept in position by a pressure bar and even in calm water in harbour still allowed some water to seep in. What was likely to happen when the ship had to encounter even the ordinary movement of the open sea had to be left to the test of experience to indicate—a test which very quickly showed results. From the time she crossed Wexford Bar she was taking in water at the rate of 2 inches per hour against the full action of the rotary pump. Her starboard engine was to all intents and purposes out of commission as were her hand-pumps. Her port engine had given trouble before she entered Wexford and gave more before she reached Arklow. In the event of it breaking down she was not merely quite helpless but was, without the aid of the rotary pump, unable to keep afloat for longer than a period of some hours, even in calm weather.

This was the condition when the vessel reached Arklow. The only repairs effected in Arklow were some repairs to the port engine and clutch carried out by K. K. who had no technical qualifications. He was one of the assistant pilots in Arklow and he said that he had some mechanical experience in connection with boats' engines. After these repairs had been carried out on the morning of 19 November 1949, K. ran the engine for some time, considered that it was working satisfactorily and, thereupon, the vessel left Arklow on her journey to Ringsend. She had only gone a short distance when the engine again failed and, as an alternative to abandoning her, the master ran the vessel on to the beach at Kilcoole.

In view of all these facts, which are not in dispute, I consider that the trial judge could not, reasonably, have failed to find that the ship was sent to sea in an unseaworthy condition.

The question then arises, was the ship sent to sea in an unseaworthy condition with the privity of the assured? In dealing with this matter I agree with the trial judge that it 'Is not essential to find that the assured posed to himself the question, "is the ship unseaworthy?"—and answered that question in the affirmative. The plaintiff was in Arklow on the morning of 18 November, and I see no reason for questioning the validity of the trial judge's finding that he was at that time fully aware of the condition of the ship. The only step he took to remedy that condition was to engage K. to repair the port engine, knowing, as the learned judge has found, that if K. could get the engine going, the vessel would leave Arklow the following morning. He knew that the starboard engine was out of commission and he took no steps to have it repaired. What is still more serious, he did nothing to repair the serious leakage in the ship nor did he do anything to supply an auxiliary means of pumping should the port engine fail. In all these circumstances I am of opinion that the ship left Arklow in an unseaworthy condition with the privity of the assured.

The only remaining question is, was the loss of the ship attributable to its unseaworthy condition?

It was clearly her unseaworthy condition which rendered it necessary to beach her at Kilcoole. The trial judge, however, has found that this was not the cause of the loss of the vessel. He says there was something superadded and proceeds:

Had the weather held as it was when she went ashore, she could have been got off under her own power and would in all probability have completed her journey to Ringsend. I am, I think, forced to the conclusion that what rendered her a total loss was not any ordinary rise and fall of the tide, or any ordinary action of wind and water, but the combined effect of strong winds and heavy seas which caused her to drag her anchor and pile herself broadside on the beach. Ignoring for the moment any other considerations, it seems to me that such agencies very obviously constitute a peril of the seas within the meaning of the policy.

As I understand this finding it means that, though the beaching of the ship was caused by her unseaworthy condition, the subsequent loss was caused by a *novus actus interveniens*, viz. a change in the weather conditions, involving strong winds and heavy seas. I am not to be taken as laying down that, if a storm of unprecedented or unusual violence had arisen and caused the loss, this might not properly be held to be *actus novus interveniens*. There seems to me to be no foundation for such a finding in the present case. There is not a scintilla of evidence that the wind (and resultant heavy seas) was in any way unusual for the time of the year when the loss occurred. The ship was beached by reason of her unseaworthy condition and, even after she had been beached, she could have been got off on the next high tide but for that condition. In these circumstances I am of opinion that the unseaworthy conditon of the ship was the dominant and effective cause of the loss . . .

Maguire C.J. concurred and while Black J. concurred that the ship was unseaworthy and the unseaworthiness was the dominant cause of the loss, he dissented on the point that the insured was privy to the unseaworthiness of the ship.

CHAPTER 18.

THE CLAIM

When the insured suffers the loss insured against, he or she is normally required to make a formal claim and to give the insurer speedy notice of the loss. The question of notice is governed by the terms of the policy and should the insured not give notice in accordance with the policy the insured may repudiate liability: *In re an Arbitration between Gaelcrann Teo and Payne* (Case 87).

The courts will not aid the enforcement of a fraudulent claim even where the party seeking the assistance is an innocent party: *Carey v W.H. Ryan Ltd* (Case 88).

Case 87. In re an Arbitration between Gaelcrann Teo and Payne
High Court [1985] I.L.R.M. 109

The arbitration concerned a dispute under an employer's liability policy between insurance underwriters and the insured. An employee of the insured had allegedly sustained injuries in 1975 and had issued legal proceedings against the insured in 1977. When the insured notified the underwriters of these proceedings the underwriters refused to indemnify the insured on the ground that the insured had failed to comply with the condition contained in clause 5 of the policy, which provided that 'the assured shall give . . . immediate notice in writing, with full particulars of the happening of any occurrence which could give rise to a claim under this insurance, or of the receipt by the assured of notice of any claim and of the institution of any proceedings against the assured . . . ' A sub-heading in relation to the conditions in that section of the policy stated 'all conditions are precedent to liability under this insurance'. The underwriters claimed to have been preju-diced by the failure of the insured to give immediate notice in writing of the happening of the occurrence which gave rise to the claim of the employee. The arbitrator stated some questions for the opinion of the High Court.

Held that the word 'or' in clause 5 was to be read in its *prima facie* ordinary and most common sense which was consistent with the rest of the condition. The insured was therefore obliged to give immediate notice in writing either of the happening of the event likely to give rise to a claim or of receipt by the insured of such a claim and was further obliged to give immediate notice in writing of the institution of proceedings in every case. Compliance with clause 5 was a condition precedent to liability of the underwriters under the policy. Unless non-compliance with clause 5 was trivial or had been waived expressly or by implication by the underwriters, they were not obliged to show that they were prejudiced by the non-compliance by the insured with clause 5.

Gannon J.:

. . . For the underwriters, counsel argues that the word 'or' where it first appears in condition 5 of the general conditions is used in a conjunctive and not a disjunctive sense so as to impose on the assured the obligation of giving immediate notice in writing of all three matters. He submitted that failure on the part of the assured to give notice of the happening of an occurrence which could give rise to a claim in relation to which notice of institution of proceedings is later given releases the underwriters from liability because the conditions as to giving notice are included in those under the heading 'All conditions are precedent to liability under this insurance'. He contended that because the condition as to giving notice is a condition precedent to liability, the question of prejudice to the underwriters by the non-compliance of the assured with such conditions is irrelevant. In presenting his argument for the assured, counsel emphasised at the outset that because the policy document was a contract drawn by the underwriters which the assured had to adopt without alteration it should be construed strictly against them. He pointed out that in condition 5 of the general conditions the word 'or' is used throughout in a disjunctive sense and that it should not be given a conjunctive meaning where first used as if the word 'and' had been intended at that point, only, but was not used where it could have been used if so intended. He argued that unless all of the conditions described as being precedent to liability can be treated as conditions precedent none should be so read, and he referred to the wording used in some of the conditions which he submitted is inconsistent with such interpretation. He contended that the requirement of giving immediate notice in writing relates only to particulars of the happening of an occurrence which could give rise to a claim but not to the receipt by the assured of notice of a claim nor the institution of proceedings against the assured. He submitted that the purpose of the requirement of giving immediate notice is to avoid any prejudice, caused by loss of time, to investigation of facts, and, where the facts are ascertained without reference to the assured there is no prejudice and liability cannot be avoided.

Some helpful observations on the principles to be applied in the construction of statutes and documents and in particular on the interpretation of the words 'or' and 'and' which are capable of different use according to context are to be found in the opinions expressed in the House of Lords in *Reg. v Federal Steam Navigation Co. Ltd* (1974). The provisions of s. 1(1) of the English statute, the *Oil and Navigable Waters Act 1955*, which creates an offence of pollution for which a ship owner or master could be liable was under consideration. The word 'or' was given a conjunctive meaning, rendering both the owner and the master liable to prosecution, on the ground that the alternative interpretation with disjunctive meaning would be absurd or unintelligible.

In stating his opinion supporting the majority Lord Salmon states as follows:

My Lords, I do not suppose that any two words in the English language have more often been used interchangeably than 'and' and 'or'. However unfortunate or incorrect this practice may be, many examples of it are to be found in all manner of documents and statutes. There are many reported cases which turn upon whether, in its particular context, the word 'or' is to be read conjunctively or the word 'and' disjunctively. There is a high authority for the view that the word 'or' can never mean 'and' although it is sometimes used by mistake when 'and' is intended: See Sir George Jessel M.R. in *Morgan v Thomas* and MacKinnon J. in *Brown & Co. v T.& J. Harrison* (1927). On the other hand, there is also the high authority of Bankes and Aitken L.JJ. on appeal in *Brown & Co. v T. & J. Harrison* that 'or' is quite commonly and gramatically used in a conjunctive sense. In *Southerland Publishing Co. Ltd v Caxton Publishing Co. Ltd* (1938) MacKinnon L.J., was able pungently to re-state the contrary view which he had expressed eleven years previously. The Oxford Dictionary seems to support Sir George Jessel M.R. and MacKinnon L.J. I do not, however, attach any real importance as to whether the one school of thought or the other is right on this interesting grammatical point. In *Brown & Co. v T. & J. Harrison* the Court of Appeal agreed with MacKinnon J., as to the effect of the relevant statutory provision. MacKinnon J. reached his conclusion by holding that the word 'or' should be substituted for the word 'and'. The Court of Appeal reached their conclusion by holding that the word 'or', on its true construction meant 'and'. The result was the same.

There is certainly no doubt that generally it is assumed that 'or' is intended to be used disjunctively and the word 'and' conjunctively. Nevertheless, it is equally well settled that if so to construe those words leads to an unintelligible or absurd result, the courts will read the word 'or' conjunctively and 'and' disjunctively as the case may be; or, to put it another way, substitute the one word for the other. This principle has been applied time and again even in penal statutes; see for example *Reg. v Oakes* (1959).

A number of cases are cited by the law lords in their opinions in that case illustrating the application of the principle of the construction in circumstances in which the conjunctive use of the word 'or' was rejected or accepted. It is implicit in these and many other judgments on the construction of statutes and documents and on the interpretation of words used therein that the court of construction will always credit the draftsman of the document with the degree of care and skill to be expected of him. In one of the cases cited in argument by counsel for the insured, *Re Diplock, Wintle v Diplock* (1941), the English Court of Apeal refused to give the word 'or' a conjunctive meaning as its use as a disjunctive is its primary use, and was suitable and made sense in the context nothwithstanding that its effect was to defeat a charitable purpose indicated in the will. The court will not look for ambiguities or inadvertencies or doubtful alternative meanings. A particularly high degree of care and skill will be presumed and attributed to the drafting of a penal statute on the one hand whereas allowance for lack of skill or inadvertenence may be made in the construction of a will drawn by a testator.

Adopting and applying the principles stated in the cited and other cases it seems to me that the word 'or' where first used in condition 5 of the general conditions of the policy can be used in its *prima facie* ordinary and most common sense consistently with the rest of that condition and with all the other provisions of the policy. An examination of the scope of the policy shows that liability could arise, for example, for damage to property from faulty or insufficient workmanship, materials or design, in respect of which it might not be possible to give notice with particulars of the happening of an occurence which might give rise to a claim. The wording of the general condition is intended presumably to comprehend in their application a wide variety of circumstances. Consequently, the use of disjunctives more probably expresses truly the intentions and purpose of the parties. The use of the punctuation commas in the first sentence of condition 5 may contribute to the difficulties of interpretation which have arisen. Had the second comma been placed after the word 'particulars' or after the word 'happening' or after the word 'claim' where it secondly appears in that sentence the meaning of the sentence would be less difficult to ascertain. The expression 'to give notice' is almost invariably followed with the word 'of' in relation to the objective matter but this is not so here with the second comma after the word 'insurance'. I can find nothing in the expressed purpose of the condition or in the sense to be derived from other terms or expressions to be found anywhere in the policy from which I should find an unintelligible or absurd meaning in the use of that word 'or' in its primary disjunctive sense where it first occurs in the first sentence of condition 5. I accept that condition 5 could also bear an intelligible and sensible meaning if the word 'or' where first used were to be given a conjunctive use, but, the mere existence of an acceptable alternative is not a sufficient reason for rejecting the *prima facie* disjunctive meaning and use of the word.

Having regard to the range of cover afforded by the policy and the variety of the nature and circumstances of the possible claims to which the general conditions are expressed to apply it seems to me the obligations imposed in condition 5 are expressed in the alternative in order to provide for the varied types of the alternatives which might be presented by the circumstances giving rise to, and the nature of, the claims. I think that the true and correct interpretation of condition 5 as expressed is that it imposes on the assured one or other alternative obligation with respect to notice of claims and in addition an obligation in respect of the institution of proceedings. The use of the conjunctive 'and' which introduces the reference to the institution of proceedings joins this obligation, to give immediate notice in writing thereof, to whichever of the alternatives in respect of notice of claim may be applicable in the circumstances. Upon this construction of condition 5 as expressed in the policy, the interpretation which I advise should be applied in relation to the obligations imposed on the insured is that:

(1) In every instance in which to the knowledge of the assured an occurence happens which he recognises could give rise to a claim under the policy, he must give to the nominated agent of the underwriters immediate notice in writing of the happening of such occurence, or alternatively give them the like immediate notice of his receipt of the claim if such be made;

(2) In the event of a claim being made or received which arises from no identifiable occurence as a happening, or of the happening of which the assured was unaware, he must give the nominated agent of the underwriters immediate notice in writing of his receipt of notice of such claim;

(3) In every case he must give to the nominated agent of the underwriters immediate notice in writing of the institution of proceedings.

The remaining two questions govern the entitlement of the assured to indemnity under the policy and the liability of the underwriters thereunder in the event of non-compliance with the condition as to notice of claim and they are interrelated. It was recognised in the course of argument that a distinction must be made between a condition expressed in a contract to be a condition precedent and one which is not so described in the contract. Counsel referred to *In Re Coleman's Depositories Ltd* (1907) and in particular to the judgment of Fletcher Moulton L.J. from which it would appear that upon non-compliance with the condition that is stated to be a condition precedent, performance of the obligations of the contract cannot be enforced by the party in default. Nevertheless, Fletcher Moulton L.J. says in reference to what he calls a trifling default:

> The courts have not always considered that they are bound to interpret provisions of this kind with unreasonable strictness, and although the word 'immediate' is no doubt a strong epithet, I think that it might be

fairly construed as meaning, with all reasonable speed considering the circumstances of the case.

In the event of non-compliance with a condition not described as a condition precedent, the party in default may be able to establish a right to the benefit of the contract, subject to an assessment in damages for the consequences of the default, or may be unable to enforce the contract. It was also accepted in the course of argument that compliance with a condition expressed in either form could be waived by the party to benefit by it either expressly or impliedly from conduct . . .

In the policy under consideration by the arbitrator, condition 5 is expressed to be a condition precedent to liability under the policy. Non-compliance with the provisions of the condition, if such there be, may be waived by the underwriters or they, the underwriters, may be found to have waived impliedly their right to rely on non-compliance. If they were found to have led the assured by their conduct to believe that their right to rely on the non-compliance was being waived by them, the matter of prejudice might possibly arise for consideration. Save in the investigation of such matters of fact it seems to me there is no onus on the underwriters to show that they are prejudiced by a non-compliance with condition 5. That is to say in the absence of waiver the underwriters are entitled without the obligation of proof of prejudice to their position to rely on non-compliance with condition 5 as releasing them from liability to meet a claim under the policy . . .

Case 88. Carey v W.H. Ryan Ltd
Supreme Court [1982] I.R. 179; [1982] I.L.R.M. 121

The plaintiff, when a minor, sustained personal injuries while in the defendant's employment and when he sued for damages, his employer's insurers lodged a sum of money in court in settlement of the claim. Subsequently the insurers became aware of fraudulent misstatements made by the employer when entering into the contract which vitiated the insurance policy, and obtained a court declaration that the policy was void. On reaching majority the plaintiff sought payment of the sum lodged in court and the insurers sought the repayment of the sum to them. The plaintiff argued that since he was not a party to the fraud he should be allowed to have the sum in question.

Held that subsequent events rendered the lodgment nugatory. While a minor the plaintiff was ignorant of the fraudulent misrepresentation but as an adult he was aware of his employer's fraud and was attempting to take advantage of it. The position might have been different if, while ignorant of the fraud, he had been allowed to take the money and had disposed of it.

Henchy J.:

The general rule is that where a person purports to pay money directly to another, or to pay it to his credit, and that other has notice that the payment has been induced by fraud, the payee or would-be payee does not get any title to the money . . . If the money has reached the payee, then, while it is in his hands, he is a constructive trustee of it for the rightful owner who had been defrauded into paying it and the payee can be compelled to repay it. If it has not been actually paid over to the payee, but remains in the hands of an intermediary who becomes aware of the fraud, then the intermediary becomes a constructive trustee of the money for the defrauded payer and can be ordered to return it to him.

In the present case the money paid into court by the insurers never reached the plaintiff and he never acquired title to it. It remained in court standing (as the certificate of funds shows) to the credit, not of the plaintiff nor of the employer nor of the insurers, but of the account specified by the title and serial number of the action. Its ultimate beneficial destination awaited an order of the court. As the plaintiff was a minor, he could not get any title to it without an order of the court . . .

The present litigation is a classical example of a case where subsequent events rendered the lodgment nugatory. When it was made, it was made under a mistake of law by the underwriters. But, as Lord Denning M.R. said in *Kiriri Cotton Co. Ltd v Dewani* (1960): 'The true proposition is that money paid under a mistake of law, *by itself and without more*, cannot be recovered back' (emphasis supplied). When the money was paid into court, both the insurers and the plaintiff were ignorant of the fraud that had induced the employer to deposit the money in court. In the absence of a contract of insurance unvitiated by fraud, the insurers were under no obligation to the plaintiff or the consequences of his accident, and therefore under no obligation to lodge any money in court in satisfaction of his claim. But when they did so, because of the rules of court (the finding to the contrary is a central flaw in the judgment under appeal), the plaintiff did not become entitled to the money. He could not become so entitled while he was a minor without getting a court order to that effect. And no such order was got.

By the time an effort was made to establish the plaintiff's entitlement to the money lodged, the situation had radically changed. The underwriters had by then established by judicial order that it was the employer's fraud that had hoodwinked them into making the lodgment in the first place. And the same judicial finding of the High Court had brought that fact home beyond yea or nay to the plaintiff, who had been made a party to that action. From being a minor plaintiff ignorant of the fraudulent misrepresentation that had led the insurers to make the lodgment, he had become a man of full age who was now thoroughly aware of the employer's fraud and of its implications to the insurers and who was nevertheless now trying to take advantage of that known fraud and of the equally known erroneous lodgment which that fraud had generated. If, while he was ignorant of the fraud, he had been allowed to take the money and had spent it or used it irretrievably, the position might be different. But the money remained with the accountant of the Courts of Justice in what was virtually a suspense account, and there it had to remain until the court exercised its discretion as to who should be held entitled to it.

In coming to court and asking to have the money paid out to him, the plaintiff in effect is asking the court to overlook the employer's fraud, to ignore the fact that the insurers would never have parted with a penny of this money if they had known of the fraud, to treat as irrelevant the fact that he now fully knows that the money he is seeking is the fruit of a tree poisoned by fraud—in short, to exercise its discretion by making an order which would have the effect or robbing Peter to pay Paul.

In such circumstances the court's discretion can be exercised in only one way: by ordering that the money in court be paid back to the insurers, who were plainly gulled by the employer's fraud into paying it into court in the first place. If the order asked for by the plaintiff were to be made and the money paid out to him, the court would thereby be wrongly exercising its discretion, for by such an order it would give efficacy to a course of fraudulent conduct on the part of the employer. It is, of course, unfortunate that the plaintiff should be left to pursue his claim against uninsured defendants, but the alternative of allowing him to take in settlement the [the sum] which the insurers were induced by the fraud to lodge in court, and which has lain there for almost four years awaiting the exercise of the court's discretion as to its disposition, would make the court virtually an accessory to the consummation of a fraudulent scheme whereby the insurers, because of a blameless error into which they were led by [a] fraudulent insured, would be dishonestly deprived of [this sum].

Griffin and Kenny JJ. concurred.

CHAPTER 19.

INDEMNITY

Contracts of insurance are construed as contracts of indemnity. This simply means that the insured cannot recover more than the actual loss. The object of this rule is to prevent the insured from making a profit from insurance which would in effect convert a contract of insurance into a contract of wagering which is contrary to law. But what is the actual loss in any given case may cause problems: *St.Alban's Investment Co. v Sun Alliance & London Insurance Co. Ltd* (Case 89).

Case 89. St Alban's Investment Co. v Sun Alliance & London Insurance Co. Ltd
Supreme Court [1983] I.R. 363; [1984] I.L.R.M. 501

The plaintiffs owned premises on which policies issued by the defendant were in force when the building was totally destroyed by fire. The policies were in the standard form of indemnity contract in that the insurers undertook to pay the value of the property at the time of its destruction, or the amount of the damage, or, at its option, to reinstate or replace the damaged property. The plaintiffs argued that the contract was for full reinstatement, or in the alternative, that if the contract was only for indemnity, that the plaintiffs were entitled to the cost of rebuilding.

Held that the contract was not one for reinstatement, and that since the plaintiff did not intend to rebuild the premises, the extent of its entitlement was only the market value of the property at the time of the fire.

Griffin J.:

The learned trial judge [in the High Court] held that there was no agreement to grant reinstatement cover, and I agree with the Chief Justice that, on the facts, he was fully justified in so holding. Indeed, in view of the evidence given at the trial, it is difficult to see how he could have come to any other conclusion.

The plaintiffs, however, claim that even if there was no reinstatement clause in the contract, they nevertheless would be entitled under the terms of the policy to the cost of rebuilding the premises, as this would be the only way in which, they allege, they can be paid the value of the property. Under the policies issued . . . the companies agreed that if the property insured or any part of such property should be destroyed or damaged (*inter alia*) by fire, each company would pay to the insured the value of the property at the time of the happening of its destruction or the amount of such damage or at its option reinstate or replace such property, or any part thereof, subject to a limit of £250,000 in the case [of one policy], and to £50,000 in the case of the [other policy]. Each of these two policies was a standard fire insurance policy.

It is well settled for upwards of one hundred years that such a policy is a contract of indemnity under which the insured may recover his actual loss, not exceeding the maximum amount specified in the policy. What is generally regarded as the authoritative statement of the right of the insured to be indemnified under such a policy is that of Brett L.J. in *Castellain v Preston* (1883):

> In order to give my opinion upon this case, I feel obliged to revert to the very foundation of every rule which has been promulgated and acted on by the courts with regard to insurance law. The very foundation, in my opinion, of every rule which has been applied to insurance law is this, namely, that the contract of insurance contained in a marine or fire policy is a contract of indemnity, and of indemnity only, and that this contract means that the assured, in case of a loss against which the policy has been made, shall be fully indemnified, but shall never be more than fully indemnified. That is the fundamental principles of insurance, and if ever a proposition is brought forward which is at variance with it, that is to say, which either will prevent the assured from obtaining a full indemnity, or which will give the assured more than a full indemnity, that proposition must certainly be wrong.

. . . In the case of such a policy, therefore, what the insurers agree to do is to indemnify the insured in respect of loss or damage caused by fire, and the insured is entitled to be paid his actual loss—no more and no less. The net question in this appeal therefore is the basis on which the amount of that loss is to be ascertained. The plaintiffs claim that they can properly be compensated only by the cost of rebuilding, whilst the defendants say that on the facts of the case the correct basis should be that of market value at the time of the destruction of the premises.

The premises in question consisted of a large five-storey sandstone building, in Maxwell Street and Howard Street in Glasgow. In 1977 these premises were approximately one hundred years old and had been built for use as a warehouse, as had many of the buildings in the same streets. When erected they were ideally situate for use as warehouse—close to the quays and almost directly opposite St Enoch's Railway Station. However, with the changes brought about in transport in modern times, this area changed significantly. The railway station closed down some thirty years ago and was unoccupied thereafter, and became a derelict building the site of which was used ever since as a car park. By 1976, many of the windows in this warehouse had been bricked up. In the middle 1950s strengthening ties had been used to keep the walls in position. In the immediate neighbourhood several other warehouses had bricked up windows and some warehouses had been vacant for some years.

Towards the end of 1976, these premises, which were then unoccupied, came on the market. The plaintiffs were sub-tenants of an adjoining building in Fox Street and . . . the plaintiffs became interested in them. The 'asking price' was £35,000 and after negotiation, towards the end of 1976 and the beginning of 1977, a price of £25,000 was agreed for all the premises for sale—these included premises in Fox Street adjoining the

Maxwell Street premises. The plaintiffs did not want these latter premises but had to take them as part of the bargain since the vendors would not sell the Maxwell Street premises without also selling the Fox Street premises at the same time. It is agreed that the price paid for the premises destroyed in the fire was £14,900 and it is also agreed that at this price they were a bargain. The floor area of these premises was approximately 17,000 sq. feet—something less than 3,500 sq. feet on each floor. The sale was closed in May 1977.

What the plaintiffs had in mind at the time of the purchase was that they would endeavour to obtain a public house licence for portion of the ground floor premises approximately 1,500 sq. feet in area, and have a discotheque on the first floor immediately over the public house. They instructed an architect to prepare a plan for the alterations and the architect obtained a preliminary estimate of the likely cost of the alterations from a quantity surveyor. Before any further steps were taken the premises, still vacant, were destroyed by fire on 15 August 1977. As what remained after the fire was dangerous, it was demolished at a cost of £9,000 shortly thereafter, and the site became and remained at all times since a vacant derelict site.

What therefore is the loss suffered by the plaintiffs as a result of the fire? As Sir James Campbell C said in *Murphy v Wexford County Council* (1921):

> . . . the principle to be applied in such a case is that of restitution, or *restitutio in integram*, as it is called, but I cannot agree that this principle is necessarily or even generally only consistent with restoration or reinstatement. It means . . . that the law will endeavour so far as money can do it, to place the insured person in the same position as if the contract had been performed, or before the occurrence of the tort.

That case was one of malicious damage, but the principle is the same. In *Munnelly v Calcon Ltd* (1978), in which the plaintiff's premises had been demolished as a result of a wrongful act of the defendant, Henchy J. put the matter thus:

> I do not consider that reinstatement damages, which may vastly exceed damages based on diminished value, are to be awarded as a *prima facie* right or, even if they are, that the plaintiff's intention as to reinstatement should be the determining factor. I do not think the authorities establish that there is *prima facie* right to this measure of damages in any given case. In my view, the particular measure of damages allowed should be objectively chosen by the court as being that which is best calculated, in all the circumstances of the particular case, to put the plaintiff fairly and reasonably in the position in which he was before the damage occurred, so far as a pecuniary award can do so.
>
> . . . a court, in endeavouring to award a sum which will be both compensatory and reasonable, will be called on to give consideration, with emphasis varying from case to case, to matters such as the nature of the property, the plaintiff's relation to it, the nature of the wrongful act

causing the damage, the conduct of the parties subsequent to the wrongful act, and the pecuniary, economic or other relevant implications or consequences of reinstatement damages as compared with diminished-value damages.

The plaintiffs claim that the loss should be evaluated by reference to the cost of reinstatement or alternatively by an equivalent modern replacement, while the defendants claim that the amount could best be ascertained by reference to the value of the premises at the time of the fire. In support of their claim that the loss should be ascertained by reference to the cost of reinstatement, the plaintiffs rely on *Reynolds and Anderson v Phoenix Assurance Co.Ltd* (1978). In that case the plaintiffs purchased old maltings some 300 feet by 80 feet for £16,000 in the summer of 1972 for the two-fold use as a grain store, and the milling of grain and other materials for the purpose of production of animal feeding stuffs. The premises were destroyed by fire in November 1973 at which time they were insured for over £600,000. Forbes J. held that on the facts of that case the plaintiffs were entitled to be compensated on the basis of reinstatement in the sum of £246,883 (together with certain architects' and surveyors' fees), which he held was sufficient, on the evidence he heard and accepted, to put the plaintiffs in the position in which they would have been had the defendants not refused to pay under the contract. The plaintiffs say that that case is on all fours with the instant case and they they should be compensated on the same basis. The learned trial judge took a different view. He evaluated the loss by reference to the value of the premises at the date of the fire, in respect of which he had been given valuations ranging from £35,000 to £130,000.

. . . In my opinion, the learned trial judge was, in the circumstances of this case, quite justified in holding that the plaintiff had refused to state, at a time when he might reasonably be expected to do so, whether he intended to rebuild, and in drawing the inference that there was not a genuine intention to rebuild on the part of the plaintiffs. *Reynolds v Phoenix* (supra) is in my view clearly distinguishable from this case. In that case, the judge made the following findings: That having heard and seen both plaintiffs in the witness box, he had no hesitation in accepting their evidence; that the plaintiffs' solicitor throughout the correspondence made it clear that the intention of the plaintiffs was to rebuild; that in the special circumstances of the case the plaintiffs did have the genuine intention to reinstate; that the maltings were ideally suitable for use in connection with the plaintiffs' business without any alteration or additional expenditure on their part apart from the provision of the necessary machinery; and that in the lengthy negotiations and correspondence which took place in the months following the fire the insurer accepted that so long as the plaintiffs intended to reinstate, the true measure of indemnity was the cost of reinstatement of which they agreed at £243,000 . . .

O'Higgins C.J. and Hederman J. delivered separate judgments. Both concurred that the contract was one for reinstalation, but O'Higgins C.J. dissented on the other point, holding that the plaintiffs were entitled to the cost of rebuilding.

CHAPTER 20.

REINSTATEMENT OF THE PROPERTY AND SUBROGATION

The primary obligation of the insurer is to provide a cash indemnity should a claim be successful. In practice many policies relating to premises give the insurer the option to either replace the value of the premises with a sum of money, or to reinstate the premises into the condition it was in prior to the damage. This clause cannot be enforced against the insurer; *St. Alban's Investment Co. v Sun Alliance & London Insurance Co. Ltd* (Case 89). Should an insured desire reinstatement of the premises in the event of its destruction, a clause to that effect, known as a reinstatment clause, must be inserted into the policy.

The cardinal principle of insurance is that the insured cannot recover more than his or her loss. The rule as to subrogation is in keeping with this policy and means that an insurer, who has indemnified the insured, stands in the place of the insured should the latter be able to sustain a claim against a third party. An insured cannot be compensated twice for the same damage but this rule only applies where the insured has been fully compensated once: *Driscoll v Driscoll* (Case 90).

Case 90. Driscoll v Driscoll
High Court [1918] 1 I.R. 152

Premises were leased which contained a covenant by the tenant to keep the premises in repair. Both the landlord and the tenant insured the premises against damage from fire. Subsequently the premises were completely destroyed by fire. Both parties were paid their full claims but these were not sufficient to reinstate the premises. The landlord sued the tenant for damages for breach of the covenant to repair and the landlord's insurance company claimed to be subrogated to the landlord's rights against the tenant irrespective of whether the landlord had been fully indemnified against the loss sustained or not.

Held that until the insured had been fully indemnified the insurer could not be subrogated to the insured's place with regard to claims against a third party.

O'Connor M.R.:

. . . I now come to the claim of the insurance company. That is based on the right of subrogation, and the contention of the company is that whatever sum is recovered by the insured must go to recoup the company the amount paid on foot of the policy, irrespective of the consideration whether the insured has been fully indemnified against the loss sustained. This is met by the insured's contention that until he is fully indemnified he is not bound to contribute anything to the company. I have no doubt that this latter view is correct. A contract of insurance against fire is only a contract of indemnity, and I think that the foundation of the doctrine of subrogation is to be found in the principle that no man should be paid twice over in compensation for the same loss. The corollary to this is that a contract of indemnity against loss should not have the effect of preventing the insured from being paid once in full. I do not think that this can be disputed. The law seems to be well settled, and is recognised in the leading text-books, and is fully borne out by the cases . . .

INDEX